Defense Addiction

DEFENSE
ADDICTION

Can America
Kick the Habit?

Sanford Gottlieb

Routledge
Taylor & Francis Group

New York London

First published 1997 by Westview Press

Published 2019 by Routledge
52 Vanderbilt Avenue, New York, NY 10017
2 Park Square, Milton Park, Abingdon, Oxon OX14 4RN

First issued in hardback 2019

Routledge is an imprint of the Taylor & Francis Group, an informa business

Library of Congress Cataloging-in-Publication Data
Gottlieb, Sanford.
   Defense addiction : can America kick the habit? / Sanford
Gottlieb.
      p.   cm.
   Includes bibliographical references and index.
   ISBN 0-8133-3119-6 (hc).—ISBN 0-8133-3120-X (pb)
   1. United States—Defenses—Economic aspects.   2. Military-
industrial complex—United States.   3. Defense industries—United
States.   4. United States—Military policy.   I. Title.
HC110.D4G67   1997
338.4′76233′0973—dc20   96-29414
                                                                    CIP

ISBN 13: 978-0-367-31537-5 (hbk)
ISBN 13: 978-0-8133-3120-1 (pbk)

CONTENTS

Acknowledgments　　　　　　　　　　　　　　　　　　　ix

Introduction　　　　　　　　　　　　　　　　　　　　1

A Witches' Brew, 2
A Clear Case of Denial, 3
Ike's Warning, 5
Soft Touch on Cost, 7
"Political Engineering," 7

1　General Dynamics Digs In　　　　　　　　　　　　11

The Battle for the Seawolf, 13
"Save Our Shipyard," 14
A Successful Campaign, 16
A Challenge to Electric Boat, 17

2　Defense Mergers　　　　　　　　　　　　　　　　19

The F-16 Cash Cow, 21
Information Services: A Growth Market, 22
Do Mergers Bring Savings? 23
From Business Links to Restructuring Payments, 25
Cozy Relationships, 26
Rewards at the Top, 27
Northrop Grumman: Operation Salvage, 28
Loral: Merger Mania, 30

3　Arms Sales Abroad　　　　　　　　　　　　　　　33

Not Any Old Product, 35
Can We Foresee Unintended Consequences? 38
Bipartisan Arms Pushers, 39

The Code of Conduct and Needed Reforms, 41
Which Way for McDonnell Douglas? 42
Which Way for Arms Sales? 43

4 **Selling to Civilian Government Agencies** 45

"Intelligent" Transportation, 46
Safer Skies, 48
High-Tech Services, 50
Local and State Governments as Markets, 51
Foreign Markets, 53

5 **Trying to Enter Commercial Markets** 55

Ahead of Schedule, 56
Head in the Sky, Feet on the Ground, 57
Saving the Tucson Plant, 58
Jobs Still Disappearing, 59
GM and Electric Vehicles, 59
The Bath Iron Works, 60
Brains as Well as Brawn, 61
"Workplace of the Future," 62
Can Hughes and BIW Make It? 63

6 **Flexibility: Key to Smaller Defense Firms' Survival** 65

The Frisby Success Story, 66
M/A-Com: "Rebuilding the Airplane
   While in Flight," 68
Gull Electronics: Breaking Down the Walls, 69
Ace Clearwater Enterprises: Director of Change, 71
Can Partnerships Prevail? 72
Small Firms Find Banks Wary, 73
Broad Range of Commercial Efforts, 75

7 **The Weapons Labs: Can Bomb Designers Help Industry?** 79

Business-Government Partnerships, 80
Troubled History, 81
Gains in Health Care and Environment, 82
Helping CRADAs Survive, 83
The Future of the Labs, 84
The Critics Respond, 85

Community Involvement, 86
Ticklish Questions, 87

8 Local Activists Pitch In   89

Only One Piece of the Process, 90
As Maine Goes . . . , 92
Slowly Building the Structures, 93
Beating the St. Louis Blues, 95
Industrial Policy, 97
New Currents in a Navy Stronghold, 98
A Mix of Backgrounds, 99
Common Threads, 100

9 State Governments Take Action   101

Connecticut, 102
Washington State, 105
Pioneering in Ohio, 107
Head Start in New York, 108
Late Start in Texas, 109
Closing the Gaps in Maryland, 110
Transitional Aid in Massachusetts, 110
The Strategy of Economic Development, 111

10 Pink Slips for Defense Workers   113

The Human Dimension, 113
The Winners, 115
Poor Prospects, 115
What if There Are No Jobs? 116
More Jobs in the Civilian Sector, 118
A New Industry, 119
A New Approach to Work, 120

11 Congress, Pork, and Defense Jobs   123

"Tip" Ladles It In, 124
Everybody But the Taxpayers, 124
Subcontractors: Lobbying Support, 125
Anchors Aweigh! 126
Aligned with Contractors, 127
The Case of Jane Harman, 129

Does Money Prevail? 130
Not All Succumb, 132
Did a GOP Majority Change the System? 133

12 The Clinton Administration and Dual Use   137

Thirty Years of Inaction, 138
Clinton's Choices as President, 139
Under Attack, TRP Bent, 140
Piggybacking, 141
Procurement Reform, 143
The Pull of the Market, 143
Underfunding Investments, 144
The Other Side of the Street, 146
Unneeded Weapons, 147

13 The Bigger Picture   149

A Survey of the Threats, 150
Stuck in the Military Rut, 152
Home-Front Weaknesses, 153
New Directions, 153
Upgraded Infrastructure, 154
A Trained, Literate Workforce, 154
Civilian R&D, 155
Achieving a Consensus, 156
Partnerships, 157
But Isn't This (Gasp) Industrial Policy? 158
Who Should Underwrite Investments? 159
Which Way Public Opinion? 162
Bucking Conventional Wisdom, 162

Conclusion   165

Good News and Bad, 166
Economic Development, 168
A Can-Do People, 169

Notes   171
About the Book and Author   195
Index   197

ACKNOWLEDGMENTS

The late William Colby was an early supporter of this book. He probably wouldn't agree with all of its conclusions, but he was deeply committed to meeting "the challenges of a new era" and was very helpful in trying to secure funding for the necessary research. Bill Colby's personal qualities of dedication and flexibility are precisely the ones needed to move the United States more firmly into a civilian post–Cold War era.

Defense Addiction is based in large part on hundreds of interviews in and around the military-industrial-congressional complex in ten states and the District of Columbia. Practitioners and analysts alike gave freely of their time and contributed greatly to an up-to-date understanding of recent developments in this key, often-ignored sector of our society.

My peripatetic fact-finding would not have been possible without the generous support of the Compton Foundation, for which I am very grateful.

The interviews, added to others conducted for the *America's Defense Monitor* television program and the information I absorbed over the decades working for nonprofit arms-control organizations, were invaluable in assessing trends and adding detail.

So were the wise counsel and insights provided by Greg Bischak, Michael Closson, Joan Holtzman, Ann Markusen, and Joel Yudken. Kevin Cassidy, Greg Frisby, Lawrence Korb, and Alexander MacLachlan offered many helpful comments on portions of the manuscript. Marcus Corbin, Victoria Holt, Lora Lumpe, Greg Stone, Paul Walker, and the research staff of the Center for Defense Information came through with timely data and leads. Richard Tirocke helped overcome technical challenges with the overworked computer. I am indebted to all of them.

Throughout, I benefited enormously from the steady editorial input, ideas, suggestions, and warm support of my wife, Gladys Gottlieb.

Sanford Gottlieb

Introduction

Back in the 1950s and '60s, American schoolchildren practiced "duck and cover" drills to prepare for the Soviet H-bomb attacks people felt sure were coming. Today, the fearsome prospect of Soviet-American nuclear war has evaporated. The Cold War is over, a development that should have ushered in a future of peace and promise.

That didn't happen.

Bloody civil wars have multiplied around the globe, and the international community has responded fitfully at best. The financially exhausted countries of the former Soviet Union, having squandered their resources on the long and losing confrontation with the West, are beset with ethnic tensions, inflation, organized crime, and all the problems of revolutionary change. No "new world order" has been built to cope with international violence.

Although the United States emerged as the sole remaining superpower, it, too, suffered the effects of nearly a half-century of Cold War. The financial costs were huge. The $4 trillion ($12.8 trillion in 1995 dollars) in military spending between 1947 and 1990[1] contributed mightily to the budget deficits of the 1990s. These deficits in turn constrain the government's ability to help solve deep-rooted, painful domestic problems.

Yet money was not the only cost of the Cold War. Secrecy exacted a toll on our democratic institutions. "Secrecy," observed Gregory Foster, a professor at the Industrial College of the Armed Forces, "is the most lasting, visible and destructive feature of the Cold War ethos. . . . Obsessive secrecy has had the unintended effects of disguising government abuse, obscuring accountability, and engendering public distrust, fear, alienation and apathy."[2]

For years, a substantial slice of military and intelligence spending, the "black budget," has been concealed even from members of Congress. Nowhere has secrecy more shamefully covered up government abuse than in the radiation experiments conducted—often in the name of "national security"—on U.S. citizens. As we have learned, seemingly benign federal agencies dealing with health and veterans' affairs experimented on more than 23,000 unsuspecting Americans. In addition, 16,000 individuals, including prisoners, mental patients, and children, were irradiated in experiments by the Department of Energy (DoE) and the Atomic Energy Commission (AEC). These figures do not include citizens subjected to tests by the Defense Department.[3]

The end of the Cold War and the breakup of the Soviet Union freed the United States to cut defense spending, especially after the surge in military outlays during the 1980s. The Bush administration undertook modest reductions, spurring hopes of a "peace dividend" that could be applied to domestic problems.

One of these problems had crept up quietly and gradually. Even though the country's gross national product increased during the final years of the Cold War, as economist Wallace Peterson pointed out, "The real weekly income of a worker in 1990 was 19.1 percent *below* the level reached in 1973."[4] This decline in real income for all except the wealthiest citizens squeezed living standards. Many Americans felt they were losing ground, and some turned to scapegoating in their frustration.

At the same time, the productivity growth rate was slowing. This was largely due to deteriorating roads, bridges, tunnels, airports, and navigation facilities—infrastructure that had been starved for public investment while the United States spent heavily on bombers, missiles, tanks, and aircraft carriers.[5] The country lacked the sturdy infrastructure a modern economy needs.

A Witches' Brew

Other, interlocking problems were more explosive. Poverty, joblessness, drugs, racial tensions, and violent crime were the stuff of a witches' brew that made many Americans fear other Americans even more than they had earlier feared communism.

The global economy, including its large U.S. component, was in recession when the Cold War ended in 1990. Ten million Americans were unemployed.[6] Eleven percent of African Americans had no jobs; the rate among white Americans was 4 percent.[7] Over 33 million Americans were living in poverty.[8] In the culture of urban poverty, drug sales became the ticket to wealth, and drug-related violence claimed the lives of many young black men. Easy availability of guns and readiness to use them made American society the most dangerous of any in the industrialized countries. Some inner-city neighborhoods became virtual war zones at night.

One unforeseen outcome of the years of military buildup was the poisonous mess left behind on U.S. soil. To dismantle nuclear and chemical arms plants and storage areas, according to one report, "will take decades and is already costing a fortune. The dismantling project, prompted both by environmental laws and international arms control treaties, is also raising so many doubts about safety that residents in more than 30 states have come to believe that they are the unintended targets of weapons once aimed at enemies."[9] Cleaning up just the nuclear weapons sites could cost more than $200 billion.[10]

The DoE is responsible for the nuclear weapons cleanup. In a remarkable booklet on the environmental problems left behind by nuclear weapons production, the DoE stated: "President Dwight D. Eisenhower warned that 'the problem in defense is how far you can go without destroying from within what you are trying to defend from without.' Meant as a warning against creating an all-powerful military-industrial complex, Eisenhower's statement is equally applicable to the environmental legacy of the Cold War."[11]

The Cold War is indeed over, but is this "winning"?

A Clear Case of Denial

When military spending started to decline from Reagan-era highs (it was still higher in constant dollars in fiscal 1995 than in fiscal 1980),[12] the downturn came as a jolt to the defense industry. Most defense contractors had no alternative plans. The Bush administration, opposed on principle to government intervention, offered no help.

Change was not welcome in the defense-industry corridors along the coasts and in other defense-dependent areas such as St. Louis and Fort Worth. For the thousands of prime contractors that supplied weapons to the Defense and Energy departments and the many more thousands of subcontractors that provided components and services, life had been good. They had produced the world's most sophisticated arms while enjoying the fruits of Pentagon-financed research, frequent cost overruns, and generous compensation for executives.

Large contractors often used government-owned plant space and equipment at little or no charge, and they did not face the risks of ordinary commerce. A Defense Department study found that, as a percentage of assets, defense-company profits between 1970 and 1983 reached 20.5 percent, compared to 13.3 percent at commercial firms.[13] Executive salaries and bonuses at a dozen large aerospace companies far exceeded those in comparable commercial companies.[14] For skilled defense workers, wages and benefits were excellent. And the stores, restaurants, bars, and real estate offices near defense plants and military bases benefited from Pentagon payrolls. In the 1990s, Chairman Alan Dixon of the Defense Base-Closure Commission found himself confronted at base entrances by parents holding children who, they said, would starve if a base closed.[15]

To ward off wrenching change after the Cold War, many defense-industry executives and employees—sometimes whole communities—did what they had often done in the past when the weapons they made were rumored to be out of favor in Washington: They called Congress for help. In addition to mobilizing their subcontractors and providing campaign contributions, big prime contractors touted their weapons systems in ads in major newspapers, especially the *Washington Post*, which members of Congress always monitor.

Across the political spectrum, members of Congress responded, voting to save weapons systems even the Pentagon did not want. They kept military-spending cuts modest. They served as a roadblock to the extensive restructuring of the armed forces that would have logically flowed from the crumbling of Soviet military power.

A funny thing happened to the "peace dividend" on the way to the post–Cold War world. The Pentagon under President Bill Clinton continued to shelter a reduced but still immensely powerful military. Its "Bottom-Up Review" called for armed forces ready to fight two regional wars almost simultaneously and without allies, a policy that would require Cold War–level budgets into the next century. President Clinton proposed spending $268 billion on the military in the year 2000. After the 1994 elections, House Republicans put forward a $270 billion-a-year military budget over a period of five years. Even in Washington, that's big money.

Lawrence Korb, an assistant secretary of defense during President Ronald Reagan's first term, commented,

Today the United States spends more than six times on defense as its closest rival, and almost as much on national security as the rest of the world combined. In 1995, Bill Clinton will actually spend $30 billion more on defense, in constant dollars, than Richard Nixon did 20 years ago and substantially more than his own Secretary of Defense argued was necessary in 1992.[16]

Yet no one at the Pentagon knew exactly how much the military spends. The director of the Defense Finance and Accounting Service told a congressional panel in 1995 that the Pentagon rates only a 3, on a scale of 1 to 10, in its ability to track these huge expenditures.[17]

Ike's Warning

The resistance to change from vested interests in the defense sector gives fresh relevance to President Eisenhower's warning in his 1961 Farewell Address:

> This conjunction of an immense military establishment and a large arms industry is new in the American experience. The total influence—economic, political, even spiritual—is felt in every city, every statehouse, every office of the Federal Government. . . . In the councils of government, we must guard against the acquisition of unwarranted influence, whether sought or unsought, by the military-industrial complex. The potential for the disastrous rise of misplaced power exists and will persist.[18]

Richard Stubbing, who spent nineteen years working on the military budget at the Bureau of the Budget at the Office of Management and Budget, saw the complex as a "battleground" where politicians, corporations, and military officers "seek to serve their personal and parochial interests."[19]

On this peculiar battleground, competition and cooperation exist side by side. The federal government, the sole buyer, cooperates closely with the defense-industry sellers. After A. Ernest Fitzgerald was named deputy for management systems for the Air Force in 1965, he made a presentation to Pentagon colleagues criticizing Air Force procurement practices. "Contract negotiations were conducted under conditions unfavorable to the government," he said, "resulting in higher-than-necessary prices. . . . Whereas the usual government team was small, composed of relatively low-ranking people, the contractor teams were large and could call on the full resources of their giant corporations. The big contractors always knew how much money the government team had to spend, and they generally held out for most of it."[20]

Within six weeks of his presentation, which was seen by his colleagues as a novice's mistake, "18 old hands, by actual count, brought up the subject of our partnership with big contractors," Fitzgerald later reported.[21] He concluded that "the easy contractual relationships and generous procurement policies had become a way of life and probably could not be changed even if we wished to do so."[22]

Fitzgerald went on to become the Pentagon's most celebrated whistle-blower, fired for "committing truth" about the cost overruns on Lockheed's C-5A military cargo plane. It took four years of legal struggle for him to be rehired by the Department of Defense (DoD), eight years for him to get his old job back. Frequently isolated in the five-sided building from one administration to the next, this soft-spoken but tough Alabaman could teach an advanced course in organizational ostracism.

One of the bits of truth telling by Fitzgerald that infuriated the old hands related to the way the Air Force chose big contractors to build its weapons. Fitzgerald made sure to mention a 1965 study by the Rand Corporation, the main think tank for the Air Force, in his book *The High Priests of Waste.* Of $30 billion worth of Air Force procurement cited by the study, "less than three percent involved formal advertising for bids, which is the strongest form of price competition."[23] The other 97 percent no doubt involved various types of coziness with the contractors.

Years later, Tom Hafer, another Pentagon cost analyst, described what happened to him when he reported to his superiors that the secret A-12 bomber would be 5,000 pounds overweight, two years behind schedule, and $500 million over budget: "I was just blasted out of the water," he said. "If you ever want to feel like David going up against Goliath, take on a major program like that sometime."[24] The information turned up by Hafer and other analysts was hidden from Defense Secretary Dick Cheney. When the contractors, General Dynamics and McDonnell Douglas, asked for more money and Cheney discovered the truth about their fiasco, he canceled the A-12. Three billion dollars had been spent. No planes had been built. Then the contractors sued the government. The taxpayers will have to pay $2 billion more.[25]

Soft Touch on Cost

Cheney's action was not typical. Although the Pentagon imposes on its contractors smothering regulations in the form of military specifications ("mil specs"), over the years it has been a soft touch on cost. It has often allowed excessive price increases when changes are negotiated after the contractor has won a bid.[26] This practice is known in the trade as "contract nourishment." Jacques Gansler, a former Pentagon official and industrial manager, estimated that the cost of a typical defense program increased at least 45 percent over the term of the contract.[27]

Eli Catran, who worked in Los Angeles defense industry from World War II until 1969, was one of those who renegotiated military contracts for his employer, Litton Industries. As Catran described the process, huge Litton staffs would travel to the Pentagon's Bureau of Ordnance, make a presentation complete with flip charts, and return to Los Angeles on the "red-eye" late-night plane exulting, "We've won another one."[28] The Defense Department was ready to be convinced and everything was renegotiable, Catran asserted. Corruption was built into the system, along with overcharging by the company, which could, for example, shift employees' time cards into the best-paid (renegotiated) government contracts.[29]

Decades later, in March 1996, agents of the FBI and the Pentagon's investigative service searched the offices of a Litton division for evidence in a probe into alleged false billings to the government.

If, despite contract nourishment, a near-monopoly on prime contracts, and other advantages, a large defense firm found itself in trouble during the Cold War, it could usually count on the Pentagon to come to its rescue with a big new contract. "A number of major weapon awards over the past 20 years," Stubbing wrote in 1986, "have gone to the firms most in need of new business."[30]

"Political Engineering"

In 1988, from his analyst's post in the Office of the Secretary of Defense, Franklin C. Spinney courageously described "political engineering" by the Pentagon. This term refers to "the strategy for aiming the money-hose at pivotal congressional districts," Spinney wrote.[31] He reported that former Defense Secretary Caspar Weinberger routinely countered threats of budget cuts by telling Congress how many jobs would be lost. The Air Force, Spinney added, sold the C-17 transport with a glossy pamphlet showing the twenty-nine states selected to receive production money and twelve others labeled as "potential" recipients.

The jobs argument was not the only one the Pentagon used with a generally friendly Congress. The U.S. General Accounting Office (GAO) found a pattern in the Pentagon's reports of foreign military threats. "DoD's threat projections were rarely if ever understated," testified Eleanor Chelimsky, the GAO's assistant comptroller general, "but rather, in the vast majority of cases, greatly overstated." The GAO found no fewer than three counts on which the Pentagon overstated its claim of a "window of vulnerability" caused by improved Soviet missile capability.[32] The exaggerated threat projections drove U.S. spending on nuclear weapons, which has accounted for more than a quarter of all military expenditures since World War II.[33]

The web of relationships among defense companies, their many subcontractors, their employees, and the military services, reinforced by a supportive Congress, remains tight and influential even in the less spendthrift climate of the post–Cold War era. Still, not everyone's interests could be protected as military spending dipped. The downturn hit the procurement of military equipment and services particularly hard.

At the end of the Cold War in 1990, over 6 million people depended directly on the DoD for their livelihood. Half worked for the defense industry, almost a million were Pentagon civilians, and 2,143,000 served in the armed forces.[34] Others living and working near defense plants and bases were indirectly dependent. Defense workers bore the brunt of the spending cuts when they came. Their employers sought to preserve profits and power through a variety of strategies.

Some large defense firms tried to hold onto the core of their business with the Pentagon, shedding the rest. Others merged, becoming larger fish in a somewhat smaller defense pond. Still others turned to arms sales abroad or looked for customers in civilian government agencies at home. A few abandoned their defense divisions. Only a handful made a serious effort to enter commercial markets.

It was hard for defense contractors to leave their cocoons and compete in the turbulent markets of the private global economy. "Their half-century marriage of convenience with the Government," wrote Les Daly, a former senior executive in the aerospace industry, "created so deep a corporate culture that the industry knows virtually nothing else."[35] Daly cited the contractors' aversion to market risks, their nonchalance about raising prices, and the Pentagon's bureaucratic oversight of every operating detail.[36]

Over the years, the Pentagon has awarded the bulk of its prime contracts to a small group of giant companies, some dedicated almost exclusively to military sales, the rest with both military and commercial divisions. The companies and divisions that worked on military contracts were steeped in this distinctive culture.

The defense-industry culture, the fear of further job loss, the competition among the military services for their slice of the budget pie, and the eagerness of members of Congress to hold onto military contracts and facilities for their constituents—together these create a defense addiction. Despite the near-universal desire to reduce government waste and budget deficits, that addiction will be hard to overcome.

What follows is a close-up look at how the various players are coping with this malady and at what other measures might be taken to help our country kick the habit.

1 General Dynamics Digs In

William Anders, the new chairman and CEO of General Dynamics, stood before the assembled guests at *Defense Week*'s twelfth annual conference one evening in October 1991 and declared, "Frankly, sword makers don't make good and affordable plowshares."[1]

The "swords" his company had forged for the Defense Department over many years included nuclear submarines, tanks, combat aircraft, missile systems, and ships for the sealift task of transporting troops and equipment. At the time of Anders's keynote address to the *Defense Week* conference, General Dynamics was the Pentagon's second largest contractor, and its top management was in no mood to make modern-day plowshares. Anders expected military spending to continue downward, "but still to be a pretty sizable market."[2] Besides, he explained, "defense industry management teams generally have little commercial experience and 'market savvy.' Most have been 'cost plus' and 'mil spec' trained."[3] In other words, defense managers were too deeply immersed in the corporate culture of weapons making to change their habits.

Armed with that rationale, Anders proceeded to transform General Dynamics into a smaller, cash-rich defense corporation committed to serving the Pentagon into the foreseeable future. Earlier, he had tried to acquire other defense businesses, but none of the parent companies was willing to sell. Then General Dynamics proceeded to sell off smaller product divisions—missiles, tactical aircraft, defense electronics, space systems, and Cessna planes (one of the firm's few commercial divisions)—and strip down to its "core competencies": submarines and tanks.

The sales of whole chunks of the sprawling company yielded a big influx of cash. At the same time, Anders and his successor, James Mellor, made a number of internal changes. They decentralized decisionmaking, preached the gospel of cost consciousness, and improved incentive pay. Senior management received more-attractive stock options. The company agreed to match purchases of General Dynamics stock, dollar for dollar, for its employees enrolled in the 401(k) retirement plan. The top twenty-five executives also received large bonuses tied to General Dynamics stock, some payable immediately, the rest payable upon retirement. Anders wanted all employees to think like shareholders.[4]

The shareholders did fabulously well. General Dynamics stock rose 553 percent between 1991 and 1993.[5] Anders assumed direction of a troubled company in 1991, but he left with a personal bonanza of $38.7 million in salary, stock options, and bonuses three years later.[6] Mellor, whose service overlapped with Anders's, earned $3,430,000 in direct compensation in 1993.[7]

Those who did not fare as well were the employees laid off in the massive downsizing. Of the 102,200 employees in the big General Dynamics of 1989, only 21,300 remained five years later. Even at the two divisions that built submarines and tanks, almost half of the jobs were cut during this period.[8] Although many of the ex-employees may have retained jobs with the firms that bought General Dynamics divisions, the downsizing left much insecurity in its wake.

General Dynamics led the post–Cold War trend among big defense contractors: shrinking employment along with strong earnings.

By 1994 the downsizing was over. Mellor was able to tell General Dynamics shareholders that the company's two main businesses had been granted a kind of privileged status by the Clinton Pentagon. They "are clearly recognized," he wrote, "as essential to America's Defense Industrial Base, and have been selected to be our nation's future sole-source suppliers of nuclear submarines and main battle tanks. Accordingly, the Department of Defense is directing programs to our Electric Boat and Land Systems Divisions to help preserve their critical capabilities."[9]

The privileged status conferred by the Pentagon on the General Dynamics Electric Boat submarine business and on its competitor Newport News Shipyard, builder of nuclear aircraft carriers, seemed to confirm William Anders's earlier prediction: "Only those operations which are number one, or in some cases number two, in their areas of expertise can remain viable businesses within their markets."[10]

The situation at the Electric Boat shipyard in Groton, Connecticut, however, was a lot shakier during the Bush administration.

The Battle for the Seawolf

Visitors arriving at the New London, Connecticut, train station can glance across the river at Groton and see one of Electric Boat's unfinished products. The hull of a Seawolf submarine sits on the riverfront like a large brown metal sausage overshadowed by big hangars and towering railroad cranes. In its unfinished state, the Seawolf doesn't look like much, but looks are deceiving. By the time it's outfitted with a compact nuclear reactor, missiles, internal-pressure seawater systems, and atmosphere control systems, this sub will cost at least $4 billion.[11]

Electric Boat, a much older company than General Dynamics, has operated a shipyard at Groton since 1911. During the Cold War, the yard specialized in building nuclear-powered submarines. The Polaris, Poseidon, and Trident subs, designed to launch undersea ballistic missiles against the Soviet Union in a nuclear war, formed one leg of the U.S. strategic nuclear "triad." The missiles of a single Trident sub carry a total of 192 H-bombs, each bomb capable of destroying a medium-sized city. Under arms agreements with the Russians, the Trident fleet will be reduced; the construction program ends by 1997.

A second type of sub is the attack submarine, of which the Seawolf is the latest model. Like its predecessors, the Seawolf was designed primarily to destroy Soviet subs in case of war. No arms agreements restrict production of attack submarines, but the Bush administration, as an economy measure, in 1992 proposed ending the Seawolf program after the first boat was launched. With the Trident program ending and the Seawolf program threatened, Electric Boat faced a bleak future. Employment at the yard had already started to decline from its Cold War peak of 25,000, and no government measures were in place to deal with large-scale layoffs.

In the 1992 Connecticut primary, candidate Bill Clinton entered the debate with supportive statements on behalf of the Seawolf. New England was critical to his electoral success.

Swinging into action to save the shipyard, Electric Boat hired a well-connected Washington, D.C., public relations firm to campaign for additional Seawolfs. The firm, Powell Tate, had been founded only a year earlier by former aides to Jimmy Carter and Nancy Reagan. Powell Tate's senior vice president, Jerry Ray, former press secretary to an Alabama senator, claimed that the firm transformed the issue from "Connecticut pork" into security for the nation.[12] The focus was on preserving the unique skills and technology assembled in Groton as key to the country's "submarine industrial base." Were the base to die, went the argument, it would take eight to ten years to build any new submarine.

"Save Our Shipyard"

Since much of the Seawolf's equipment is manufactured by subcontractors, Electric Boat was able to mobilize 450 companies in its supplier base in forty-four states. Congress quickly began to hear from them. Simultaneously, retired admirals were out stumping before community groups and newspaper editorial boards.[13]

Neil Ruenzel, director of communications at Electric Boat, was a key player in the campaign. He visited newspapers, radio talk shows, and industry representatives. Sometimes he traveled with retired admiral Bud Carter, who later became head of the Navy Submarine League. In some places, Ruenzel reported,[14] it was uphill work arguing for the submarine industrial base. Milwaukee, Ruenzel's hometown, was skeptical. At the *New York Times*, he "ran into some people who didn't care to understand." The editorial board of the *Boston Globe* "grudgingly accepted" the argument that if the United States is to have a capable sub force, "these are not skills you can put on the shelf."[15]

While Ruenzel was making the rounds of the newspapers and the Electric Boat subcontractors were contacting their legislators, Connecticut's generally liberal congressional delegation was making a jobs pitch on behalf of their constituents. In the Senate, Chris Dodd (D.–Conn.), who had vigorously opposed Reagan administration support for the Nicaraguan contras, led the effort to head off pink slips for the Electric Boat employees. One close observer said, off the record, that Dodd "called in years of chips" with his colleagues to solicit support for the Seawolf.

David Pryor (D.–Ark.), a member of the Democratic leadership team in the Senate at the time, was frank in a TV interview with me about the nature of his support for the submarine: "I voted for the Seawolf on economic grounds," he said,

> and the fact that I did not believe that this area of our country could absorb that economic loss in that period of time. I also hope that I never have to vote for it again because I don't think I can support the Seawolf.
>
> I also hope, though, that when the time rolls around, that when my military jobs get in trouble, if we have not made that transition, I hope that they will know that Arkansas, my home state . . . is having economic transition problems, and I hope the same people that asked me for my help will remember me.[16]

Other senators, always off the record, admit to voting for the Seawolf out of friendship for Dodd. "Friendship over principle," admitted a West Coast Democrat. Yet Dodd was hardly the only member of Congress trying to save Electric Boat's main shipyard in Groton and its facility in Quonset Point, Rhode Island. Electric Boat is Rhode Island's largest private employer. The whole New England delegation, according to John Isaacs of the Council for a Livable World, "ardently backed the Seawolf and traded votes" on the submarine's behalf.[17] If vote trading did indeed take place, it was among powerful members of Congress who were supporting their own favored weapons systems.

In the House, liberal Sam Gejdenson (D.–Conn.) represents a southeast Connecticut district where thousands of workers build subs and thousands more make other military products. Gejdenson knows something about survival. He was born in a displaced persons camp in Europe at the end of World War II. In 1994, he barely won reelection to an eighth term, and his opponent challenged the outcome. In championing the Seawolf, Gejdenson was open about trying to save his constituents' jobs. And like all Seawolf advocates, he also cited other arguments. Among them were the high cost of shutting down production and the need to preserve sub-making skills until the next generation of attack submarines could be authorized in fiscal 1998.

Some of the members of Congress who presented these arguments, as well as some of those who found them persuasive, were no doubt sincere. But would these arguments have been made in the first place if the underlying fear of constituent job loss had not propelled Dodd, Gejdenson, and their New England colleagues into a spirited defense of Seawolf? As early as December 1991, Dodd had sounded the alarm: "As veterans of the Cold War, these defense workers deserve more than our debt of gratitude. We owe them our pledge that their jobs and their livelihoods will not be jeopardized by the very peace they helped bring about."[18]

During the campaign for the Seawolf, a hot-pink sign reading "Save Our Shipyard" adorned the gray building of the multiunion Metal Trades Council, which represents many of the Electric Boat submarine builders. In the absence of alternative plans by their employer, these workers continue to look to the federal government to preserve their jobs and their livelihoods.

An editorial in the *New London Day* commented on southeast Connecticut's defense dependence at the end of 1992: "In its prosperity, the area ignored its growing incapacity to build products for a civilian marketplace. Its economic development plan consisted of stationing its congressman outside the Pentagon."[19]

A Successful Campaign

"Political support is essential," according to one knowledgeable observer. "It gets you in the game." General Dynamics' Electric Boat Division had so much political support it *was* the game. In Congress, there were votes to spare. Thus, the House in 1992 defeated by a vote of 266–150 the Bush administration's effort to halt construction of the sub; it then voted 412–2 to continue funding the Seawolf. Later, Congress and the Clinton administration authorized construction of three Seawolf submarines. The shipyard was saved, at least for the time being.

"Now people talk about preserving unique skills," claimed Jerry Ray of Powell Tate. "There's not much talk about pork. We beat them back with good, strong intellectual arguments. Truth was on our side."[20] But without the mobilization of Electric Boat's many supplier companies and the political clout of the bipartisan New England delegation to Congress, "truth" might not have prevailed.

General Dynamics wielded additional means of influencing Congress. In the fifteen-month period ending March 31, 1992, Electric Boat's parent company contributed $306,641 to 180 lawmakers—

about a third of Congress's entire membership. Some members were more equal than others. The powerful chairman of the House Defense Appropriations Subcommittee, Representative John Murtha (D.–Pa.), was the leading recipient at $10,000. Dodd received $8,000. Murtha's Senate counterpart, Daniel Inouye (D.–Hawaii), received $5,000.[21]

There's no precise way to measure the influence of campaign contributions. Are they just a way to gain access to members of Congress? A reward for favors done or anticipated? Support for a common philosophy? (See Chapter 11.) All that is certain is that Murtha, Dodd, and Inouye played important roles in winning funding for additional Seawolfs.

Despite the successful campaign, employment at Electric Boat continues to decline. According to Ruenzel, Electric Boat employed about 16,000 workers toward the end of 1994, with a projected drop to 6,000 by 1998. Despite wages of up to sixteen dollars an hour, the anxiety level is very high.[22] Within the declining labor ranks, the number of skilled craftsmen will decrease while the number in design and engineering is expected to go up.

For a brief time after the Cold War ended, Electric Boat departed from Anders's policy of spurning commercial markets. The shipyard studied ocean thermal energy projects and explored a joint venture in marine diesels. Electric Boat actually won a contract to clean up sewage in Boston Harbor. Unfortunately, the company lost several million dollars by overbuilding metal tanks with overqualified people.[23] Today, Electric Boat is totally aligned with its parent company as a downsized military-serving firm, dependent on future Defense Department contracts.

"It's not hard to understand why companies such as General Dynamics have shied from commercial work," editorialized the *New London Day* in 1992. "They're used to dealing with one customer who sets the rules. They have huge overheads, and are weak in commercial marketing skills."[24]

A Challenge to Electric Boat

The Newport News shipyard, claiming it can save the government money, has challenged Electric Boat as the Navy's sub-maker of the future. From May through August 1995, in the weeks before critical decisions on military spending are annually made in Congress, the two shipyards dueled, sometimes daily, in the pages of the *Washington Post*. The weapon of choice: paid advertisements touting their respective talents. Newport News Shipbuilding reiterated its accusation that the administration planned "to award the 20-year, $50–$60 billion New Attack Submarine program *without a competitive bid*"[25] to an unnamed Connecticut shipyard. On a day when both companies paid for ads in the *Post*, Newport News enlisted the support of fifty-five subcontractors to "affirm both the need for the New Attack Submarine program and the need for competition in awarding the contract."[26]

Newport News Shipbuilding went so far as to ask the Pentagon for help in buying Electric Boat in 1995. But the Clinton Pentagon, which had helped finance the merger between Lockheed and Martin Marietta, turned down the Virginia shipyard. The Navy appears committed to keeping Electric Boat as a sub maker and Newport News as the builder of aircraft carriers.[27]

Electric Boat has been challenged from other quarters. Senator John McCain (R.–Ariz.), the first lawmaker to call for cancellation of the Seawolf, was joined by Senator John Warner (R.–Va.) in December 1994 in proposing termination of the program. Veteran members of the Senate Armed Services Committee, McCain and Warner cited the submarine as an example of "wasteful pork barrel spending."

Nonetheless, General Dynamics holds some sturdy assets to help it survive in the military-industrial sector: powerful friends in Congress; lots of cash; an experienced workforce anxious to hold onto its jobs; a program, somewhat belated, to trim costs while maintaining skills; and a flair for touting the varied missions an attack submarine can accomplish beyond blowing enemy subs out of the water.

In August 1995, in a radical departure from its policy of stripping down to its core competencies, General Dynamics used $300 million of its assets to buy a shipyard: the Bath Iron Works (BIW) in Maine. (See Chapter 5.) The purchase gave General Dynamics the capability of building destroyers for the Navy, a move that strengthened the company in its competition with Newport News. In buying BIW, General Dynamics switched to a strategy that became increasingly popular among other big defense companies: consolidation.

2 Defense Mergers

Norman Augustine didn't get to head the world's largest defense firm by accident. An imposing six feet, three inches tall, a Princeton graduate, an aeronautical engineer, an amateur photographer, and a writer of novels and books on business and military procurement, Augustine had a vision of the direction the American defense industry should take in the post–Cold War era. As president and CEO of Martin Marietta, a fast-growing aerospace giant, he single-mindedly pursued consolidation. A few years earlier, he might not have predicted Martin Marietta's merger in 1995 with rival Lockheed, but the logic of Augustine's vision led to the marriage of these two, the second and third biggest defense contractors.

With declining military budgets, Augustine saw four options[1] for Pentagon contractors. First, they could try to convert to commercial production. Noting past failures, he suggested that it would be very hard for defense companies to break into commercial fields already dominated by civilian firms. Second, defense contractors could "hunker down," a choice Augustine associated with business failure. Third, they could liquidate. This, he said, would make the shareholders rich, but "that's tearing things apart, not building." Fourth, they could consolidate, a path leading to growth and lowered costs. This is the path Martin Marietta followed by buying General Electric (GE) Aerospace and the General Dynamics Space Systems Division.

Maryland-based Martin Marietta almost doubled its assets with the 1993 purchase of GE Aerospace,[2] even with the resulting layoff of 11,000 workers. For Augustine, size is clearly a key to survival.

Augustine tried to expand further by buying Grumman, the troubled Long Island combat aircraft manufacturer. Grumman, however, rejected Martin Marietta and accepted a more favorable bid from Northrop Corporation. But even as Augustine's courtship of Grumman unraveled in 1994, Lockheed chairman and CEO Daniel Tellep approached with an offer of a more rewarding relationship.

Lockheed, the veteran producer of warplanes, missiles, and military transport vehicles, and Martin Marietta, the younger defense conglomerate, engaged in secret negotiations—complete with code names for the two companies and individual executives—in locations across the country.[3] When the talks were successfully completed and the two sets of shareholders had approved the merger, Lockheed Martin emerged in March 1995 as the largest defense corporation in the world. By agreement, Tellep assumed the top post until his retirement nine and a half months after merger. Augustine became CEO January 1, 1996.

The merged company started out with 170,000 employees in all fifty states.[4] Although 19,000 employees would later be cut from the payroll because of consolidation,[5] the sheer size and geographic spread of Lockheed Martin guaranteed it political and economic clout, even more clout, for example, than General Dynamics' Electric Boat Division and all its suppliers in forty-four states could muster. Lockheed and Martin Marietta had had a combined total of $22.51 billion in 1993 sales. No defense firm had higher sales except Boeing, and it is largely a producer of commercial aircraft.[6]

Separately, the two companies had sold to approximately the same customers. In 1993, Martin Marietta had done 67 percent of its business with the Defense Department, 13 percent with civilian agencies of government, including the National Aeronautics and Space Administration (NASA), 13 percent with foreign purchasers (largely of arms), and 7 percent with commercial customers. Lockheed's comparable figures were 64 percent with the Defense Department, 13 percent with civilian government agencies, 13 percent in foreign military markets, and 10 percent commercial.[7]

Martin Marietta and Lockheed brought to the merger a range of production specialties and complementary skills. A major difference between them was Lockheed's product line of fighter planes: the stealthy F-117; the futuristic F-22, whose soaring overhead costs were a source of concern to the Air Force; and the relatively low-cost, popular F-16. Lockheed had acquired the F-16 production line through its 1993 purchase of General Dynamics' Fort Worth Division. As one of the three principal contractors on the F-22 program, with General Dynamics and Boeing, Lockheed was also able to assume a two-thirds share of the project's management through the General Dynamics deal.

It was the purchase of General Dynamics' immense Fort Worth plant for $1.525 billion that propelled Lockheed into second place, just ahead of Martin Marietta, among the Pentagon's prime contractors.[8]

The F-16 Cash Cow

At Fort Worth, one can't tour the mile-long factory on foot. One needs an electric golf cart. The plant employed 31,000 people in 1990, the equivalent of two army divisions. At the end of 1994, when I visited, the Lockheed Fort Worth Division still employed 13,000 people.[9] They were at work on the F-16, "the most profitable fighter in history."[10] The plane was bringing Lockheed about $3 billion a year in sales, earning a healthy return on investment within the first twelve months.

The F-16 is reputed to be the only fighter plane that is both efficient and low cost, at least by comparison with its competitors. "Critical action teams," small groups of employees, work full-time to solve problems on the shop floor and improve efficiency. This innovation has reduced the ratio of supervisors to workers.[11] The pace seemed steady and relaxed in 1994 at the individual workstations, presses, machining areas, and assembly lines. With four European countries plus Israel, Turkey, Korea, Taiwan, and the U.S. Air Force as customers, the Fort Worth employees had more job security than many other defense workers. Yet Lockheed Martin management could contemplate farming out some of the work to lower-wage areas, although not enough to threaten the existence of the highly profitable plant or to anger the members of Congress from the Dallas–Fort Worth area.

Lockheed management was delighted with the acquisition of Fort Worth. The two top officers told shareholders: "The benefits are exceeding expectations in nearly all respects. . . . With its firm backlog of nearly 600 F-16 aircraft, the Fort Worth Company will continue to have a positive influence on our earnings and cash flow."[12]

Apart from Lockheed's fighter plane production and a crushed stone, sand, and gravel business owned by Martin Marietta, the two defense giants had covered similar bases before the merger. Both had specialized in defense electronics, with Martin Marietta's Electronics Group its largest and most diverse division. Both companies had participated in important space ventures for the military, NASA, and commercial firms. Lockheed had been part of the Hubble Space Telescope team; Martin Marietta had built the Titan family of rockets. Lockheed had forged a joint commercial venture with two Russian aerospace firms, while building missiles for Trident submarines designed for nuclear retaliation against the former Soviet Union. Lockheed also was developing the Theater High-Altitude Area Defense (THAAD), a system that critics charged could violate the Anti-Ballistic Missile (ABM) Treaty of 1972 between the United States and the Soviet Union.[13]

In little more than a year after the merger, Lockheed Martin won the primary role in the future of the space shuttle program.

Information Services: A Growth Market

Martin Marietta and Lockheed both sold information services to federal, state, and local governments in transportation, traffic violations, law enforcement, and medical care (a subject covered in Chapter 4).

One offshoot of Martin Marietta's military training equipment was designed by the firm's Information Group to appeal to teenagers. Using virtual reality simulation from fighter-pilot and tank-commander training, Martin Marietta created an electronic car-racing game that Sega Enterprises marketed to amusement arcades as "Daytona USA." Players sit behind the wheel and, facing a fifty-inch screen, experience realistic dashes around dizzying turns. The challenge is to win the high-speed race while avoiding collisions with the other cars crowding the course. This may not be a great contribution to the quality of American life, but electronic games have become a source of commercial revenue to the merged Lockheed Martin.

Daytona USA broke income records for Sega, the $4 billion entertainment heavyweight that is now a partner to Lockheed Martin in bringing new electronic games to the arcades. A team drawn from both companies designed Desert Tank, based on a Gulf War scenario, and Sega has used the same technology to produce a third game, Virtua Cop.

Such simulation has become a growth industry for Lockheed Martin, according to a company spokesman.[14] But the top defense company may have entered a fickle commercial marketplace.

Two Daytona USA machines are in use in the dark confines of the Family Amusements arcade center in Wheaton, Maryland, just a few miles from Lockheed Martin's suburban headquarters in Bethesda. When the arcade owner bought the first of the two machines, it increased his weekly returns, but the addition of a second proved a poor investment. Novelty-seeking young customers quickly lost interest. After eight months, the two machines brought in less than the original one had alone.[15]

A more stable market in the information field has been found in a $650 million job to bring wireless telephone service to Southeast Asia. Lockheed Martin has struck a deal with a consortium of companies from the Philippines, Indonesia, and Thailand to erect a satellite-based system that would reach 2 billion people. The system will permit people in the region to use car- and briefcase-mounted wireless telephones to connect with the satellite if they are out of range of ground-based cellular phones. At home, Lockheed Martin plans to launch a satellite-based system that can rapidly deliver voice, video, and data to businesses, schools, and health-care facilities. The company estimates the system would cost $4 billion to develop and implement.[16]

In the health field, a socially useful transfer of military technology is taking place in the fight against breast cancer. Lockheed Martin and Rose Health Care System of Denver in 1995 established a joint company, MedDetect, to help radiologists screen mammograms faster and more effectively. Technology originally developed to locate military targets is being converted to reveal tiny cancerous breast lesions. MedDetect, which started as a small firm, expected the new technology to be ready eighteen months after the creation of the joint company. Eventually, it hopes to expand its detection to chest X-rays and pap smears.[17]

Do Mergers Bring Savings?

The consolidation of Martin Marietta with GE Aerospace, Norman Augustine estimated, will lead to $1.5 billion in savings over five years.[18] Martin Marietta's purchase of the General Dynamics space division will add another $500 million in savings, according to a Lockheed Martin spokesman. Lockheed Martin estimated that its merger will produce additional savings of $1.8 billion.[19] The big merger eliminates duplicate headquarters (Lockheed gave up its headquarters in California) and field offices and twelve facilities and laboratories.

Before the management decided which plants and offices to close, "officials from as far away as California, Georgia and Massachusetts made impassioned, sometimes desperate pitches to Augustine and company chairman Daniel Tellep." In the most unrestrained pitch, Senator Alphonse D'Amato (R.–N.Y.) "flared up on the phone, industry officials said, hollering and cursing at Augustine" in an effort to keep open plants in Utica and Syracuse.[20]

Augustine asserted that consolidation will permit defense firms to reduce prices on weapons and telecommunications, become more competitive in the global market, and achieve critical mass in commercial markets. He believes that the merged firm's information services division, for example, will be able to compete commercially with IBM.[21]

Norman Augustine was not alone in promoting defense-industry mergers. Early in the Clinton administration, the late Les Aspin, then secretary of defense, flanked by his second and third in command, William Perry and John Deutch, called in the heads of major defense companies. Citing a recent study, the Pentagon chiefs concluded that U.S. defense industry had about 50 percent more capacity than needed in the post–Cold War environment. The Defense Department officials told the industry representatives to do something about it, reported Augustine, one of the participants.[22] "I believe it should be done by those who know the firms," Augustine said, "not Wall Street."

Augustine went on to do something about it, but he exacted a price from the Defense Department in the form of "restructuring payments." As Augustine told a congressional hearing in 1994, "It is very unpleasant to lay off able, dedicated employees for lack of work. Companies frequently try to soften the blow for such persons by offering some form of severance pay. That pay is a restructuring cost. Reducing facilities isn't much easier."[23] Arguing that the government would realize most of the savings from defense mergers, Augustine proposed that the government pay most of the restructuring costs. By the time Augustine presented this argument, Martin

Marietta had already benefited from a controversial Defense Department ruling that awarded it restructuring payments.

From Business Links
to Restructuring Payments

As reported by Patrick Sloyan of *Newsday*, both William Perry and John Deutch had business links to Martin Marietta before becoming Pentagon officials. Martin Marietta was a client of Perry's consulting firm, Technology Strategies & Alliances. Deutch was a member of Martin Marietta's advisory board and received $42,500 in consulting fees in 1992.[24] Once in the Pentagon, Perry and Deutch obtained waivers of ethics regulations against dealing with former employers. Then, Sloyan wrote, Deutch approved the restructuring payments to Martin Marietta.

Deutch, who later became head of the Central Intelligence Agency (CIA), acted after Augustine complained in a June 1993 letter to Perry about Defense Department regulations prohibiting reimbursement of merger costs. The letter was co-signed by the heads of Lockheed, Hughes-GM, and Loral. A month later, Deutch reversed previous interpretations of the regulations, thus permitting restructuring payments to Martin Marietta and other companies caught up in the swirl of defense-industry mergers. Perry and Deutch refused repeated requests by *Newsday* for interviews, but Pentagon statements on their behalf "confirmed that they approved the agreement without the usual notification of Congress or the public through the *Federal Register*."[25] The Pentagon said that since the decision was only a clarification of existing policies, no announcement was necessary.

Lawrence Korb, former assistant secretary of defense, disagreed. He told the House Armed Services Oversight Subcommittee that the Pentagon's political leadership had made a significant policy change. "This unprecedented subsidization of the defense industry," Korb testified, "is not a clarification of existing policy, and no amount of semantic jiu-jitsu can make it so. As we used to say in reference to taxes, if it walks like a duck, and quacks like a duck, it is indeed a duck."[26]

What "walked like a duck" in 1994 was only the latest of many concessions made over the years to the defense industry by the federal government. "Progress payments" flowed to companies regardless of the state of progress in the production cycle. So did funds for research. As I indicated in the Introduction, defense firms earned a good share of their profits by negotiating changes in their contracts with a compliant Pentagon. When Lockheed encountered serious problems with its C-5A military cargo planes and commercial jetliners in 1971, the Nixon administration bailed it out with a guaranteed loan and restructured military contracts.

A. Ernest Fitzgerald, the Pentagon civilian analyst who blew the whistle on the C-5A's defects, wrote a year later:

> The American taxpayer probably will never know exactly how much Lockheed was given in return for vastly degraded military hardware in the "restructuring" of their military contracts, including the C-5A, the Cheyenne (helicopter), the SRAM (missile), the shipbuilding claims, and miscellaneous spurious additions to contracts during 1970 and 1971, but the immediate giveaway of at least a billion dollars represented the largest single theft in history.[27]

In the 1990s, Martin Marietta received a total of $350 million in restructuring payments from the Pentagon to compensate for its costs in acquiring GE Aerospace and the General Dynamics Space Systems Division.[28] Lockheed Martin requested $31 million in reimbursements to help fund the $92 million in bonuses that top executives gave themselves in their merger.

To block payments such as this, Congressman Bernie Sanders (Ind.–Vt.) succeeded in having an amendment passed that prohibited the use of fiscal 1996 appropriations to reimburse government contractors for compensation costs in excess of normal salary. In reviewing the Lockheed Martin request, the Defense Contract Audit Agency (DCAA) disallowed $15 million.[29] Although the Pentagon claimed DCAA had allowed the remaining $16 million, Sanders's staff asserted in January 1996 that DCAA had not yet reached a judgment.[30]

Cozy Relationships

Did the professional relationship among William Perry, John Deutch, and the top management of Martin Marietta prior to 1993 tilt the Defense Department's decision in favor of restructuring payments? In addition to their other dealings, Perry, Deutch, and Augustine had served together on the Defense Science Board, and Augustine had chaired an advisory panel for MIT's Lincoln Laboratory while Deutch was MIT provost.[31] Perhaps Perry and Deutch, who became secretary of defense and deputy secretary, respectively, when Les Aspin resigned in 1994, were simply eager to accelerate defense mergers. But the secrecy with which they surrounded their actions created doubts.

By the end of 1994, the top three civilian officials in the Pentagon were former defense consultants with ties to each other, to Martin Marietta, and to other major defense contractors. Paul Kaminski, Perry's successor at Technology Strategies & Alliances, was named undersecretary of defense for acquisition and technology. Kaminski had advised a who's who of contractors on such issues as defense mergers, according to *Newsday*. Secretary Perry approved a waiver of ethics regulations for Kaminski, thus permitting the number three man in the Pentagon to deal with his former clients.[32]

Although it was a unique situation for former defense consultants simultaneously to occupy the Pentagon's three top civilian posts, close relationships among defense-industry managers, Pentagon civilian leaders, and retired military officers are nothing new. Some industry executives have taken top Pentagon posts; the late David Packard is a prime example. Many more officials and officers have moved in the opposite direction, leaving the Pentagon for lucrative jobs with defense firms. Almost 20,000 Pentagon employees went to work for defense contractors between 1975 and 1985. Over a fifth of those who resigned or retired from the Pentagon in 1983 and 1984 went to work in the defense industry on the same projects they had worked on in the Defense Department.[33]

Retired Colonel Howard Bodenhamer, who headed the Air Force's plant representative office at the Fort Worth General Dynamics plant, spelled out the military-industrial dynamics: "You wear the rank of colonel or commander, and literally the next day, you're working for the same contractor at the same plant—and they expect the American people to believe that we're not all in the same bed together."[34]

Rewards at the Top

Some former Pentagon chiefs serve on the boards of directors of major defense companies, much more rewarding than working in

the plant, and with less work involved. Former Defense Secretary
Melvin Laird and John Vessey, Jr., retired chairman of the Joint
Chiefs of Staff, served on the Martin Marietta board until the
merger with Lockheed. The former chief of naval operations, retired
Admiral Carlisle Trost, served on the Lockheed board.

Five members of the Martin Marietta board elected to retire at the
time of the merger to accommodate the limited size of the consoli-
dated governing body. Among the retirees were Laird and Vessey.
Martin Marietta compensated them with checks of $427,000 and
$428,000, respectively, based on the number of meetings they would
have attended in their unfilled terms. In all, Martin Marietta paid
out $1,853,000 to its five retiring board members, including
$236,000 to Republican presidential candidate Lamar Alexander.[35]

The compensation was part of an $82-million payout by Martin
Marietta to 460 of its top officials. Shareholders holding 27 percent
of the company's stock expressed unhappiness over this largesse and
voted against the payment plan at their final meeting before the
merger. Norman Augustine was paid $8.2 million but said he would
donate $2.9 million of it to charity.[36] Lockheed's payout to its exec-
utives was much smaller, amounting to $10 million in all.

Norman Augustine acknowledged that there is a downside to defense mergers: the disruption in the lives of employees and the layoffs of the thousands whose jobs are penciled out of the new organizational charts. But, he adds, "in the long term we'll be more
competitive and will be able to hire more people."[37]

But in the long term, will the Defense Department and the taxpayers get to see lower costs for weapons? Will Lockheed Martin hire
more employees in the future? It may be just as likely that consolidation, having produced fewer defense companies, will lead to less
competition, no lowering of military prices, and a continuing erosion in the number of jobs. One thing that has already been produced by the Lockheed Martin merger, however, is a surge in its
stock—a 59-percent increase from March to October 1995.[38]

Northrop Grumman: Operation Salvage

Hollywood gave Grumman's F-14 fighter plane the starring role in
the movie *Top Gun*, planting among the public a romantic image of
derring-do. As of 1989, however, this image no longer carried
weight with President Bush and the chairmen of the two congres-

sional armed services committees. They were ready to scrap the F-14 as not worth its cost, threatening the core of Grumman's business.

The bipartisan congressional delegation from Long Island, where the F-14 was made, united in defense of the company's interests. The delegation, Republican hawks and Democratic doves, met with Grumman lobbyists Wednesday mornings in the Longworth House office building to plan congressional strategy.[39] With the aid of solid technical arguments put together by the office of Democratic Representative George Hochbrueckner, a former Grumman engineer, and support from their colleagues, the Long Islanders were able to preserve funding for the F-14—at least for a while.

Facing continuing opposition to the F-14, Grumman had decided by 1993 to abandon its sixty-year tradition of building Navy jets. The company prepared to focus instead on defense electronics, surveillance, and information systems. At that point, Grumman was in financial trouble and ripe for a takeover.

When Northrop Corporation won the bidding war for Grumman in April 1994, the former had 28,500 employees, Grumman 16,700. The newly merged company, called Northrop Grumman, bought Vought Aircraft, with its 5,000 employees, a few months later. From this total of 50,200 employees in August 1994, Northrop Grumman had downsized to a workforce of 41,300 by the end of the following March.[40] Like most other large defense contractors, Northrop Grumman gave pink slips to many of its employees. But it retained the services of influential board members.

Among those who had served on the Northrop board and continued to serve on the merged board are Brent Scowcroft, former national security adviser; retired Air Force general John Chain, Jr., former head of the Strategic Air Command (SAC), and Jack Edwards, former ranking Republican on the House Defense Appropriations Subcommittee.

Northrop, builder of the B-2 bomber (which is sold to General Chain's old outfit) and the F/A-18C/D fighter plane, needed the presence of national security luminaries to help restore its reputation. The Justice Department had indicted the company and some of its executives on charges of falsifying tests and padding bills and accused it of paying bribes to win foreign contracts. Northrop was also found to be entertaining generals at hunting lodges on Maryland's eastern shore.[41] The Air Force concluded in a 1990 report that Northrop had no program to develop and train program managers and no system for managing subcontractors and that it was steeped in a culture that emphasized loyalty to the company over ethical conduct.[42]

Following the departure of Northrop's longtime chairman Thomas Jones in 1989, the company cleaned up its act and reorganized under new management. By the time it purchased Grumman, Northrop was in shape to implement its corporate strategy: "to remain a significant part of America's defense technology base while expanding its commercial aircraft structures business."[43] And to proclaim its public-spiritedness, Northrop Grumman provided support to the *MacNeil, Lehrer Newshour* on PBS.

Its public-spiritedness notwithstanding, Northrop Grumman robustly pursued its own self-interest as prime contractor on the B-2 stealth bomber. In the face of a Pentagon decision to cap production at twenty planes and a GAO draft report revealing technical shortcomings, the company went on a political and public relations offensive in 1995. Northrop Grumman "has engaged in a very aggressive campaign," wrote the *Washington Post*,

> running newspaper and television ads extolling the B-2, organizing subcontractors to lobby congressional representatives, hiring retired senior Air Force officers to promote the plane, offering rides in the bomber to Hill members and proposing to provide 20 more B-2s at a "flyaway cost" of about $570 million per plane.[44]

Under the price cap mandated by Congress in 1994, the cost was about $2.2 billion each.

None of this disturbed Northrop Grumman's winning ways with Wall Street; its stock rose 41 percent during 1995.[45] Then, with $3 billion, it bought Westinghouse's defense business.

Loral: Merger Mania

After Bernard Schwartz, an accountant, took the helm of a sinking firm named Loral in 1972, he turned it into the defense industry's fastest-growing company. Schwartz had bought sixteen defense firms as of March 1995, increased Loral's sales to $5.4 billion, and presided over a workforce of 41,000 employees.[46] As of Loral's 1994 fiscal year, the company had twenty-two years of successive improvements in operating earnings.[47] Among Loral's acquisitions were the defense arms of such major corporations as IBM, Ford,

Honeywell, Xerox, and Goodyear, which were trying to shed their ties to the arms industry.

Schwartz left the management and employees of the acquired firms in place, one of the reasons Unisys agreed to sell its defense division to Loral in 1995 despite offers from Raytheon and Hughes. The newly acquired firms even keep their names, prefixed by "Loral."

Loral's leader bears little resemblance to typical defense-industry top management. He is Brooklyn-born, Jewish, and a liberal Democrat who opposed the Vietnam War. Before accepting his post in 1972, he raised the question of whether his "adamant" opposition to the Vietnam War would hurt the firm. He discussed the problem with Pentagon customers and "concluded it probably wouldn't affect our business."[48]

Schwartz stunned the defense industry in 1996 by agreeing to merge Loral with Lockheed Martin. The latter thus became a $30-billion behemoth, adding to the economic and political power it already wielded. The growing concentration of power among the biggest defense contractors will no doubt enhance their profits. But if these big contractors remain in close partnership with a still well-nourished Pentagon, this concentration also increases the danger that they will continue to have undue influence in the councils of government.

3 Arms Sales Abroad

To overcome the impact of cuts in U.S. military spending after the Cold War ended, some big defense contractors turned to increased weapons sales abroad. Although both the Bush and Clinton administrations piously called for restraint in the international arms trade, foreign sales have soared, satisfying the separate goals of the government, worried about unemployment, and the defense industry, seeking customers.

McDonnell Douglas is a case in point. The foremost Pentagon supplier until it was edged out by the Lockheed–Martin Marietta merger, McDonnell Douglas sells combat aircraft to all four branches of the U.S. military. Its top management concluded early on that military business would continue to be profitable even in the post–Cold War world. As Chairman John McDonnell said in 1991: "Even in decline, the U.S. defense market will remain very large. McDonnell Douglas is in a uniquely favorable position: With the F/A-18 Hornet, the C-17 military transport and the T-45 naval trainer, we have all three of the major aircraft programs in production today that are included in DoD's procurement plans beyond 1993."[1]

Despite these brave words, McDonnell Douglas was in a financial bind in 1991. The Navy had canceled the A-12 bomber program, which McDonnell Douglas coproduced with General Dynamics. The C-17, with its massive cost overruns and delays, faced congressional opposition. McDonnell Douglas's commercial aircraft business, meanwhile, although temporarily on the upswing, was also facing hard times because of the global airline recession.

Under these pressures, John McDonnell had asked the Air Force in January 1991 for as much as $1 billion in advance payments on nine projects, including the C-17.[2] The Pentagon, ever protective of its major suppliers, bailed out McDonnell Douglas with two payments totaling $220 million. An audit by the Pentagon's inspector general deleted any reference to the payments. "If the Defense Department has nothing to hide," the *Los Angeles Times* later editorialized, "why is it acting as if it does?"[3]

Big arms sales abroad helped keep the company afloat. Although McDonnell Douglas had closed down its St. Louis assembly line for F-4 Phantom fighters within days of the shah of Iran's overthrow in 1979, the company's annual reports in the late 1980s increasingly emphasized arms sales to the turbulent Middle East.[4] McDonnell Douglas aircraft performed well in the Gulf War, and Chairman John McDonnell reported afterward that four models "are scheduled to go out of production in the next two or three years, barring new export orders." He added, "We are working on potential international sales for each of these product lines."[5]

One of those product lines was the F-15E fighter bomber, which can deliver twelve tons of bombs to targets a thousand miles away. McDonnell Douglas worked feverishly to sell seventy-two of them to Saudi Arabia in what was to become a $9-billion deal, including construction of a military base for the Saudis. The sale required government approval. John McDonnell wrote to President Bush in July 1992, warning that 20,000 workers would be laid off by the following year unless the F-15 sale was approved. "The layoffs we predicted [in a letter in March], have begun," McDonnell asserted. "Last month more than 1,000 highly skilled aerospace workers associated with the F-15 lost their jobs."[6]

That letter to the White House revealed both the crux of McDonnell Douglas' sales blitz—jobs—and its penchant for exaggeration. According to the company's own press releases, the number of F-15 layoffs in June 1992 was 448, not "more than 1,000." There were 207 additional layoffs at the Tulsa plant, which were due to declining commercial jetliner production as well as to the slowdown in the F-15 program.[7]

McDonnell Douglas formed a coalition with other companies and labor unions, mobilized its 2,000 suppliers in forty-six states, flooded Congress with videos and promotional literature, bought newspaper ads, organized rallies, and generated 20,000 letters to decisionmakers.[8] The company increased its claim of the number of jobs affected to 40,000.[9]

Two critics of foreign arms sales, the Federation of American Scientists (FAS) and the National Commission for Economic Conversion and Disarmament, disputed these job-loss claims. In an annotated version of a McDonnell Douglas promotional brochure that the two groups prepared, they stated: "Using multipliers put out by the Department of Commerce and a model of the industrial impacts of spending for combat aircraft and engineering, we estimate that this sale [to Saudi Arabia] would generate 13,000 direct and 14,000 indirect jobs."[10] The critics noted that record U.S. arms sales in 1990 and 1991 did not prevent nearly 300,000 industry workers from losing their jobs. "If Washington is seriously concerned about jobs," they suggested, "it should be promoting the conversion of military industry to civilian production."[11]

The McDonnell Douglas brochure proclaimed: "A Middle East Ally Wants 72 F-15s . . . But Will Buy from Europe if Refused," to which the FAS and the National Commission replied that the European arms industry viewed aggressive U.S. marketing in the Middle East as justification for its own continued sales. The critics further noted Russia's recent announcement that it was getting back into the arms trade because other major suppliers were increasing rather than cutting their arms exports.[12]

The critics' arguments did not prevail. The jobs appeal overwhelmed calls for arms restraint. The Bush administration and Congress approved the export of forty-eight F-15E Strike Eagles to Saudi Arabia in 1992. It was the first time the F-15E had been exported to any nation, although the exported planes lacked some of the missiles and radar on the U.S. Air Force version. A year and a half later the Clinton administration and Congress agreed to supply Israel with twenty-one F-15Es possessing greater capabilities. The United States had assured Israel that its military-technological edge over its neighbors would be preserved.

James Caldwell, who led the multifaceted campaign in support of the Saudi sale, was promoted in 1994 to McDonnell Douglas vice president and general manager of F-15 new business.[13]

Not Any Old Product

Weapons should not be seen as any old product to be bought and sold in the global marketplace. They kill people and destroy things. High-tech conventional weapons can kill and destroy with a range and precision unimaginable earlier in this century. Just since the end of World War II, more than 23 million people have been killed by conventional arms.[14] Although it is understandable that contractors and workers who manufacture weapons want to maintain profits and jobs, governments and citizens should give serious thought to the consequences of arms sales abroad.

The most glaring example of unintended consequences of arms shipments to an "ally" was the massive U.S. sale of $19.5 billion worth of weaponry to Iran between 1972 and 1978. Because of the lack of trained Iranian personnel to operate the equipment, wrote arms-trade expert Michael Klare, the shah of Iran recruited thousands of Western technicians. They aroused the hostility of Iranians, both military and civilian, "who felt that their culture was being subverted by Western values."[15] The shah's passion for expensive weapons, which he continued to indulge even as oil revenues dropped, Klare wrote, led to higher inflation, lower living standards, and resentment among poorer and middle-class Iranians. "This economic resentment combined with religious animosities to spark the revolution of 1978–79."[16]

The flow of U.S. arms to Iran was undertaken in pursuit of the "Nixon Doctrine," which had been spawned in Vietnam and was applied globally. President Nixon quietly designated a number of countries, including Iran, to serve as regional surrogates of the United States. Most had authoritarian governments, but Nixon armed them all. The purpose was to encourage them to act on behalf of U.S. interests without sending American troops. And, coincidentally, the arms exports meant good business for powerful American companies.

Warning voices were raised and ignored. In May 1975, Senator Edward Kennedy (D.–Mass.) criticized U.S. arms exports to the Persian Gulf at a UN conference in Geneva and a week afterward in Tehran. Later that year Senator Hubert Humphrey (D.–Minn.) introduced a bill to tighten controls over arms transfers. He decried "an alarming and steady escalation of exports, many . . . to unstable and volatile areas of the world, such as the Persian Gulf."[17]

The Iranian revolution unleashed a chain reaction of military responses. The fundamentalist revolutionaries in Iran inherited an arsenal of U.S. and Western weapons. Western countries tried to counter Iran by tilting toward Iraq during the ensuing eight-year Iran-Iraq War, adding to the weaponry already supplied to Iraq by the Soviet Union. Saddam Hussein took brilliant advantage of this tilt by importing arms, including the technology for a nuclear weapons program, from West European and U.S. firms through a covert purchasing network. A well-armed Iraqi military probably emboldened Saddam Hussein to attack Kuwait. That attack led to war with the very governments that had been leaning toward Iraq only a few years earlier. French troops and possibly others who fought in the Gulf War faced weapons produced in their own countries. Today the United States, having helped arm Iran and Iraq in the not-too-distant past, considers them the countries most hostile to American interests.

Among other sorry consequences of U.S. weapons transfers: the arming of Guatemalan death squads; the perpetuation of Ferdinand Marcos's dictatorship in the Philippines and the Mobutu dictatorship in Zaire; Jonas Savimbi's long refusal to end the civil war and accept the result of elections in Angola; the arming of Somali warlords with equipment supplied to U.S. Cold War "ally" Siad Barre; and the private resale of Stinger missiles beyond the borders of Afghanistan, where they had originally been used to shoot down Soviet planes.

Clearly, over the years American defense contractors, with the support of government officials, sold arms to more than just the Middle East. Nor did they wait for the Nixon administration to pursue worldwide sales. In 1961, Robert McNamara's Pentagon set up an arms-selling agency, International Logistics Negotiations. Washington "could now be prodded into exports from three separate directions—from the Treasury to earn foreign currency, from the separate states to maintain employment, and from the armed forces, to reduce costs by increasing production," wrote British scholar Anthony Sampson.[18]

Even earlier, beginning in the 1950s, Lockheed and other big U.S. companies started to open the European market to a flood of American arms. Bribery became a way of doing business. Lockheed was accused of bribing Prince Bernhard of the Netherlands and Christian Democratic politicians in Italy, among others.[19] The Securities and Exchange Commission found that during the 1960s and 1970s, nearly four hundred U.S. companies had made questionable payments or engaged in questionable sales practices overseas. Lockheed admitted to over $200 million in improper payments to officials in Indonesia, Italy, Japan, Saudi Arabia, Turkey, and West Germany.[20] Years later, in 1995, Lockheed pleaded guilty to bribing an Egyptian politician and paid a $24.8 million fine.[21] The sleazy side of the arms trade as well as its unintended consequences linger for a long time.

Can We Foresee
Unintended Consequences?

Arms sales to such peaceful and democratic countries as Finland and Switzerland, which bought McDonnell Douglas weapons in the 1990s, present few political problems. Can the same be said of arms sales to Saudi Arabia? A repressive regime whose human rights abuses the State Department has termed "pervasive," Saudi Arabia faces dissidents in exile in London, embarrassing accusations by a defecting diplomat, terrorism directed against the U.S. presence, and reports of high-level corruption.[22]

In 1994, dissidents belonging to Saudi Arabia's Sunni Muslim majority set up shop in London, charging that they had been forced into exile by repression at home. These Sunnis want to create a "true" Islamic state. According to the *Washington Post*'s Cairo correspondent, the group has support from disaffected professionals and clergy and ties to the Saudi bureaucracy.[23] Only months earlier, King Fahd had reached an agreement with exiled Shiite Muslims, a minority in Saudi Arabia. The Shiites agreed to halt antigovernment activities in exchange for government promises to address their complaints of discrimination and human rights abuses.

Mohammed Khilewi, a young Saudi diplomat at the UN, defected at about the time the Sunni dissidents began operating in London. He received a grant of U.S. asylum three months after applying. Khilewi said he had collected many pages of Saudi documents showing that his government finances Islamic terrorists, spies on Jewish activists in the United States, and smuggles bombs and firearms across international borders. The Saudi vice consul in Houston also denounced the regime and defected in London.[24]

The most sensational of Khilewi's charges involved Saudi involvement with Iraq's nuclear weapons program. He said he had attended a 1989 meeting at which Iraqi nuclear specialists requested $200 million from the Saudis in exchange for information on Iraq's nuclear weapons program. Teams of Saudi scientists, Khilewi reported, secretly received training in nuclear technology in Iraq during the 1980s.[25] Was the training in civilian nuclear power or in nuclear weapons? And why the secrecy? Although Saudi Arabia signed the Nuclear Non-Proliferation Treaty in 1988, it has refused to negotiate a comprehensive safeguards agreement as required by the treaty. Does the Saudi royal family, not content with the $67.7 billion worth of conventional arms bought between 1986 and 1993,[26] harbor nuclear ambitions?

Twenty American soldiers and four civilians were killed by bombs in Saudi Arabia during a seven-month period in 1995–1996. They were among the estimated 5,000 American military personnel and the large number of defense-contractor employees who train Saudis in the use of U.S. weapons and help modernize, train, and equip the Saudi national guard.[27] Americans operate in semisecrecy because of Saudi sensitivity toward foreigners on their soil. Several Sunni Muslim leaders criticized the presence of U.S. troops in Saudi Arabia during the buildup to the Gulf War.[28]

Despite these questions about the monarchy's reliability and stability, the trade of oil for arms has frozen U.S. policy toward Saudi Arabia. Political upheaval on the Saudi peninsula may jolt Washington in the future. Despite its oil wealth, its generous social welfare policies, and the links between the royal family and the country's elite, the Saudi regime could be overthrown. If revolution breaks out, would the United States intervene militarily to prevent the F-15s and other U.S.-made weapons from falling into the "wrong" hands?

Bipartisan Arms Pushers

McDonnell Douglas nailed down a sale of Apache helicopters to the Netherlands in May 1995, over European competition. Commerce Secretary Ron Brown, with help from President Clinton and Defense Secretary William Perry, persuaded the Dutch government to buy the American products, according to a Commerce Department official.[29] He explained that it was Clinton administration policy to vigorously promote American exports, both military and commercial, so long as the government doesn't have to choose among companies.

Ron Brown's predecessor in the Bush administration, Robert Mosbacher, had also energetically promoted military and commercial exports. At the same time, Bush's State and Defense departments institutionalized the practice of serving in effect as the overseas sales force of U.S. arms makers. The Pentagon even agreed to pay the costs of transporting and displaying U.S. aircraft at international air shows. Previously, manufacturers bore this expense. Active-duty military personnel were flown at taxpayer expense to the 1991 Paris Air Show—and to several air shows since then—to tout the performance of American arms during the Gulf War.[30] Charles Duelfer, the chief of the State Department's Center for Defense Trade, made it known that in future department evaluations of specific embassies, help in marketing U.S. military products would be "one of the things they'll be graded on."[31]

At the end of the Gulf War, President Bush spoke of the need to curtail the world arms trade. But after massive sales to the Middle East in the wake of Operation Desert Storm, the Bush administration continued down the path of marketing rather than restraint. In fiscal 1991 and 1992, U.S. foreign military sales reached a total of almost $38 billion.[32]

As a presidential candidate in 1992, Bill Clinton watched as George Bush went to Fort Worth to announce the sale of F-16 fighter planes to Taiwan (thus violating a 1982 agreement with China) and to St. Louis to announce the sale of F-15s to Saudi Arabia. Although both sales had serious international implications, Clinton did not take issue with Bush's actions. In fact, he supported the arms sales, issuing a press release headlined "Governor Clinton Supports F-15 Sale to Saudi Arabia." This was not just the traditional appeal for votes in a key electoral state, wrote arms-trade specialist William Hartung. One of the board members of the Progressive Policy Institute, the think tank for the centrist Democratic Leadership Council formerly led by Clinton, heads McDonnell Douglas's Washington office. A McDonnell Douglas lobbyist told Hartung after the election that he felt confident his firm could "do business" with President Clinton.[33]

As president, Clinton has spoken of restraint, but his administration's actions belie the words. The heavy lifting on behalf of McDonnell Douglas's sale of Apache helicopters to the Netherlands was a truer indication of administration practices. After two years in office, Clinton finally signed off on a written arms transfer policy. It stated that "Transfers of conventional arms [are] a legitimate instrument of U.S. foreign policy—deserving U.S. government support—when they enable us to help friends and allies deter aggression, promote regional stability, and increase interoperability of U.S. forces and allied forces."[34]

That had all been said before, many times by many administrations. But, as the Federation of American Scientists pointed out, the Clinton policy added a feature "saying the government will now explicitly consider the impact on the arms industry when deciding whether to approve an export."[35] Since U.S. friends and allies are not now threatened with aggression, this policy reveals the main motivation for continued high levels of arms sales: jobs and profits in the defense industry.

With a strong push from the Bush and Clinton administrations, the United States by 1993 had captured 73 percent of arms sales to the Third World and 70 percent of those to the entire world.[36] In fiscal 1994, the U.S. government approved the export of $38.5 billion of arms and related services to over 150 countries, including both the deals made through the Foreign Military Sales program (negotiated by the government), and the State Department–licensed sales negotiated directly by U.S. manufacturers.[37] By the end of 1993, the United States was sending arms to twenty-six out of the fifty areas where wars were being fought.[38]

The Code of Conduct and Needed Reforms

Senator Mark Hatfield (R.–Ore.) and Representative Cynthia McKinney (D.–Ga.) in 1995 introduced for the second time legislation that would set standards for U.S. arms sales abroad. The Code of Conduct on Arms Transfers Act would block arms sales to governments that attack their neighbors, violate the human rights of their own citizens, come to power undemocratically, or refuse to participate in the UN arms register that monitors the worldwide arms traffic. Sales to countries that do not meet these criteria could continue if Congress affirmed a presidential waiver.

Opposed by the Clinton administration and most Republicans, the Code of Conduct failed by one vote in the House International Relations Committee and by a vote of 262–157 on the House floor. Sixteen House Republicans voted for it. The measure did not come to a vote in the Senate in 1995 but was defeated there in 1996.

The unilateral Code of Conduct would be a step toward a responsible arms-export policy. For it to pass, however, the executive branch would have to recognize that arms sales to regions of conflict and repressive regimes can prove to be a danger as well as an economic opportunity. And the code's advocates would have to provide a practical answer to the argument that "if we don't sell arms someone else will."

The answer can only come from the exercise of U.S. leadership combined with cooperation among the arms-exporting countries. Curbing dangerous arms sales cannot be achieved by any single nation, even the dominant arms merchant; restraints must be negotiated internationally. Without the leadership of the United States, nothing will change.

There are precedents: When the United States exercised its leadership and leverage to block exports of ballistic and cruise missiles, Lora Lumpe of the Federation of American Scientists points out, the worldwide traffic in these weapons declined.[39]

Several unilateral actions would make the U.S. government more credible in persuading other nations to accept limitations. As William Hartung suggests, the executive branch could provide Congress with fuller, more timely information on arms sales; Congress could require the Pentagon and CIA to file annual reports on the use of U.S. arms in current conflicts, and it could outlaw covert arms shipments. It was such shipments that strengthened Saddam Hussein in Iraq, turned Afghanistan into an arms bazaar, and escalated civil wars in Central America.[40]

Yet those measures do not address the powerful pressures coming from defense industry. Even with a huge backlog of arms sales abroad and substantial company profits, defense employment is declining. As the number of jobs declines, the remaining workforce becomes more insecure. Individual workers, their unions, and their employers are motivated to press for still more military contracts and arms sales, whether justified or not by military or foreign policy requirements.

McDonnell Douglas, despite its lucrative arms sales to Saudi Arabia and Europe, in a cost-cutting drive slashed employment from 121,000 in 1989 to 70,000 in 1993.[41] That loss of 51,000 jobs exceeds the size of the workforce at all but a handful of individual American companies. McDonnell Douglas's shareholders and executives are doing well, but its employees are bearing the burdens imposed by modest cuts in military spending.

Clearly the need is for large numbers of new jobs, not necessarily within defense firms, a subject to which we will return.

Which Way for McDonnell Douglas?

While McDonnell Douglas may be indifferent to the use of its military products sold abroad, top management did consider expanding its commercial work at the end of the Cold War. It looked for opportunities close to its core competencies—utilizing the same personnel and machines—and decided it didn't like what it saw. There are not a lot of commercial uses for the technologies that produce combat weapons, according to Fred Whiteford, McDonnell Douglas's director of strategic planning and analysis.[42] He emphasized that defense electronics firms like Hughes Aircraft Company and TRW can more easily convert to commercial work than can the makers of fighter planes and missiles.

"We're not good at low-cost, low performance," Whiteford said. "We don't have marketing. Our customers distribute for us. They fly the planes from St. Louis." Whiteford reported that the company was looking hard at commercial space projects, but in that field it would face numerous competitors and high risk.

Therefore, McDonnell Douglas is likely to follow the course it took in 1994, when 59 percent of its $13-billion income came from military aircraft, many sold abroad, and 14 percent came from missiles, space, and electronics, much of it military.[43]

As of 1995, the company was in good financial shape. Its prospects were buoyed by the Defense Acquisition Board's recommendation that the Pentagon buy eighty more C-17 cargo planes. Representative Elizabeth Furse (D.–Ore.), charging that billions could be saved by modifying existing Boeing 747s, asked the GAO to investigate.

McDonnell Douglas started looking at the possibility of buying other firms and even discussed with Boeing the possibility of a merger or of selling each other assets. At the same time, its current chairman, Harry Stonecipher, warned about the trend toward bigness in the industry. Stonecipher predicted that the big, merged, military-oriented companies would have to split themselves into smaller units to preserve an entrepreneurial edge.[44] But, large or small, they could continue to count on friends in high places at home and abroad to keep them prosperous.

Which Way for Arms Sales?

An advisory board named by President Clinton warned in 1996 that the global trade in increasingly destructive conventional weapons threatens U.S. security. "A disturbing image is forming," the panel reported. "Ever more transfers driven by shrinking defense industries placing increasingly more weapons in troubled regions. The exporting states in turn feel compelled to develop and produce even more advanced weapons to counter this proliferation."[45]

Stressing the primacy of foreign-policy criteria, the adivsory board opposed arms sales "simply to preserve jobs or keep a production line open." "Unwise arms sales remain unwise no matter how many jobs are involved; moreover, those jobs are protected only in the short term."[46]

The panel, chaired by Janne Nolan of the Brookings Institution and including two former directors of the Arms Control and Disarmament Agency, advocated "a new culture among nations, one that accepts increased responsibility for control and restraint, despite short-term economic and political factors pulling in other directions."[47]

4 Selling to Civilian Government Agencies

Since the dawn of the space age, big American defense contractors have worked on NASA's civilian space projects. "We're privileged to have been part of the adventure since Project Mercury in the early 1960s," Lockheed Martin boasted in a full-page ad in the *Washington Post* in July 1995. "We look forward to the challenges of the next 100 missions."[1] Over those three decades, NASA contracts frequently opened when Defense Department contracts ended,[2] in a Pentagon-NASA effort to keep the big companies permanently busy.

As the Cold War drew to a close, defense firms large and small began to step up sales to earthbound nondefense customers in the federal government, as well as to state, local, and even foreign governments.

Some of these companies sold a variety of mundane products to civilian government agencies. Grumman, for example, provided more than 142,000 trucks to the U.S. Postal Service between 1986 and 1994.[3] But the strong suit of the big defense firms was technological expertise, and that had many applications.

The Justice Department and the Immigration and Naturalization Service needed a computerized system for determining whether particular aliens living in the United States are entitled to federal services. Martin Marietta won a contract to develop such a system. Martin Marietta also established a computerized linkup for the Department of Housing and Urban Development and its ninety field offices. The merged company, Lockheed Martin, took over both contracts. TRW holds the prime contract for a DoE program to dispose of spent nuclear fuel and high-level radioactive wastes. By means of a robot that can enter a "hot" room and take photos, TRW can construct a three-dimensional training model of the room revealing every crack and wire in the walls. Thanks to the model, workers know exactly what to look for once they enter and can thus minimize their exposure. TRW has also created technology that helps the Internal Revenue Service ferret out tax cheating. In the field of transportation, the Federal Highway Administration awarded Hughes a contract in 1993 to install an automatic system for identifying trucks along a major corridor stretching from Florida to Ontario, Canada. Indeed, the transportation sector offers defense companies one of their biggest opportunities in nonmilitary government markets.

"Intelligent" Transportation

Advances in surface transportation that only recently were the stuff of science fiction are already within reach and could become commonplaces of everyday life early in the twenty-first century. For example: "driving" on a freeway with no hands on the steering wheel in an electronically controlled convoy that maintains a fixed distance between vehicles; passing toll booths without stopping, the fare automatically charged to the correct account; receiving up-to-the-second travel information at home via cable TV or, in the street, at electronic kiosks; police, firefighters, and ambulances proceeding swiftly to an accident scene, having been alerted by Mayday alarms from the affected vehicles.

Some of these technologies are ready now; others are still on the drawing board or nearing completion. With the Intermodal Surface Transportation Efficiency Act of 1991, President Bush set in motion a long-range program combining modern communications, electronics, and information processing to create a national transportation system that would carry people and goods safely and efficiently.

The need is obvious. Congestion along heavily traveled intercity corridors and in urban areas, where rush hour traffic often moves at the pace of a camel caravan, costs the nation about $100 billion a year in lost productivity.[4] In a 1995 survey of Long Island businesses, many respondents complained about highway congestion, the lack of public transport, and the cost these conditions imposed. They emphasized that "highly paid professionals lost valuable time and missed business opportunities in stalled traffic."[5]

Furthermore, some 40,000 persons are killed and 5 million more are injured annually in traffic accidents, at a financial cost of over

$137 billion.[6] The annual toll in lives amounts to more than two-thirds of the total U.S. war dead in Vietnam and may increase as speed limits are raised.

Large defense companies—Hughes, Lockheed Martin, Loral, Northrop Grumman, Raytheon, Rockwell International, TRW, and Westinghouse—have joined with government at all levels, commercial firms, universities, and research laboratories in planning "intelligent transportation systems" and furnishing the components for such systems. The Department of Transportation (DoT) works closely with these groups, which have organized Intelligent Transportation Society (ITS) of America, a nonprofit consortium, in an active public-private partnership.

Each defense company is seeking its own piece of the action in a complex, interconnected market valued at $210 billion over the next twenty years.[7] Public agencies will be among the main customers. Westinghouse hopes to supply the transportation industry with a system for dispatching and locating driverless vehicles. Lockheed Martin has begun work on "intelligent highway" systems in Georgia, New York, and California and is developing an advanced system for Denver. The Denver system features automatically triggered warnings to drivers of vehicles that exceed permissible emission levels.

According to Walter Faulconer, the manager of Lockheed Martin's Automated Highway System Division, the company is still seeking its niche.[8] Among the possibilities are specialization in traffic-control centers that draw on the company's experience in space and the military and manufacture of driverless snowplows, a spinoff of automated highways.

Rockwell set up an executive-level board in 1991 to coordinate its various intelligent highway activities. "We just feel like strategically it's a market we can't afford not to be involved in," said Roger Stevens, general manager of Rockwell's automotive electronics division.[9]

The DoT heads the public-private effort whose mission is to define the framework and standards for a national surface transportation system. Teams led by Loral and Rockwell beat out teams from Hughes and Westinghouse in competition for the contract to do this work. Loral and Rockwell are now collaborating on the system's final "architecture," as the planners call it.

Much remains to be done, however, before a more automated, safer, more efficient transportation system becomes a reality. Consensus on a range of key issues must emerge among consumers, public agencies at all levels, fleet operators, manufacturers, and other participants. And public officials have to weigh the importance of transportation against other basic needs, as well as the importance of highways against railroads, in the increasingly tough competition for tax dollars. If support for deficit reduction continues to swamp the need for public investment, "intelligent transportation" could be delayed for years.

Nonetheless, the budget-cutting Congress of 1995 appropriated $223 million for the federal share of the program, only a small decrease from the previous year's appropriation. This amounted to a vote of confidence, given the prevailing political climate.

Safer Skies

Compared with surface transportation, the skies are friendlier. "By far the most dangerous part of a trip," said Robert Vaage, "is between the home and the airport."[10] Vaage directed Martin Marietta's work in helping modernize the nation's air traffic management system, a system in which air traffic controllers utilize ground-based radars and computers. Airline accidents are relatively rare, and even rerouting a passenger plane, he observed wryly, makes the front page.

Vaage made his comments shortly before the Federal Aviation Administration (FAA) announced in August 1995 that aging computers would be replaced at five major air traffic control centers in 1997. Yet Martin Marietta, beginning in 1984, had a decade-long contract to lead the systems engineering group in modernizing the nation's airspace management for the FAA. The group was responsible for deciding what equipment to buy for an advanced automation system, procuring it, and making sure it worked well. Systems engineers, radar specialists, computer experts, and meteorologists worked on the $1 billion FAA contract. GE Aerospace, acquired by Martin Marietta, held a separate FAA contract worth $350 million.

Why, then, the air traffic problems in 1995 near Chicago (the world's busiest airport), Washington, Dallas–Fort Worth, Cleveland, and New York after completion of Martin Marietta's contract? And why the loss of radio and radar contact between the air traffic control center that handles flights over northern California and a large part of the Pacific Ocean? The National Air Traffic Controllers Association pinned the blame on the FAA officials who let the contracts and ran them in the 1980s. It was a bungled, uncoordinated effort, said the association's safety director, Mike Connor. He added: "They're using 25-to-30-year-old equipment to keep a vastly expanded system running."[11]

Because of a $1.8-billion cost overrun by the contractors, the Clinton administration FAA had canceled by 1994 the advanced automated system on which Martin Marietta had worked and struggled to catch up through incremental improvements.

Roger Martino, an FAA procurement analyst, claimed the contractors shared the blame with the agency. Most of the problems, he explained, related to the development of computer software, and the contractors often didn't deliver the software on a timely basis.[12] Later, a panel named by the FAA drew up a longer list of problems: old equipment, poor training, leaky roofs, and miscommunication.[13]

As the FAA struggles to upgrade the air traffic system with the help of outside contractors, wind shear—a sudden change in wind speed or direction that is especially dangerous during takeoffs and landings—remains a serious flight hazard. The FAA settled on Doppler weather radar technology as the best means of coping with this problem and commissioned Raytheon to produce forty-seven Doppler radars for major airports throughout the country. Looking like a huge white ball sitting atop a metal tower, Raytheon's Doppler radar is already providing warning of wind shear at airports from San Juan to Phoenix—although some of these radars are sometimes out of commission.

TRW, like Raytheon, is a major defense contractor whose nondefense business with government agencies is expanding. In 1990, the FAA chose TRW to lead a sophisticated multicompany effort to mesh complex navigation and surveillance systems. Three years later, TRW received a contract to improve the FAA's weather-monitoring system, including rapid transmission of Doppler radar data to air controllers.

TRW, along with Hughes and Wilcox Electric, will design the FAA's conversion of the ground-based air traffic control system to one based on satellites in stationary orbit. The new system, to begin phasing in at the turn of the century, will permit planes to make precision approaches into almost any airport with the proper equipment, fly more direct routes, and save fuel.

High-Tech Services

Some smaller—but not necessarily small—high-tech defense firms have prospered by applying their expertise to services for civilian government agencies. Many of these firms are headquartered in the Washington, D.C., suburbs. Unlike the defense giants, they are not laying off personnel; some are adding to their workforce.

BDM International is a prime example. "For BDM, as for other technology services companies," its top officers wrote in 1994, "the 'assets' go home every night. There isn't any production machinery or inventory, nothing being manufactured. Just a lot of very bright men and women using their brainpower to create solutions, design and integrate advanced systems, manage and operate large enterprises, and provide other services and support to literally thousands of clients."[14]

Between 1991 and 1994, BDM's defense work dropped from 70 percent to 57 percent of total sales. In the same period, sales to federal, state, local, and foreign governments rose from 23 percent to 29 percent. Private commercial business was the company's other growth sector.[15] The workforce was 3,000 in 1991, 7,000 in 1995.[16]

BDM manages five Job Corps centers for the Labor Department, providing education and training as well as administrative services. The company serves the Food and Drug Administration by streamlining the process for bringing new drugs to market. Publicly traded corporations can file reports with the Securities and Exchange Commission by computer, thanks to BDM software.

In the nation's capital, BDM has designed the central control system for all rail and bus operations. Contracts valued at more than $100 million have brought new BDM information systems to state governments in Alabama, Iowa, Missouri, and Puerto Rico. Before congressional attempts to change the federal welfare system, BDM was helping Missouri design and implement an integrated, federally certified method of delivering Aid to Families with Dependent Children, food stamps, Medicaid, and other services.

Child welfare is becoming a key focus for the company. In Iowa, BDM is designing and implementing the first fully automated system capable of handling all data on foster care, adoptions, and immunization of children.

In less of a departure from its military-oriented past, BDM has a research contract with the DoT dealing with intelligent highways. The DoT wants to know how an automated highway would affect people. Who would be sued, for example, if the computers failed and caused a pileup? In seeking answers, BDM can put to use the methodology it created for a study it once did for the Pentagon on the weaknesses of Soviet highways.

PRC, another information-technology firm with an alphabet-soup name and 7,000 employees, has lengthy experience with military command, control, communications, and intelligence work. But public safety and criminal justice now constitute a big share of its growth market. Working with the Justice and Treasury departments, PRC is consolidating a computerized system that tracks seized criminal assets throughout the world. For the Drug Enforcement Administration, the company has built an information system that identifies drug and smuggling operations.

PRC estimates that 66 million people in North America live in areas reached by the company's computer-aided dispatch systems that form part of 911 emergency services. Municipal and college campus police departments and fire-fighting and emergency agencies use PRC's products.

For these information-technology companies as well as some of the largest defense contractors, state and local governments are a significant source of potential customers.

Local and State Governments as Markets

A huge expansion of Lockheed Martin's business in the field of child support, which generated "substantial revenues" from a dozen states in 1995, can be expected in the future. So says Ed Gund, the senior vice president for marketing in the company's Information Management Services division.[17] Faced with a host of "deadbeat dads" and mothers on welfare because fathers are absent, the states have been looking for new strategies to bolster collection of child-support payments. The financial scale of the problem has been estimated at wildly diverse levels—ranging from $34 billion in 1993 to $5.8 billion in 1995.[18]

Six years before its merger with Martin Marietta, Lockheed entered the child-support field and became an industry leader. It specialized in helping state governments privatize their collection systems. Today, Lockheed Martin recruits the best child-support experts from government, according to Gund, and asks them to shape less-expensive private collection systems that the company can staff, manage, and operate.

Unlike other projects in which defense contractors shift military technology to civilian uses, Lockheed's involvement in child-support problems arose from its purchase of a commercial company, Datacom Systems. The expertise for dealing with "deadbeat dads" was not developed from experience in building sophisticated weapons systems.

Alliant Techsystems, the nation's largest munitions maker, on the other hand, is trying to transfer into law enforcement some of its imaginative ordnance-based ideas. Aided by a grant from the Pentagon, Alliant is developing equipment that would enable police to instantly distinguish gunfire from other urban noises. Thus alerted, police could reach the scene of violence very fast.

To create an appropriate database, Alliant has recorded D.C. policemen discharging various weapons at an open-air firing range and FBI and U.S. Marine marksmen firing weapons in a mock city at Quantico, Virginia, that more closely resembles an urban environment. A prototype of the system will be tested in Washington, where the company hopes to sell the equipment to the city government.[19]

TRW is another defense conglomerate that targets state and local law enforcement authorities. For the state of California, the company tracks prisoner records and links forensic labs by computer. For the city of Atlanta, TRW provides part of the 911 emergency services.

In the transportation sector, San Francisco is the hub of a multi-county venture that translates military technology into improvements for mass transit users. The partnership of Hughes, Bay Area Rapid Transit (BART), and Morrison Knudsen, a train manufacturer, is converting a battlefield communications system into automatic train controls. The new equipment is expected to track the exact locations of all trains, shorten the intervals between them to one minute, and safely speed up passenger service during rush hour.

Marvin Swensen, Hughes program manager for the joint project, predicts a near-doubling of BART's passenger capacity by 1998, without disruption of service, and a vast increase in reliability. "If BART tried to double the passenger capacity through conventional methods by constructing new lines, tunnels and stations," he said in 1994, "it would probably cost $5 to $10 billion today." If successful on BART's tracks, Swensen said, the system could be used in other urban areas at a savings of billions in construction costs.[20]

Raytheon, a source of both military and civilian products for many years, is making a vigorous effort to sell transportation equipment and services to public agencies. The Dallas Area Rapid Transit has ordered forty light rail vehicles assembled by Raytheon. The company bid on but failed to get a contract to construct one hundred light rail cars for the Massachusetts Bay Transit Authority. Raytheon's most unusual entry in the transportation field is an automated people mover called PRT 2000. The Northeastern Illinois Transportation Regional Authority has chosen Raytheon to develop the system on elevated guideways that will link the suburb of Rosemont with a Chicago transit line. On the way, four-person vehicles will be able to stop at hotels, office buildings, and a convention center.

Architects of the automated system describe its operation this way:

> At each station, a map of the system of lines and stations is posted near a ticket machine similar to a bank cash machine. A patron selects a destination on the network, whereupon a display verifies the destination and indicates the fare, which may be paid by cash, a prepaid card, or a credit card. The machine then dispenses a ticket on which the destination is magnetically encoded. The patron takes the ticket to the loading platform and inserts it into a slot in a stanchion in front of the first empty vehicle in a line of usually three or four vehicles, like a sheltered taxi stand. The ticket is read and the destination is transferred to a microprocessor aboard the vehicle. The door then opens, the patron, or a group of two to four patrons traveling together enter, sit down and close the door.[21]

That signals readiness to depart. A computer senses an opening, and the vehicle merges into traffic and goes nonstop to the destination.

After buying E-Systems, a defense and government electronics firm based in Dallas, Raytheon's business was more than half commercial in 1995.[22] With construction and engineering businesses booming, and with its long track record in high technology, Raytheon has recently found foreign governments to be valued nondefense customers.

Foreign Markets

Among its far-flung construction projects, Raytheon is building a big tank farm and truck-loading facility for the Portuguese state-owned oil company, a barge-mounted gas turbine unit on the coast of the Dominican Republic, and a fertilizer plant in China.

Those projects, however, are dwarfed by a $1.3 billion contract with the Brazilian government. The objective is to protect the Amazon basin, which contains a third of the earth's tropical forests. An international team of contractors led by Raytheon will use radars, sensors, aircraft, and telecommunications to preserve forests, combat illegal mining and drug trafficking, protect indigenous tribes, and monitor traffic on the Amazon. The project is known as SIVAM. The Clinton administration spared no effort to land the contract for Raytheon. SIVAM will continue until 2002, becoming in the process one of the world's most ambitious environmental projects.

On the other side of the globe, Alliant Techsystems is engaged in low-tech joint ventures with the governments of Ukraine and Belarus. The job there is to dismantle artillery shells and sell the metal for scrap on the world market.

Raytheon may have the biggest foreign project and Alliant the lowest tech, but Hughes gets points for the best-named. Hughes's Smog Dog, a remote sensor system being tested in Toronto, sniffs out tailpipe emissions. Pollutants in the exhaust are measured, first as the vehicle passes by three Smog Dogs, then as it is driven onto a kind of treadmill. This mechanism analyzes exhaust as the vehicle accelerates, cruises, and slows down. Hughes has also sold the Czech Republic a fixed wireless network that will serve 50,000 telephone subscribers in the Prague area.

Air traffic control systems appear to be one of the hottest items in nondefense sales to foreign governments. Hughes has logged sales to Canada, China, Germany, Indonesia, Russia, and Switzerland. Raytheon has comparable contracts with China, Germany, Hong Kong, India, the Netherlands, Norway, and Oman. Likewise, Lockheed Martin's air traffic control contracts span the globe.

Clearly, defense companies, some of which already had a track record in selling to civilian government agencies, perform much useful work for public authorities in the United States and around the world. That work represents a significant growth market. With two exceptions, however—Raytheon's Amazon basin project and the FAA's long-term modernization—the dollar value of the individual nonmilitary contracts is lower than that of most weapons-production contracts. Therefore, defense contractors are likely to see work for the civilian side of government as a supplement to but not an alternative to their business with the Pentagon.

5 Trying to Enter Commercial Markets

French Guiana is usually not considered a trendsetter in any league. But the launch of a Hughes Aircraft space satellite from a remote site in Kourou, French Guiana, on December 17, 1993, could be considered a post–Cold War landmark. The satellite launch, the first of three, was the start of a high-tech commercial challenge to the cable TV industry by a major American defense company. Hughes, which had provided radar to the B-2 bomber and night-vision equipment to troops in the Gulf War, was making a bold pitch to consumers through DirecTV, telecasting up to 175 channels via satellite, with exceptionally clear digitized pictures for the viewers.

Hughes teamed up with RCA in this joint venture. RCA makes the eighteen-inch satellite dish that can be fixed to the side of a house and the electronics box that sits atop the TV set. Sony and AT&T later joined the Hughes-RCA partnership.

DirecTV in particular and telecommunications in general represent one of the two main paths to commercialization staked out by Hughes. The other is the transfer of military technologies into General Motors (GM) vehicles. A wholly owned subsidiary of GM, Hughes Aircraft evolved into Hughes Electronics Corporation in 1995. A division that is still called Hughes Aircraft handles the company's military production.

Once Hughes management made the decision to diversify in 1988 because it saw military spending heading downward, GM capital and credit helped speed the shift into commercial work. Without a firm commitment from top Hughes management, however, the long-time defense contractor would not have been able to manage the shift by money alone. Malcolm Currie, former Hughes chairman, and C. Michael Armstrong, his successor, moved decisively to enter commercial markets while keeping the company a strong player in defense. Hughes trained key supervisory employees in the basics of commercial markets, without trying to transform the culture of the entire decades-old defense corporation.

Ahead of Schedule

Hughes had roughly 85 percent defense and other large government business in 1985. The company is wary of using percentage goals today, but in 1993 Robert Dankanyin, its then–vice president for diversification, said: "With the growth we project, we will have more non-defense work than defense work by the year 2000."[1] By the end of 1995, only 40 percent of Hughes's business was generated by its defense and aerospace division.[2]

By 2000, Hughes and its partners hope to reach 10 million DirecTV subscribers. There were over 700,000 in DirecTV's first thirteen months and 1.2 million by the end of 1995, with an international market just opening. The advertising seen by potential customers focuses on RCA, but Hughes as the creator and organizer stands to reap big profits if the consortium reaches its sales goal.

Armstrong originally believed that DirecTV would be most attractive in rural areas not reached by cable TV. DirecTV's sponsors have noted, however, that almost half of the first subscribers were dissatisfied cable users.[3] Many of the crossover customers live in cities and suburbs. "Satellite has become the first true national competitor to cable," according to Bob Sherman, publisher of *Satellite Business News*, quoted by the *Washington Post*'s enthusiastically pro-DirecTV television critic, Tom Shales.[4]

DirecTV offers subscribers a long menu of recent movies, sports, and special interest programming, much of it pay-per-view. Customers cannot receive local stations, however. Subscribers who vow over the phone that they are not cable TV users and cannot receive acceptable pictures over the air from their local stations can add the major networks to the menu, for a fee.

No doubt the digitized pictures of DirecTV are a great technological leap forward. And no doubt the range of entertainment offered viewers surpasses anything previously beamed to or wired into American living rooms. But beyond popular entertainment, the 175 channels of DirecTV are unlikely to make a measurable difference in improving the generally poor quality of American television. Nonetheless, Hughes has to get high marks for taking the big financial risk involved in shifting into the unknown world of broadcast television and challenging the cable owners.

There were fewer risks involved in selling commercial communications satellites, which Hughes had been doing for years. The worldwide desire for rapid communication provided Hughes with a booming market. The company sold satellite network equipment and cellular phone networks to businesses and governments in scores of countries in the 1990s.

Head in the Sky, Feet on the Ground

In its DirecTV venture, Hughes made use of its experience manufacturing military satellites. With its more earthbound commercial products, intended for GM vehicles, Hughes also tapped into its store of military technology. The "head-up display" (HUD), which electronically projects a car's speed and other information onto windshields, was first used on fighter planes. Pilots in combat could see the information they needed on the plane's windshield without having to look down at the control panel.

In addition to some Pontiac Bonnevilles and Oldsmobile Cutlasses that incorporate the HUD, police and fire departments are using it to project vital information onto windshields while their vehicles head into action. GM sold nearly 140,000 vehicles with HUDs through the end of 1995.[5]

Radar sensors that Hughes made for the military have been transformed into a warning system for school buses. Called Forewarn, the system alerts the drivers to moving objects in front of or underneath a bus when it is stopped. Hughes has also teamed up with Texas Instruments to market Nightsight, a six-pound thermal vision camera that permits law-enforcement personnel, boaters, and private security personnel to detect people and objects in the dark.

The shift from high-cost military production to affordable commercial production has not been easy. The HUD for a warplane, for example, cost $100,000; it had to be produced for cars at only $200. This estimate comes from Howard G. Wilson, a retired GM vice president who became the link between GM and Hughes after the latter was absorbed by the auto giant. Wilson says the transfer of radar from planes to school buses was even more challenging. Military radars cost over $1 million apiece; they cost a few hundred dollars for autos and buses.[6]

Saving the Tucson Plant

Robert Walkup dealt with the challenge at Hughes's Tucson, Arizona, plant, an immense former IBM building. The Tucson plant, which makes sophisticated tactical missiles, was in danger of going under in the early 1990s until Hughes brought thousands of ex–General Dynamics missile workers from California following a corporate buyout. Arizona helped lure Hughes to Tucson with tax-incentive legislation known locally as "the Hughes bill."[7] At the time of threatened shutdown, Hughes management asked Walkup to help save the factory. He began to explore the possibility of transferring some of the technology used on tactical missiles into civilian products.

Knowing that GM had an electrical vehicle program, Walkup asked defense engineers at the Tucson plant to design components for an electric car. They did. But the projected cost reached astronomical levels. Walkup says it took three years to change the defense engineers' cost-is-not-our-concern mind-set into one geared to consumers in the marketplace.[8]

Currently in charge of commercial operations and government relations at the 8,000-worker Tucson plant, Walkup has missile engineers utilize their slack time to try to commercialize military technology. The results have been promising, if not yet profitable. The technology that permits the Maverick missile to "see" where it is going can help the Post Office read handwritten addresses. The same system can help insurance companies read handwritten claims forms and enable law-enforcement agencies to compare local fingerprints with a huge database of prints from around the country.

Hughes has a contract with the city of Tucson and the University of Arizona to design a system that would scan all vehicles at intersections, transmitting data to determine the most efficient traffic flow. Walkup estimates that there could be a 40 percent reduction in the length of time drivers remain behind the wheel, as well as a drop in air pollution.[9] This Tucson project is a small local variation on the futuristic intelligent transportation system outlined in Chapter 4.

Another Hughes-Tucson commercial product, the motion detection radar system, almost made history in Waco, Texas. The radar system's three-dimensional version permits the operator to look through walls and see if anything is moving on the other side. The Justice Department had one during the government's blockade of and attack on the Branch Davidian compound in Waco, but it decided against using an untested system.[10] Local police departments are using less-advanced versions.

Jobs Still Disappearing

Despite the business potential of these Hughes products, even with commercial success they will do little to increase employment. Once designed in Tucson, these products use components that come largely off the shelf. Some Hughes employees work on computer software for these products, and others have been added to the sales force. But few are needed to manufacture the new goods coming from the Tucson plant.

At the national level, employment at Hughes fell from 93,000 to 78,000 between 1991 and 1993 even as the company diversified.[11] In subsequent years, the workforce at Hughes began slowly to expand. Job loss remains the biggest problem in the transition to a less-militarized economy, even among the companies with the greatest potential for commercial success.

Hughes Electronics now includes five major divisions: automotive electronics, telecommunications and space, defense electronics, DirecTV, and commercial technologies. Any serious upturn in future jobs there could depend in large part on the investment of the parent company, GM, in electric vehicles.

GM and Electric Vehicles

GM has specialized in producing the power systems for electric vehicles and the equipment to charge them and keep them running. GM electronic drive systems for buses are in use in four California locations and in Chattanooga, Tennessee. A two-year nationwide field test involving over a thousand consumers in twelve cities began in 1994. The consumers test-drove GM's Impact electric vehicles for two- or four-week periods. At the same time, GM, Chrysler, and Ford have opposed government mandates to require that a given fraction of vehicles be pollution-free by a certain date.

"Detroit," Jessica Mathews of the Council on Foreign Relations wrote in January 1995, "wants to keep a technological competition between conventional and electric cars from ever occurring, by keeping the struggle political, so it has been working to undo California's requirement that beginning in 1998 a rising fraction of new cars be 'zero emission vehicles' and to prevent other states from following suit."[12]

Why would an automotive giant that is investing in the new technology—a technology that is the only near-term alternative capable of seriously cutting air pollution and demand for oil—oppose the very mandates that would boost the electric car industry? Former GM vice president Wilson, now a consultant, told me in 1994 that the corporation wants the market, not the government, to drive production. He spoke of uncertainty over the price of electric cars and predicted that they won't become competitive until at least the year 2005.[13]

Yet GM surprised the industry by announcing the introduction of an electric car in 1996, powered at first by traditional lead-acid batteries. A more efficient nickel metal-hydride battery manufactured by Energy Conversion Devices in Michigan will soon become the alternative fuel. (See Chapter 10.)

Whatever the outcome of GM's entry into the electric vehicle market, Hughes remains the largest defense contractor making a major effort to become a robust diversified enterprise, part commercial, part military. A handful of other big contractors, such as TRW and Raytheon, have significantly increased their nondefense sales, but they started the process with much more commercial business than did Hughes.

A defense electronics firm whose technologies can be readily adapted to commercial use, Hughes is in a better position to shift gears than are companies that build military aircraft, tanks, and naval ships. There are very limited civilian uses for submarines and tanks, and building fighter planes under the heavy hand of military specifications doesn't prepare the manufacturer for life in commercial global markets.

The Bath Iron Works

There is one exception: the Bath Iron Works, a key naval shipyard and the largest private employer in Maine. The Navy has been the shipyard's only customer since the 1980s, and BIW has worked hard to learn how to compete for commercial business around the world.

After a century of building half its ships for private customers, half for the Navy, BIW was pushed into total defense-dependence by two decisions of the Reagan administration. First, President Reagan abandoned subsidies for commercial shipbuilding. Second, he set the goal of a huge six-hundred-ship navy. The six-hundred-ship navy was never to be, and the end of the Cold War found BIW in a bind. It was burdened with a heavy fixed overhead from big military programs like the construction of Aegis destroyers. It had no civilian work. And foreign shipyards had a near-lock on global commercial shipbuilding.

Led by its progressive president and CEO, Duane "Buzz" Fitzgerald, BIW decided to reinvent itself. While continuing to build complex, high-cost destroyers, the shipyard tried to relearn the skills of building lower-cost, simpler commercial ships. BIW won a two-year matching-fund grant from the U.S. Technology Reinvestment Program to study commercial shipbuilding abroad and bring the know-how home to Bath.

Internally, BIW management signed a pioneering collective bargaining agreement with its production and clerical employees that established joint decisionmaking at every level of the shipyard. The contract, ratified in 1994, provides for joint union and management teams and committees to plan work and iron out problems. Fitzgerald said that problems that became grievances in the past are now dealt with on the spot by these joint teams.[14] John "Stoney" Dionne, president of International Association of Machinists (IAM) Local S6, which represents 5,700 BIW production workers, explained that management still assigns work and supervisors help bring in the supplies workers need. But "the workers determine how it's done, with less supervision."[15]

The agreement guarantees no involuntary layoffs for three years, a rare commitment in either defense or commercial industry. The contract also provides for continuous upgrading of employee skills. Within a few months of contract ratification, 99 percent of Local S6 members had agreed to expand their existing skills as carpenters, ship riggers, and so on, and 90 percent had committed to learning new skills.[16]

Brains as Well as Brawn

American management, says Buzz Fitzgerald, tended to assume that all the wisdom comes from the top, all the doing from the bottom. At BIW, on the other hand, management understands that workers have brains as well as brawn. "Our joint goals," says Fitzgerald, "are to emphasize the importance of people, save jobs, and maximize efficiency."[17]

The agreement wouldn't have happened, according to Fitzgerald, without joint training. Even before the contract was signed, some forty union and management representatives attended joint two-day sessions on conflict resolution. They agreed on ground rules for the negotiation. Later, all management and union representatives named to the joint committees were trained together.[18]

The new forms of cooperation at BIW also benefited from constructive leadership on both sides of the labor-management divide. The IAM, parent union of Local S6, for years has been the most defense-dependent labor organization in the United States. By the end of 1994, the IAM had lost 300,000–400,000 members, many of them laid off by defense industry. Since the 1970s, the IAM has also been the union most committed to planning for defense conversion. When IAM's president, George Kourpias, met Buzz Fitzgerald at a 1993 conference, the latter stressed the importance of union and management partnerships. Kourpias asked the officers of IAM Local S6 if Fitzgerald was serious. When assured that he was, Kourpias replied, "If he means it, let's go."[19]

Fitzgerald later invited Kourpias to address the entire workforce at BIW's three sites. Kourpias encouraged workers to pursue the partnership concept. It was the only time a corporate CEO had ever suspended operations to allow Kourpias to address IAM members throughout a workplace.[20]

"Workplace of the Future"

Kourpias calls BIW "the workplace of the future." The IAM had been suspicious of most corporate "total quality management" efforts, Kourpias says, because many were designed to weaken unions. But he promises full IAM cooperation with any company that is, like BIW, serious about making the union "full partners."[21] The IAM expects to merge with the United Auto Workers and the United Steelworkers by the year 2000.

Through the two-year grant from the Technology Reinvestment Program, BIW is also cooperating with a different set of partners. Working with Japanese and Finnish shipyards and two American shipping lines to learn and apply the latest commercial shipbuilding processes, BIW expects to produce two new ship designs. One, a cargo ship, would carry cars in one direction and refrigerated food on the return trip. The second would carry trucks and cars. Great American Lines and American Automar, partners in the grant, could purchase the newly designed ships.

Another matching grant, from the government's Maritech program, will enable BIW and GE Engines of Ohio to design a futuristic monohull, a long, thin ship with a wave-piercing bow. It would be able to carry cargoes or people at higher speeds than today's vessels can achieve.

Can Hughes and BIW Make It?

Can BIW and Hughes Electronics adapt to the rigors of the post–Cold War marketplace? These two firms are mavericks among the community of larger defense contractors that see their future mainly as suppliers to the Pentagon.

BIW clearly has a much tougher struggle. The shipyard was owned primarily by Prudential Insurance Company before its purchase by General Dynamics in 1995. At the end of 1994, BIW was worth $310 million less than what Prudential and its partners paid for it in 1986.[22]

The shipyard, unlike Hughes, has no technologies available for transfer to commercial products. Moreover, building complex destroyers is very different from building cargo ships. Under military specifications, it takes at least six times as long to build a destroyer as it does to build a commercial cargo ship. BIW's workforce had shrunk from 12,000 in 1990 to 8,700 by the time the labor-management contract was ratified in 1994.[23]

With its potential South Korean competitors tightening their grip on the global shipbuilding market, BIW will have a tough time translating new ship designs into profitable commercial ships. Another naval shipyard, Newport News, has sold four commercial tankers, but it lost $14 million on the first two. The Avondale, Louisiana, shipyard may turn a profit on tankers, Buzz Fitzgerald reported, but it had not "strayed so far" from commercial shipbuilding.[24] The more defense-dependent a shipyard, the harder it is to shift gears.

General Dynamics, known primarily for stripping down to its submarine and tank business and rejecting commercial work before the purchase of BIW, has agreed to allow the shipyard to pursue commercialization—if Buzz Fitzgerald and his management team can make a dollars-and-cents case for it. General Dynamics will also respect the labor-management contract.[25]

For its part, Hughes has the strength of GM's abundant assets behind its efforts to break into commercial markets. Among these assets is the existence of automotive outlets for defense technologies adapted by Hughes. On the other hand, Hughes has nothing comparable to BIW's involvement of employees in decisionmaking, certainly one of BIW's greatest strengths. Joint decisionmaking in the shipyard began to improve the company's productivity within a year after it began.

Both Hughes and BIW benefit from the strong leadership of their corporate chiefs. Armstrong, who came to Hughes after a long career at IBM, has championed competitiveness and especially the DirecTV challenge to the cable TV industry. At BIW, Buzz Fitzgerald's support for cooperation with the workers has led to greatly improved labor-management relations. It has also led to frequent joint appearances with Stoney Dionne. These appearances have been dubbed "the Buzz and Stoney Show." Dionne joshes the balding Fitzgerald, asserting that if their closeness is to continue, Fitzgerald will have to emulate his own biker style: Grow a beard, wear an earring, and "ride a Harley."

Buzz Fitzgerald may not ride a Harley motorcycle, but neither is he a typical defense contractor. In addition to advocating partnerships with the union and foreign shipyards, Fitzgerald publicly embraced the Nuclear Weapons Freeze Campaign in the 1980s. "Even though I didn't foresee the downfall of communism," he says, "I thought the Cold War would end because you can't have arms you can't use. We couldn't afford it. We squandered the most important security of all: financial."[26]

The Cold War did end, but most of the defense companies that seriously hunted new commercial business—with the main exceptions of Hughes and BIW—were the smaller subcontractors that showed much more flexibility than the bigger firms they supplied.

6 Flexibility: Key to Smaller Defense Firms' Survival

John Hoops, director of a Massachusetts agency that helps firms and workers hit by Pentagon procurement cuts, visited a family-owned machine shop in 1991. The company, in central Massachusetts, was 100 percent defense dependent. Hoops told a congressional subcommittee:

> This company had been in the military business for a number of years and was doing quite well; however, the owners fully realized that all they could do was military sales. Its engineering department was geared to writing specifications according to standard military specifications, many of which are not used in commercial production. The company had no commercial sales strategy and did not retain manufacturers representatives. . . . The company president showed me a part that was almost done but had been held for 10 months for a clarification on a detail. The president was not concerned, however, because he had already been paid for about 90 percent of the job.[1]

Unfortunately, Hoops's testimony accurately described the culture in which many smaller defense firms have operated: mil specs guiding every production detail; ignorance of commercial markets; progress payments from the Defense Department regardless of progress in production. As the GAO recognized in 1994, "Defense firms have historically depended on progress payments for financing and lacked experience preparing business plans needed to obtain financing from banks or venture capital firms."[2] Hardly the preparation needed for the tough realities of commercial competition.

Aerospace Technologies, a small Fort Worth defense contractor, decided that to prepare for the world of commerce it had to replace much of its personnel and build a new company. "Most people in the plant had a military products background," explained CEO James Shortt. "Even some of our key managers didn't like the new atmosphere. Some just couldn't stand the pressure of working for commercial companies, making deliveries on time."[3]

Nonetheless, many smaller defense firms have shown flexibility in adapting to commercial markets. Those that reinvent themselves account for most of the successes, however tentative, in defense conversion. Survival demands no less. Bigger companies can afford to downsize and still retain access to credit, a sizable if diminished share of military contracts, and healthy profits. Most smaller firms don't have the resources demanded by first downsizing and then trying to rebuild. Diversifying into commercial production becomes a case of sink or swim.

The Frisby Success Story

In the early 1980s, family-owned Frisby Airborne Hydraulics, having served for decades as a subcontractor to Long Island's Grumman and Fairchild-Republic defense aircraft companies, was 95 percent military. In 1995, it was 70 percent commercial.[4] How did they manage the turnaround?

At a symposium in 1981, the firm's president, Jeff Frisby, heard a talk by Tom Peters, author of *In Search of Excellence* and other books on modern management. Jeff Frisby told me in a TV interview: "He basically lit a fire under me that made me believe those crazy ideas that I had been having for years were not lunacy but were, in fact, workable management philosophy. . . . Actually communicating with your people . . . talking to customers and going out of your way to satisfy them, creating a sense of ownership in the company by your employees."[5]

Jeff Frisby and his brother Greg, the company's CEO, slashed a layer of management in the hundred-person plant and brought employees into the decision-making process. "What we wanted to do," Greg Frisby said, "was to get back to as basic an operation as we could, having people who actually work the machines tell us how best to make the changes necessary to bring the cost down on the job."[6] Since then, employees have been meeting several times a week on shop floor problems and reaching a consensus on how they should perform a job.

Referring to a discharged foreman, veteran production worker Wayne Lester commented, "We just had a general running the place, and we had to do it the general's way. Well, unfortunately, the general didn't always know what he was doing. Any business, no matter how small or how big, you have to go to the people who are doing the work and get better ideas."[7]

Now, in addition to their traditional work, machinists perform inspections, and engineering and manufacturing personnel work with customers to design new, cost-effective products. A profit-sharing plan has further boosted the employees' sense of commitment. Costs, debt, and the amount of scrap generated by manufacturing processes have declined dramatically.

At first, Frisby Airborne searched for new military customers. But as the two young executives recognized early signs of the downward trend in military procurement, they set their gaze on long-term commercial relationships. Their first such venture was with Boeing, making parts for its commercial projects. Gradually, Frisby Airborne branched out into other fields, sometimes developing new technologies, sometimes applying existing ones. The company produced a valve for the oil industry; thermal items such as cold weather boots, firefighters' outfits, and a cooling mechanism for computers; environmental products such as an advanced water filtration system and a process for cleaning up oil-contaminated soil. Most of the technologies used in the firm's varied products have both commercial and military applications.

Frisby Airborne has expanded from its Long Island home base to facilities in North and South Carolina to accommodate a 30-percent growth in a two-year period. A spin-off company in North Carolina, Frisby Technologies, now adapts the company's technologies to commercial uses.

Yet for all the progress, in 1993 Frisby Airborne had to lay off employees—25 percent of the workforce—for the first time in over half a century.[8] The layoffs were due to a lack of working capital needed for its expanding commercial contracts, where progress payments were no longer forthcoming. This lack is one of the major hurdles in the path of small and medium-sized defense firms that seek to shift into commercial work, a subject we shall return to.

M/A-Com: "Rebuilding the Airplane
While in Flight"

Young women in white coats, many of them recent immigrants from Vietnam and other Southeast Asian countries, peer into double microscopes at their workstations. At M/A-Com's large modern building on the outskirts of Lowell, Massachusetts, they are turning out wireless products for everyday use: phones that allow sunbathers to make calls from the beach; tags on garments that speed up store inventories; equipment to prevent collisions on intelligent highways.

In 1989, most of the workers at M/A-Com (pronounced MAY-com) Microelectronics Division were producing components for missile guidance systems. As a subcontractor to Hughes, Raytheon, and other major defense companies, M/A-Com's business was 95 percent military. By the end of 1994, over 60 percent was commercial.[9]

James Fallon, who is shepherding the transition, compared the process to "rebuilding the airplane while in flight."[10] Management devoted much time to reengineering the workforce and transforming the company's military-industrial culture. The process began with brown paper sheets plastered on walls. The sheets listed everything individual employees did in the old culture. Under the new system, engineers were taught to design for individual consumers and workers upgraded their skills. Eight separate divisions were moved into a single building. "Virtual partnerships"—ad hoc employee groupings—were formed, project by project.

Fallon likes images. He has another one for M/A-Com's commitment to change: "We went to the New World," he said, "and burnt the boats." Then the company went around the world to find customers and build a sales force that enables it to compete globally. Its biggest growth is abroad, especially in Japan and Sweden.

M/A-Com paid for most of these changes with its own money. Later it applied for and received six research awards—an unprecedented number—from the federal Technology Reinvestment Project (TRP). One was as prime contractor, the leader in a joint research project. With industrial and university partners, M/A-Com is re-searching commercial and military uses of microwave technologies for wireless communications and air transportation safety. It is also engaged in setting up partnerships for modern manufacturing in New England, and it is cofounder of an engineering academy and a consortium for electromagnetics research.

The company had 4,200 employees in 1989, 3,500 five years later.[11] M/A-Com is not a small business by ordinary standards, but compared to the giants that dominate military production it qualifies as "smaller." Like virtually all defense contractors shifting away from near-total dependence on the Pentagon, M/A-Com will try to keep some military business. Still, it appears well able to compete in the worldwide commercial marketplace. It helps to have topflight veterans at the controls. M/A-Com's board chairman is Thomas Vanderslice, former CEO of the Apollo space project and a protégé of GE's Jack Welch, a leader in corporate restructuring.

Gull Electronics:
Breaking Down the Walls

It took six months to sell the concept of low-cost commercial com-petition to employees of Parker Hannifin Corporation's Gull Elec-tronic Systems Division on Long Island. Half of the company's work in the late 1980s consisted of building cockpit instruments for fighter planes. But Gull had delivery problems. The components it made for its biggest customers, major defense contractors, often did not arrive on time. As a result, Gull lost its supplier status with Boe-ing. Gull was bedeviled by engineering and other problems as well.[12]

When management moved to promote commercial sales and transform working arrangements, employees were initially confused. "But we communicated well, in advance," said Gull's vice president John Stadelmann.[13] Three to four employee meetings a year were just the beginning. Gull broke down the walls among departments, creating new teams and work groups that mixed engineers, produc-tion workers, and other employees. Each product line has an engi-neer on the design team, plus business contract administrators and another engineer who knows how to market. Team leaders are chosen by management and an industrial psychologist after interviews with potential candidates. The supervisory role of engineers has been ended, with no cut in pay. Almost all production workers have been formally certified as inspectors, and all employees now inspect their own work.

Today there are fewer bureaucratic layers at Gull Electronics, and management invites comments from everyone in advance of plantwide "communications meetings."

Like M/A-Com, Gull looked abroad for new opportunities. Most of the $94 million in new business the firm won during the year beginning in fall 1993 was both commercial and international. Gull sold flight inspection systems to Brazil (as a subcontractor to Raytheon in its Amazon basin project), Japan, Canada, and Israel and explored sales to Greece, Thailand, and Russia.

Marketing began with in-house talent. An employee who speaks some Hebrew became the salesman to Israel. Team members who look for markets in Japan read up on that country's culture, and a few have learned some Japanese. Gull has hired local agents in order to open doors in South Korea, but the regular company staff handles the actual marketing there.

Buoyed by international commercial sales, Gull expects to reduce the military share to 25–30 percent of its total business.

In the early 1990s, when its sales were dropping and before it undertook sweeping changes, Gull talked with the New York State agency that runs the Industrial Effectiveness Program. The state brought in consultants on a cost-sharing basis and arranged for a five-year reduction in the firm's electricity bills with the local utility company. The consultants were particularly useful in organizing worker-training and blueprint-reading courses.

These initiatives are paying off for Gull. Speed in filling orders is the key to reducing costs and increasing sales. The firm's motto is "twice the speed, half the cost." By the end of 1994, said John Stadelmann, Gull employees had reduced by a third the time from customer's order to delivery. This opened the way to new business. Sales per employee more than doubled, costs are down, and quality is up.

Gull Electronics is freeing itself from dependence on Pentagon purchases, but it has not escaped the all-too-familiar penalty of lost jobs. Employment plummeted from 1,250 in 1988 to 470 in 1994. Nevertheless, as a result of growth in commercial sales, the company expects to increase its workforce by 5–10 percent annually for the foreseeable future—a rare prospect for American manufacturers.

Ace Clearwater Enterprises:
Director of Change

Kellie Dodson and Gary Johnson, a young married couple, serve as president and vice president, respectively, of Ace Clearwater Enterprises in Torrance, California. A small job shop that filled orders for components for the aerospace industry, Ace Clearwater began in the late 1980s to replace its military business (35–45 percent at the time) with commercial work. To smooth the transition, the position of "director of change" was created, and King Lum was chosen to fill it.

With an MBA in marketing and finance and lengthy experience as an industrial engineer, project engineer, and business manager, Lum was ideal for the job. First, he found out what tasks the workers performed and then determined how much of their work was necessary. What followed was similar to the "breaking down the walls" approach at Gull Electronics, but it was described by a different image: "taking down fences." Work cells were organized with a mix of production workers, engineers, estimators, and contract administrators. Employees received training in new skills.

Initially, workers were resentful, feeling they were being asked to do more without extra pay. Later, they felt a sense of ownership. Today, suggestions flow from staff meetings and the shop floor, where work cells meet daily. The meetings have helped the company chart its new direction.[14]

Ace has adopted a strategy it calls "gain sharing" to raise productivity. A bonus based on the value of shipments per man-hour is awarded to all employees; management decides when the bonus is due. The first one was paid in 1995, after a quarterly jump in productivity of 13 percent.

Ace found new customers and reduced military sales to 10–15 percent of its business by 1994. The company has added a design capability and is trying to differentiate itself from the thousands of other small job shops that dot the industrial landscape of southern California. There have been no layoffs. A few new hires brought the workforce to 185 in 1995. Job applicants go through a series of interviews, including at least one group interview with prospective peers and subordinates.

Can Partnerships Prevail?

Many of the missiles and bombers at the heart of the U.S.-Soviet arms race were made in California. With barely a pause after World War II, the state's profitable defense industries provided hundreds of thousands of well-paid jobs, in the process creating new bedroom communities, opening housing and employment opportunities to minorities, and generally fueling an economic boom. That boom peaked in the 1980s as California's former governor presided in Washington over record levels of military spending.

The decline began in 1988–1989. All of the major aerospace contractors, largely concentrated in southern California, laid off thousands of workers. Contractors moved some of these defense jobs to low-wage areas in the South and Southwest. And when the big defense companies sneezed, their smaller suppliers caught cold. By the end of 1991, California had lost 60,000 aerospace jobs.[15] The downturn in military procurement was an important contributor to the state's serious and lengthy recession. Los Angeles County, particularly hard hit, lost almost 11 percent of its job base.[16] As of 1994, the job loss in California aerospace had reached 198,000.[17]

In defense-dependent southern California, District Lodge 725 of the IAM suffered a membership drop from 10,000 to 1,900.[18] The union, which represented the production workers at HR Textron, a defense subsidiary of the $9-billion Textron Corporation, in 1992 asked the firm to machine metal parts for a showcase electric car being built by a consortium. HR Textron, whose workforce had dwindled from 1,300 to 750, agreed. From that limited collaboration blossomed a broad partnership, encouraged by Congressman Howard Berman (D.–Calif.), encompassing large and small defense companies, the union, universities, and a national laboratory.[19]

Those various elements worked together through the Regional Advanced Manufacturing Project (RAMP), anchored at HR Textron. RAMP was set up as a three-year program to develop new ways of transferring military technologies to commercial industries. Thirty of HR Textron's subcontractors, some of them minority owned, signed on. Hughes Aircraft agreed to share certain of its patents that had potential commercial use. The Los Alamos National Laboratory and the Allied Signal Kansas City plant agreed to share technology for environmentally clean, advanced manufacturing. California State University undertook to provide consulting services for small businesses and to develop a curriculum for a training center in a Los Angeles enterprise zone. Glendale Community College was to handle the training.

IAM District Lodge 725 participated in the planning process from the outset. In addition, the union received a Department of Labor (DoL) grant for a pilot project at HR Textron that would retrain 118 workers. Productivity gains traceable to the training succeeded in salvaging some thirty-five jobs at HR Textron.[20] The company is acutely aware of the workers' need for training. It has found shop floor, engineering, and purchasing employees, both foreign- and American-born, who cannot read or write. Some can't read blueprints. The company will provide computer-based training, in which the employee does not have to publicly admit a lack of skills.[21]

The broader partnership, however, which was to reorient a whole train of HR Textron's subcontractors, is shaky and may dissolve. And the transfer of military technologies into commercial products may die for lack of supplementary funding. Despite grant proposals to federal agencies, backed by local members of Congress, RAMP has received no government money. A Republican-controlled Congress made that prospect even more remote. The organizers of RAMP find themselves unable to fund this ambitious project without some outside help. The shift of key HR Textron personnel to other posts has further weakened RAMP. Thus, a promising partnership of southern California defense industry, labor, and universities may become a casualty of underfunding and lack of follow-through.

The failure of such a hopeful project would remind us that the road to defense conversion is strewn with obstacles. The process, once begun, can be reversed. In fact, a study of defense industry in the Los Angeles region found that dependence on military sales *increased* from 58.8 percent to 64.9 percent in the first post–Cold War years of 1991–1993.[22]

Small Firms Find Banks Wary

One of the biggest obstacles small defense firms face in entering commercial markets is a lack of ready money. "The banks are not there for you," Greg Frisby said in 1993 as he joined with fellow

Long Island subcontractors to solve the problem of working capital.[23] In testimony before a House subcommittee the following year, Frisby estimated that $500 million in long-term commercial contracts had been lost or passed up by 125 small and medium-sized Long Island defense firms because of lack of capital.[24]

These Long Island firms were accustomed to the pay-as-you-work progress payments of military procurement, whereas commercial contracts typically pay upon delivery. Long Island companies had received $5.28 billion in Defense Department contracts in 1985; that figure dropped to $2.86 billion in 1992.[25] The banks, according to Greg Frisby, were reluctant to fill the gap because of defense industry's "layoffs, mergers, and thousand-dollar hammers."[26] Frequently, the same banks that had readily lent to companies engaged in military production found their new commercial ventures too risky. A spokesman for Business Executives for National Security (BENS) suggested additional reasons for the banks' skittishness: skepticism about the market savvy of defense firms and fear of future downturns in commercial aerospace.[27]

The Defense Department in 1994 released a national survey of small defense firms' strategies for dealing with a shrinking military market. The study, prepared by the Logistics Management Institute, found that firms trying to enter commercial markets reported significantly more difficulty obtaining financing for product development than did the overall group of respondents. Firms trying to go commercial also had trouble securing credit for market assessments, marketing, and retooling.[28]

The solution, says Jon Kutler, a former Navy officer, lies in setting up a venture capital fund, with the federal government putting up 10–15 percent and private investors the rest.[29] Kutler heads Quarterdeck Investment Partners, a venture capital company that seeks to transfer appropriate technologies from major defense contractors to small, start-up commercial firms. Since the Defense Department "has already spent $30-, $40-, $50 million developing that technology and you can acquire it basically at no cost," Kutler said in 1994, "it becomes very economical to do that."[30] The transfer of technology can be effected through licensing arrangements.

Quarterdeck has invested in a number of such small companies. One in Florida, for example, uses antisubmarine warfare technology in the manufacture of devices for underwater viewing. The device can be used to search for toxic materials dumped in the ocean—or buried treasure.

Kutler believes a venture capital fund should lend money not only for research and development but also to finance acquisitions that could help small firms grow. The 10–15 percent share from the federal government, he suggests, should not be Defense Department money.[31]

A variation on Kutler's proposal came in 1994 from Eric Pages, then working for BENS. He urged creation of a privately run Fund for Defense Conversion that would provide low-interest, long-term loans or loan guarantees, with the government as initial investor; the recipients would be required to put up a third of the capital. "Fortunately, the creation of financing mechanisms does not require massive funding or new government bureaucracies," Pages said. "By leveraging private funds and utilizing existing financial institutions, we can create new forms of public-private partnerships that create new jobs and new companies."[32]

Congress did vote $50 million for a loan guarantee program in fiscal 1995 in an attempt to generate $2 billion in loans to defense companies. Under the program, run by the Small Business Administration (SBA), $30 million in loan guarantees would be reserved for smaller firms. Through leverage, the $30 million is expected to raise about $1 billion.[33]

On Long Island, Greg Frisby and colleagues in more than a hundred small and medium-sized defense companies organized the Aerospace and Defense Diversification Alliance in Peacetime Transition (ADDAPT). In 1995, ADDAPT began to set up a Small Business Investment Corporation, under another SBA program, with venture capital provided by local companies, banks, and ADDAPT members and with matching funds from the federal government. An independent board makes the lending decisions.

Broad Range of Commercial Efforts

The small and medium-sized defense firms whose initiatives are summarized here are hardly the only businesses engaged in vigorous efforts to break into commercial markets. There are many others throughout the military-industrial sector. They range in size from Cletronics in northeastern Ohio, with 36 employees, to AM General in South Bend, Indiana, with a workforce of 1,700. One in between is Sonalysts in Connecticut, which converted its facility for making Navy sonar into state-of-the-art recording studios for music and the movies.

Cletronics, which made magnetic parts for military surveillance cameras, switched to manufacturing pocket-sized magnetic detection devices for the health-care industry and sensors for pacemakers. By 1990, this small firm had decreased its military business from 85 percent to 15 percent of its sales and has since managed to maintain that ratio. Cletronics made good use of Ohio's government services, especially one that introduced small defense companies to private firms in their own backyard.[34] These firms could be suppliers, partners, or customers for defense companies.

AM General manufactures the Humvee all-terrain vehicle made famous in the Gulf War. By producing a civilian version of the Humvee, the company expanded commercial sales from nothing to 60 percent of its total sales within three years. AM General is exploring the production of emergency vehicles. The owners invested their own money in commercialization.[35]

Control Knobs, Inc., a small Long Island manufacturer of knobs for military equipment, also took advantage of state government services to overcome its problems adapting to consumer markets. Control Knobs tried unsuccessfully to move "from a candystore operation to the big leagues" before connecting with New York's Industrial Effectiveness Program. "The program saved our lives," confessed president Andrew Franzone.[36] With the aid of state consultants, the company initiated basic workplace reforms. Instead of carrying out repetitive, assembly-line production, pairs of workers now move around U-shaped stations performing a variety of tasks while seated on chairs with rollers. Workers' suggestions are actively solicited. One down-to-earth suggestion was to raise the height of the chairs. That simple idea increased efficiency. A quarter of the Hispanic, Haitian, and Polish workforce are studying English, thanks to a Department of Labor grant. Quality is up; the return rate is down. Making knobs for guitars and gas grills as well as weapons, the company has increased its commercial sales from 8 percent to 35 percent.[37]

In Atlanta, Electromagnetic Sciences laid off an eighth of its employees when the Navy canceled the A-12 bomber in 1991. The company was stuck with millions of dollars' worth of antenna positioning devices for the planes. Yet Electromagnetic Sciences recovered rapidly because it had not waited for the Cold War to end before developing civilian products. It built handheld devices that allow workers in large warehouses—including one Ford facility the size of fifty-five football fields—to update inventory figures without leaving their forklifts. Commercial sales went from 23 percent of the business in 1987 to 60 percent in 1991 and are expected to reach 80 percent in 1997.[38]

LAU Technologies in Acton, Massachusetts, followed two principles in making the transition from 99-percent dependence on military sales: adapting the electronics technology it used as a subcontractor for the Bradley fighting vehicle and teaming with "big brothers."[39] LAU joined a consortium of twelve companies to make driver's licenses that electronically reproduce an individual's photo. The licenses resemble credit cards and are designed to thwart fraudulent reproduction. The states of Massachusetts and Ohio were the first to buy the new product. LAU also works with Raytheon on its northern Illinois people mover and other transportation projects. Commercial sales reached 30 percent in 1994; the goal is to reach 50 percent. LAU invested its own money in the change. The banks came in after initial success was achieved.

These stories of budding successes share a number of characteristics: The companies all engage in self-help, sometimes with a hand from outside. A key ingredient of self-help has been employee participation in the decision-making process as firms remake the workplace. The changes have generated enthusiasm, better performance, and lower prices but have not stemmed the decline in jobs. And even as they learn the ways of commercial markets, these firms continue to face a major hurdle in access to capital.

Outside aid, whether from federal or state governments, has been modest. Nonetheless, this aid can be crucial in helping reorient the firm. Apart from working capital, the smaller companies most need practical advice from individuals with experience in the private sector. That aid may not be costly, but it does have to be there when needed.

7 The Weapons Labs: Can Bomb Designers Help Industry?

As the rain tapered off one December day in 1994, thick fog shrouded the approaches to the Los Alamos National Laboratory, which sits atop a mesa two hours' drive north of Albuquerque. Unable to see much on the mountain road, I mused on the otherworldly isolation of that famous center of nuclear-bomb design. So I was somewhat taken aback to hear Los Alamos employees referring to their once supersecret facility as a "campus."

Los Alamos, like its sister weapons laboratories Lawrence Livermore National Laboratory in California and Sandia National Laboratories in both New Mexico and California, was trying to shed its old fortress mentality and find new missions.

The three weapons labs, along with seven major nonmilitary labs, have been administered by the DoE and its predecessors. During the Cold War, the weapons labs designed and engineered the U.S. nuclear arsenal. Total production reached a staggering total of 77,000 nuclear warheads of all sizes.[1] The weapons labs also played a leading role in conducting the nuclear tests that caused public concern and controversy for decades. The three facilities, employing over 24,000 scientists, engineers, technicians, and support personnel as of 1990, constituted a formidable storehouse of expertise and equipment.[2]

Not all the research at the weapons labs was devoted to doomsday arms. In 1988, the nuclear weapons share was 53 percent at Los Alamos, 46 percent at Livermore, and 62 percent at Sandia.[3] The labs could pull together multidisciplinary teams to do modeling, design, engineering, and prototyping of new technologies. The national laboratories occupied a niche between universities with narrowly focused research and big corporations that have been cutting back on research.

Building on their enviable assets and on legislation that Congress passed in 1989, the weapons labs in the early 1990s undertook a mission no one could have predicted: In peacetime, they would help American industry become more productive.

Business-Government Partnerships

The 1989 legislation authorized the labs to form technological partnerships with companies and universities so long as their joint projects benefited both the government and the private partners. Many of the partnerships took the form of Cooperative Research and Development Agreements (CRADAs). CRADAs (pronounced CRAY-das) are financed on a matching basis, with the private contributions in kind rather than cash.

The idea of CRADAs both attracted and repelled private industry. Attracted, in the words of Alexander MacLachlan, who became DoE deputy under secretary after working thirty-seven years at DuPont, because "in today's industry, even the big guys don't have enough money to keep up with the proliferation of new technologies. . . . When you're lean and mean, you can't do it yourself."[4] Repelled, because most businesses want less contact, not more, with government bureaucracies. And Gilbert Marguth, a key official at Sandia's California branch, told me, "Businesses were very suspicious of the labs; they couldn't trust anything Not Invented Here"[5]—in their own research facilities.

Formidable problems plagued the CRADAs at the outset. They began with small regard for priorities or for the mandated benefit to the government, whether in defense or civilian areas.[6] These omissions undermined the public stake in the new partnerships. The private sector, for its part, encountered an even graver problem: The weapons-making culture was oblivious to cost, and DoE had no managerial experience of "how to make it happen."[7]

Ray Kidder, a veteran physicist at Livermore, cautioned in 1992 against expecting too much benefit to the civilian sector from military work. He called it "terribly inefficient" as a way to help increase the country's industrial strength. "You spend $10 on your research, of which maybe 50 cents is a useful result" for civilian industry, he said.[8]

Just a month later, as though to rebut Kidder's criticism, Livermore announced a new machining system developed in partnership with a small California firm. The CRADA with Industrial Tools, Inc., produced equipment that could cut materials such as ceramics and silicon wafers to within 150th the width of a human hair. The process had particular significance for the computer industry. High-precision slicing could vastly improve the capacity of disk drives.

Livermore's press release stated that Industrial Tools contributed $440,000 toward the project, with $249,000 coming from the lab and DoE. "It's been a very good partnership," said Livermore engineer Tom Vercelli, the project's leader. "Industrial Tools is a small company and they needed our expertise. At the same time we've learned how to function more effectively in an industrial, high-production environment."[9]

A different picture emerged from my conversation in 1995 with the board chairman of Industrial Tools, W. R. Nielsen. "The people at Livermore," he asserted, "didn't know how to steward labor and costs." They had originally estimated the company's costs to be $500,000–700,000. According to Nielsen, Industrial Tools actually spent $1,500,000 of its own money on the equipment, in addition to labor costs. The machining system was indeed developed, but it still had problems three years later.[10]

Troubled History

In light of widespread practices uncovered at major DoE laboratories, Nielsen's criticism of Livermore is not surprising. More than fifty audits have revealed mismanagement, inadequate financial and cost controls, huge legal fees, excessive overtime, fraud, and abuse at the labs. At Sandia in 1994, inspectors discovered large numbers of computers, printers, and other pieces of equipment sitting outdoors in the desert sun.[11] Private contractors and universities operate the labs for DoE.

And yet despite this seamy management record, potentially useful projects are emerging from the weapons labs' collaboration with industry. GM, for example, which has many more CRADAs with DoE than does any other corporation, has found the overall experience "very positive."[12] In addition to cooperative projects at the civilian labs that deal with energy efficiency, auto safety, and emission controls, GM is a partner with Los Alamos in that laboratory's single biggest CRADA. In a joint effort directed at hardening the surfaces of common materials, GM will spend $8 million in its own labs. Los Alamos will put in $5 million.[13] The process involves ionizing gases in an eighteen-foot machine that resembles a giant, sawed-off yellow caterpillar located in the Los Alamos Physics Division. GM has also worked with Livermore on applying laser expertise to industrial welding.

GM is part of a consortium with Chrysler, Ford, and DoE to develop advanced technologies for electric vehicles. Sandia and the consortium are collaborating on electric-car batteries. The Big Three automakers' consortium has sped up the interminable process of negotiating new CRADAs by forging a standardized agreement with DoE. Some large companies have followed suit, but smaller firms, on their own, have had to engage in lengthier negotiations. In Europe, governments help small businesses apply for partnership agreements.[14]

Gains in Health Care and Environment

Some of the more intriguing CRADAs at the weapons labs are pursuing innovations in health care. At Sandia, scientists are working with researchers from Massachusetts General Hospital to improve burn treatment. They hope to use lasers to remove burned skin, minimizing the loss of live skin and blood. A Florida firm, Fonet, Inc., came to Los Alamos looking for a way to monitor cancerous cells. A fiber-optic method was developed at the lab. Fonet created alliances with other companies to produce and market a medical device based on fiber optics, which is being tested pending FDA approval.

The Perkin-Elmer Corporation of Connecticut joined Lawrence Livermore in a CRADA to speed the sequencing of DNA, a process that could help diagnose and ultimately prevent genetic diseases. Livermore is also enrolled in the fight against breast cancer. Using special X-rays that once peered into hydrogen bombs, the lab and Fischer Imaging of Denver are developing a highly accurate mammography device. Under the agreement, a new type of electronic X-ray camera will be produced that eliminates film; digital X-ray images will be stored in a computer capable of studying the picture and displaying the color-coded results on its screen.

Safety is the objective of a Livermore-generated device that could help drivers avoid automobile collisions. A tiny radar has been licensed to Los Angeles–based Amerigon, which hopes to install it in vehicles by 1997. The radar would beep to warn drivers if any cars approached their blind spots. The device can be set to detect objects within a twenty-foot radius, a much shorter range than conventional radar.

A number of weapons lab partnerships hold promise for both the environment and industry. At Sandia, scientists helped Industrial Solar Technology of Denver develop a more efficient receiver tube for its solar collector system. They developed a coating that reflects light while increasing the amount of light energy absorbed by the tube.

Another boost to a cleaner environment could result from the introduction of high-speed magnetically levitated trains (mag-lev) propelled by an electromagnetic field a half-inch above a guideway. The United States has been slow to introduce mag-lev trains, which were pioneered by Germany and Japan. But Los Alamos signed a CRADA with Grumman (now Northrop Grumman) and Bethlehem Steel to explore the use of superconducting materials to power these trains. A superconductor is a material that conducts electricity without resistance. Superconductors have a host of other applications in new industry that will, it is estimated, be worth $200 billion by the year 2020.[15]

Helping CRADAs Survive

Hazel O'Leary, President Clinton's secretary of energy, championed industrial partnerships. DoE had over 1,500 CRADAs as of September 1995, with those in manufacturing and advanced materials and instrumentation leading the other categories. Industry had contributed 57 percent of the $2.1 billion expended on the collaborative projects under way in 1995.[16]

Early in 1995, industrial partnerships as well as the entire DoE were targeted by zealots among the resurgent Republican majorities in Congress. The agency survived, but it and the CRADAs suffered spending cuts. The future of the DoE partnership program will depend in large part on whether the agreements with industry are sufficiently rooted to weather continuing attacks from the Right.

MacLachlan, lured out of his retirement from DuPont by O'Leary, has applied his business and technical background to helping the partnerships survive. He focused the CRADAs on stricter adherence to DoE missions and economic benefits to the nation. The agency's criteria for new partnerships emphasized improvements to the environment (including weapon-site cleanup), energy, national security, and economic growth. A significant number of joint projects benefited more than one core mission.

By 1995, the processing time for forming new CRADAs had been cut in half, and DoE began to provide aid to small firms in mastering the paper work.[17] MacLachlan was able to tell a congressional subcommittee in March 1995 that relations with industry had improved dramatically in pursuit of these "pre-competitive stages of new knowledge development."[18]

One goal officially absent from this pursuit is job creation. The DoE R&D agreements are both long-term and high risk. Down the road, there may—or may not—be new processes, patents, licenses, products, and companies. If successful, a CRADA could generate new jobs, perhaps many new jobs, but only after some years of joint federal-private efforts to perfect an embryonic technology, followed by private efforts to turn it into a product to fit a market niche.

The Future of the Labs

Pete Lyons, the director of the Los Alamos Industrial Partnership Office, told me it should remain as a defense-centered, multipurpose lab for a decade or two—until the world "has no nuclear concerns." The lab's defense mission, Lyons said, should include management of the nuclear stockpile (with the capability to resume testing if necessary) and measures to prevent the spread of nuclear weapons to other countries. As for industrial partnerships, he added, they should increase from 5 percent of the lab's work to 20 percent. "It would take four to five years. It's culture change for both of us."[19]

Lyons's vision is not very different from the conclusions of the Galvin Commission, an advisory body on the future of the labs appointed by Secretary O'Leary and informally named after its chairman, Robert Galvin, the former CEO of Motorola. The commission, however, recommended closing Lawrence Livermore and strongly emphasized that the remaining two weapons labs should be limited to their traditional missions of national security, energy and environmental science, and fundamental science.[20] As for relations with industry, the commission recommended that "the economic impact of R&D performed for such general benefit by the national laboratories should be viewed as a derivative, or outcome, of the other core missions."[21] The Galvin Commission warned the labs against becoming short-term "job shops" for the private sector and insisted that they continue to perform long-term, fundamental research.[22]

While supporting the labs' traditional focus on nuclear research, the commission also urged that "the highest priority" be given to applied research in the areas of energy efficiency, conservation, renewable energy sources (including photovoltaics, biomass, wind, geothermal energy, and hydrogen), and more efficient recovery of gas and oil resources.[23]

Finally, the Galvin Commission recommended that the civilian labs be converted into a not-for-profit R&D corporation, funded by Congress, with the DoE as the customer.[24]

DoE concurred with all the recommendations except for the privatization of the civilian labs and closure of Lawrence Livermore. In September 1995, President Clinton announced that all three weapons labs would continue to operate. He no doubt feared closing Livermore because of California's importance in the 1996 election year.

The Critics Respond

Dissatisfied with the commission's recommendations, critics published their own views. William Weida of the Colorado College and Ann Markusen of Rutgers University coauthored a response on behalf of a coalition of thirty-seven citizens' groups. They contended that "where taxpayers pay for research and private companies are given proprietary rights," technology-transfer programs either should be transformed over time into public-private projects financed entirely by the business enterprises involved or should have their personnel, facilities, and creative ideas spun off into the private sector.[25]

Some spin-off of personnel from the weapons labs into the private sector is taking place. Sandia, for example, is training some employees to become entrepreneurs. They can take a two-year leave to prepare to start their own firms. Martin Marietta (now Lockheed Martin), which operates Sandia, created the Technology Ventures Corporation to assist start-up firms with financing, management support, relocation, or expansion. Martin Marietta committed $1 million a year for five years to fund this effort.[26]

On a different tack, the National Commission for Economic Conversion and Disarmament, one of the country's premier think tanks on defense-conversion issues, proposed a community-based alternative to "corporatizing" the civilian labs. Director Gregory Bischak and his associate, James Bridgman, looked to the Netherlands for a model. There, government-financed universities have evolved a network of Community Research, Policy, and Assistance Centers that respond to the concerns of community groups, small businesses, labor unions, and public interest organizations. "Such a network of science shops could serve as an alternative model for converting the labs to serve the public interest," Bridgman and Bischak wrote.[27]

An article in the *Chronicle of Higher Education* has reported that the staff and volunteers at the Dutch centers have "helped workers evaluate the consequences of new production processes and helped environmental groups document sources of industrial pollution."[28] While such assistance at the local level would be useful, this model is not a sufficient guide for making the best national use of the impressive talent and technology amassed, at taxpayers' expense, in the three weapons labs.

Community Involvement

One of the civilian labs, Brookhaven on Long Island, moved toward community involvement in response to an appeal for help. A local citizens' group was determined to get Brooklyn's Gowanus Canal cleaned up. The Gowanus flows into New York Harbor and adds to its pollution. Keith Jones, a Brookhaven lab physicist, went to the aid of the Gowanus group, then broadened his objectives. Today, working with four universities in New York and New Jersey and an array of subcontractors, Brookhaven directs a demonstration project aimed at decontaminating sediment harborwide.

Jones, founder of the project, soon found that decontamination required more than new technologies. It took persuasion. He now deals with politicians, officials, and community leaders in two states. Jones has explained the project to a neighborhood meeting in a Brooklyn Catholic church and has reassured citizens in New Jersey concerned that the cleanup process might endanger their area.[29] Funding for the project has come from the Environmental Protection Agency (EPA) and the Army Corps of Engineers.

On the West Side of Chicago, Argonne National Laboratory and a community development corporation are working together to apply technology to the solution of urban problems in an African-American neighborhood. Argonne provides energy-efficient techniques in the rehabilitation of local housing, explores a means of converting recycled newspapers into wall insulation, identifies ground contaminants and suggests cleanup methods, and encourages the establishment of local businesses to convert waste products into building materials. The DoE has financed this effort in a neighborhood where a community group, Bethel New Life, developed almost 1,000 housing units in its first fifteen years.[30]

Another means of bringing DoE's environmental mission to the grass roots was initiated by Lawrence Livermore in the western states. The lab partnered with community colleges in the region to provide technical training on the environment to interested individuals. A network of partnerships between individual labs and nearby community colleges has since been established across the country. Modest funding comes from DoE and regional EPA offices.[31]

The examples of Brookhaven's harbor project, Argonne's work in Chicago, and the partnerships with community colleges suggest that the weapons labs can share their resources not only with private industry but with the general public as well.

Ticklish Questions

Working for local community development is clearly a public good, but the weapons labs' partnerships with private industry raise difficult policy questions. Is aiding individual private companies with publicly funded research an appropriate national mission? Is this a valid mission for the weapons labs? And will the results offer a fair return to the public investor, the taxpayer? For private companies, there is potential profit in the joint projects. For the public as a whole, is the view worth the climb?

The answers should emerge only after serious debate inside and outside government. But this has not yet happened. Indeed, the public is largely unaware of DoE-industry partnerships. Without a clear consensus on these questions, the civilian resources of the labs could fall victim to congressional budget cutting or to a drive to sell off government facilities. The latter approach would deliver pieces of the labs to those best able to pay, the large corporations.

If and when the debate takes place, I offer several thoughts for consideration. Helping industry become more productive holds the promise of new, socially useful products and processes—plus some modest job creation. These results can be accelerated by continuous interaction among government researchers and business personnel working on common projects. If American living standards can be boosted over time with a relatively small additional investment, I think these partnerships are legitimate. And federal participation should not be confined to DoE.

As for the specific role of the weapons labs, there is the lingering question of whether their weapons culture can be replaced by the civilian mind-set new missions would require. There are two parts to the answer: First, even during the Cold War a significant amount of nonmilitary research was conducted at the weapons labs, so the changeover would not be total. Second, these labs now have a track record with CRADAs. After an undisciplined and profligate start, the combination of experience and a firmer hand at DoE seems to have made the weapons labs more focused and efficient. CRADAs are already demonstrating that taxpayers can benefit as consumers from new technologies and products that diagnose illnesses, prevent auto accidents, and improve solar collectors.

What they have yet to prove is that they can improve industry productivity and U.S. living standards when they focus on DoE's core missions of energy and the environment. Since public needs in these two areas are immense, the CRADAs have ample scope to justify themselves.

Two decades after the oil crises of the 1970s, the U.S. stock of fossil fuels is dwindling and imports of foreign oil are rising. Alternative clean, safe fuel sources, recommended for priority research by the Galvin Commission, remain underdeveloped.

Meanwhile, our air and water, both made cleaner as a result of government regulation, could become more polluted if Congress rolls back environmental measures. Nor do environmental problems stop at borders—global warming is an example. A working group of the International Panel on Climate Change agreed in 1995 that "the balance of evidence suggests that there is a discernible human influence on global climate."[32] (See Chapter 13.) Weapons labs' research, some of it in partnerships, could speed the development of energy-efficient technologies to counter the greenhouse effect.

If DoE interprets benefits to the government from its industrial partnerships as benefits to the nation as a whole and if it continues to promote cost reduction, the weapons labs' collaboration with industry could contribute significantly to America's energy and environmental needs.

8 Local Activists Pitch In

"Don't have anything to do with Roz Boxer," a local beer distributor warned members of the Tucson business establishment in 1991. "She doesn't shave her legs or underarms, she wears Birkenstocks, and they sent her here to close the Air Force base."[1]

The object of these bizarre accusations—all untrue—was Rosalyn Boxer, a divorced mother of two in her late forties who had been working as a dental assistant for more than twenty years. Boxer had come to Tucson from New York in 1973, time enough to be accepted by the local community. But what riled some of Tucson's business people and no doubt triggered the beer distributor's paranoia was Boxer's public advocacy of defense conversion.

A big Hughes Aircraft missile plant, a Lockheed facility, a multitude of defense subcontractors, and the Davis Monthan Air Force Base had made this desert city almost as economically dependent on the military as on tourism. In 1991, the conservative business establishment was still denying that the good old Cold War days were over. The following year a spokeswoman for the Greater Tucson Economic Council told the *Arizona Daily Star*: "Conversion is not a popular thing. People have been used to doing business a particular way for quite a long time, and change is not easy."[2]

Clearly, advocates of change must be prepared to persevere. Roz Boxer, who admits "patience was not one of my virtues," discovered inner reserves in Tucson.[3] A 1989 speech by Lloyd Jeffry Dumas of the University of Texas–Dallas first rallied her to the cause of converting defense plants to civilian production. As a one-day-a-week staff member for Physicians for Social Responsibility, she persuaded the Tucson chapter to create a defense-conversion project. The project soon evolved into the Tucson Council for Economic Conversion. Responding to expressions of interest statewide, the council incorporated and replaced "Tucson" with "Arizona" in its title.

The Arizona Council for Economic Conversion (ACEC) started small, with a trickle of cash, in 1991. At first Roz Boxer searched unsuccessfully for government programs that would provide hands-on advice to worried defense-firm CEOs. She contacted government agencies, universities, and private organizations. "I was a maniac on the phone," she said, recalling her efforts.[4] In her spare time—she was working three part-time jobs at that point—Boxer read everything she could find on a subject that had few experts.

As one of its first projects, ACEC organized the Technology Exchange Forum, which brought together defense and nondefense business people with community leaders and local politicians. The forum brought in outside speakers and encouraged networking. It received enthusiastic reviews. Buried in an ACEC collection of testimonials is a 1992 letter from Mary Ann Chapman, the president of EcoElectric Corporation, who wrote:

> Reading name tags in the breakfast line, I found one belonging to someone whom I've unsuccessfully tried to contact in the past. I followed him to a table, where I learned that his company was about to buy a converted electrical vehicle from out of state! Be assured that they have now been apprised of Arizona's emerging electric vehicle industry. They promise that we'll be on the bid list for future purchases. Thank goodness for the Forum!

The forum gave ACEC visibility. Later, its skill in securing federal grants helped overcome hostility from some business and political leaders. A first grant, from DoL, paired ACEC and its surrounding Pima County in a demonstration project with Sargent Controls, a small firm that depended heavily on the Seawolf submarine program. "Efforts to convert the Pima County defense sector would start with one firm," DoL reported.[5]

Only One Piece of the Process

County officials and ACEC's volunteer trainers soon discovered that worker retraining—their original focus—was only one piece of the conversion process for Sargent Controls. They added assessments of workers' skills and of company systems and equipment. The expanded effort was led by a management consultant who served on ACEC's board and a laid-off worker with thirty years' experience in defense industry. Neither they nor their team members received compensation for their six months of work.[6] But they were successful. A manager of Sargent's Marine Division told me, "If it hadn't been for ACEC, we couldn't have gotten the training, which led us to become more streamlined, efficient, and commercialized."[7]

Over the next few years, ACEC was instrumental in securing a second DoL grant to Pima County and one from the Defense Department, which went to the Governor's Office. The federal grants totaled $938,000, of which $493,000 was sent to ACEC. These awards required ACEC to raise matching funds, which Boxer obtained from large defense contractors, small machine shops, the county, and the city of Tucson.[8]

These funds enabled ACEC to hire a temporary field staff, as many as twenty at one point, with defense-industry and management backgrounds. Under the terms of the federal grants, the staff helped prepare fourteen Arizona defense firms to operate in the commercial world. Boxer later estimated that these firms had hired two hundred new workers after the training program began.[9] Impressed by this performance, the city of Tucson asked ACEC to come up with a plan detailing how the communities around the air base could become less defense-dependent. The mayor and city council accepted all of ACEC's recommendations. Later, Arizona's Republican governor, Fife Symington, designated ACEC as a representative to the state development zones, thus permitting it to receive grants directly rather than through state or local agencies.

By 1994, a Hughes executive told Rosalyn Boxer at a meeting, "Roz, you're no longer controversial."[10] That half-joking compliment reflected admiration for Boxer's accomplishments—all the more impressive in view of the fact that her formal education had ended with high school.

By April 1996, the conservative, part-time Arizona legislature had passed a $250,000 appropriation for hands-on aid to small defense firms wanting to convert. The funds will go to ACEC via the state Department of Commerce. Because of her persistent one-on-one lobbying of legislators, the measure was known informally as "the Roz Boxer bill." A Republican state senator, Larry Chesley, led the effort, which included his impassioned speech before the Senate Appropriations Committee. Committee members gave Boxer a standing ovation.

As a fledgling practitioner in the field of defense conversion, Boxer says she learned that you have to deliver something specific that those directly affected can use. And, she adds, it's not enough to work with companies and labor; the local political structure and economic development officials must become part of the process.[11]

"People think anyone can do a conversion," Boxer told a visiting Connecticut reporter. "No. Communities have to give their general support. A company has to know if there is a university that can help. Is there a computer network they can plug into? What is the banking industry willing to do to help a company that has a good track record but can't overcome the barriers to make these changes?"[12]

Yet impersonal, institutional forces are not the whole story. Frank Barton, the project manager for the Defense Department grant, told me, "ACEC's success was due wholly to Rosalyn Boxer's drive, dedication and creativity." Creativity was needed, he explained, "in order to obtain political and financial support in spite of a very difficult political climate."[13]

Boxer's creativity consisted partly in getting people to work together across economic, political, and geographic lines—no small achievement in today's fragmented society.

ACEC is one of four local organizations I will describe briefly in which activists have served as community catalysts in pursuit of defense conversion. All those described here, are, interestingly enough, led by women. They toiled in different defense-dependent environments but shared common experiences.

As Maine Goes . . .

Susie Schweppe came to Maine with her husband the same year Roz Boxer arrived in Tucson. A native of New Jersey, she had worked in New York's advertising industry in the 1960s. Today, the Schweppes and their three children live in a graceful, converted farmhouse in Falmouth that until January 1996 had sheltered the tiny office of the Maine Economic Conversion Project (MECP).

In a sense, Susie Schweppe's eight-year-old son propelled his mother on the path she was later to follow. Worry in his voice, he asked her in the early Reagan years about the danger of nuclear war. His anxiety spurred Schweppe to start a peace education program in their local church. From that base, she helped organize a statewide interdenominational church group that sent weekly delegations to

Congress to discuss military issues. They met weekly with Democratic Senator George Mitchell, about half as often with Republican Senator William Cohen. Schweppe says her son, Jesse, young as he was, "lobbied very effectively."[14]

Even as the prospect of nuclear war dissipated later in the 1980s, the financial costs of the U.S.-Soviet military competition continued to mount. Schweppe and her colleagues began to advocate cuts in military spending and investment of the savings in the domestic economy. They sounded out Maine opinion leaders about the feasibility of working for defense conversion. Buzz Fitzgerald, who was to become BIW's CEO, encouraged them. They visited the State Planning Office and "found nothing moving," but they came away with one invisible ally deep in the bowels of the state bureaucracy.[15]

During the 1990 gubernatorial campaign, Governor John McKernan and challenger Joseph Brennan had vied to adopt an idea advanced by Schweppe's group: the creation of a state task force to research defense dependence and layoffs. When he was reelected, McKernan created a task force—but with no financial resources. It was a learning experience for Schweppe. Not only did new institutions have to be established and funded, but politicians needed constant prodding by concerned citizens. The MECP was founded to mobilize these citizens.

From the outset MECP, with Susie Schweppe as unpaid director, fostered partnerships and networks among people who had not before worked together. MECP's board, with members from business, banking, defense industry, labor, research groups, churches, and peace organizations, reflected this cooperative approach.

The organization had its work cut out for it. Maine was vulnerable. The state's largest private employer, BIW, laid off several thousand workers before its 1994 labor-management contract called a halt to layoffs. A major air base in Maine was slated to close, along with another just across the New Hampshire border. Eight percent of the workforce was employed in defense jobs that provided 10 percent of total Maine income in 1993.[16]

Slowly Building the Structures

Bit by bit, nudged along by growing citizen pressure, Maine established a task force on defense realignment, created an office of economic conversion and a council to stimulate the economy, and received federal grants to strengthen manufacturing and marketing skills and provide loans to defense firms. Although the Office of Economic Conversion had only one employee and a two-year budget of $200,000, Maine slowly built the structures needed to begin shedding defense dependence.

Progress was not smooth. As Susie Schweppe organized on behalf of MECP's goals, she encountered resistance, both to change and to the practice of cooperation. And no one seemed to have a long-term strategy for change. What she doesn't talk about and perhaps didn't know about was the whispering campaign to impugn her motives in state government and business circles. I heard about it from a sympathetic state employee. Perhaps this was a milder Maine version of the pathological resistance Roz Boxer initially met in Arizona. Perhaps it came from people who felt threatened by uncertainty, jealously guarding their turf.

Schweppe found her work all consuming. The endless meetings in a sprawling and decentralized state, monitoring activities of the legislature and executive agencies, serving on state advisory councils, distributing questionnaires to congressional and gubernatorial candidates, publishing a substantive newsletter, building a mailing list of 2,500—all this was hard on her family. In the process, however, the Schweppe children became more self-reliant. As two of them approached college age and her husband's income dipped in the recession of the early 1990s, Susie Schweppe concluded she needed a salary and sought and won foundation support. Later, her one-person operation doubled in size when a former employee of a Maine defense firm hired on for two years.

MECP's advocacy of policies to help defense-dependent firms, workers, and communities led to a broader, longer-term perspective. The organization embraced sustainable development, which stresses the interdependence of economic growth, environmental protection, and social equity. MECP also sought partnerships with the Maine Chamber of Commerce, among others, in order to generate new jobs through manufacture of zero-emission vehicles, establishment of transportation hubs around the state, and work on intelligent highways. The State Department of Transportation invited Schweppe to address these issues at its annual conference in 1995.

As MECP discussed its financially uncertain future that year, the path from fear of nuclear war to support for electric cars may have looked long and winding. But for those who think globally and act locally, the path was as direct as it was logical. That path, however, will have to be pursued by others; foundation support dried up and

MECP had to close its doors. At the end, Schweppe was proud that "individuals and organizations that worked in isolation of each other in the past now work together as a team. Out of these partnerships has grown a statewide structure of public, private and nonprofit organizations to do the work of economic conversion and sustainable development."[17]

Beating the St. Louis Blues

Sister Mary Ann McGivern had deep roots in the St. Louis community. The oldest of seven children in a midwestern Irish-Catholic family that viewed John L. Lewis as a hero, she had only two female roles as models. There were mothers and nuns. Fresh out of high school, she became a nun. Her order, the Sisters of Loretto, sent her to attend Webster College in St. Louis.

After graduation and years of teaching at Loretto schools (the current mayor of St. Louis was one of her pupils), McGivern received two M.A.'s from Stanford and returned to St. Louis in the 1970s to work at the Institute for Peace and Justice. The institute had a project on defense conversion, which hired an engineer from McDonnell Douglas to run it when it received a Ford Foundation grant in 1980. The project, unfortunately, did not last out the decade. Meanwhile, Mary Ann McGivern had founded a coalition of religious orders to introduce resolutions at McDonnell Douglas shareholder meetings.

The giant defense contractor—its civilian aircraft operation was located elsewhere—dominated manufacturing in the St. Louis region. Its management scorned the annual appeals from the religious group working for defense conversion, public participation in the conversion process, and an end to arms sales abroad. Nonetheless, year by year, minority support for these resolutions slowly grew among the shareholders.

In 1988, McGivern and a handful of activists revived the moribund St. Louis Economic Conversion Project (SLECP). It became functional shortly before recession and defense cuts struck, eliminating thousands of manufacturing jobs in the St. Louis region. McDonnell Douglas was not spared.

Cassell Williams, a former director of IAM District 837, had foresightedly urged McDonnell Douglas in the 1980s to begin building rapid transit cars. His advice went unheeded. McDonnell Douglas employees, a union spokesman commented, are now paying the price for their company's rebuff to defense conversion.[18]

The SLECP helped introduce the concept of defense conversion to a troubled region. It worked with the Economic Adjustment and Diversification Committee, a coalition of business, labor, academic, and citizen leaders that had received the blessing of the area's political leadership. New training, loans, and technical assistance programs were initiated with the aid of federal grants in a drive to keep good jobs in St. Louis.

Mary Ann McGivern wrote the original proposal for one of those programs, the Management Assistance and Technology Transfer program (MATT). A Department of Labor demonstration project, MATT helped smaller defense firms diversify by transforming their management practices. SLECP served on the MATT board.

Seyer Industries was one of more than twenty firms aided by MATT before the program ended in 1995. The company produces equipment for the military that hoists heavy weapons and lifts aircraft for maintenance work. A Rush Limbaugh calendar displayed in CEO Christopher Seyer's office presumably indicates where his political sympathies lie. But a month after the 1994 congressional elections he told me, "We decided to commercialize because growth is not in the military even though the new Congress will enhance readiness."[19] Since readiness involves considerable weapons maintenance, Seyer could have chosen to remain glued to the Pentagon's long coattails. Instead, he is looking for customers who install commercial equipment.

Before MATT consultants introduced Seyer Industries employees to "workforce activity-based management," they were frustrated by a lack of communication with management. Now they participate in decisionmaking through teams that track work processes and cost on storyboards. Through colorful symbols and codes, employees can see at a glance what is being done and what should be done in the plant. Seyer's fifty-two employees decide, in teams that unite different skills, the "should-be" activities of the plant. By identifying areas of waste and duplication, this process yielded almost $300,000 in cost savings within months.[20]

Another small defense contractor echoed Christopher Seyer's commitment to conversion after the 1994 elections. "It does not affect me," he said, "that the Republicans have come to power promising more military spending. I know now that SLECP was right and that my business must aggressively convert because I cannot count on military contracts for either stability or growth."[21]

Industrial Policy

As SLECP intensified its efforts, it broadened its own view of what was required to make St. Louis and its environs a region of long-lasting jobs that pay a decent wage. Bucking the trend represented by freshman Republicans in the House of Representatives, SLECP advocated a community-based industrial policy with light manufacturing as the region's economic anchor.

"Taxpayers want fiscal responsibility," a SLECP working paper stated. "In order to achieve it, we need to do some financial planning. We need to establish some policies about how we will use our tax monies to do the work of government: create jobs, build infrastructure, educate ourselves and maintain a safety net for those in need." Anticipating the objections of those who argue that industrial policy obliges government to pick winners and losers, the draft pointed out that "the Pentagon has been picking winners and losers for 50 years. In its choices for computers, for miniaturization, and against development of ceramic engines and solar and wind energy, the Pentagon has driven both military and commercial research and development in particular directions."[22]

To a city that offered financial incentives to riverboat gambling and to the Los Angeles Rams to lure them to St. Louis, SLECP suggested an alternative strategy: technical aid to small firms; employee buyouts; worker participation; and consortia of small companies tackling common problems. As an honest broker, SLECP convened eight meetings of economic development officials, companies, and labor in 1994 to discuss industrial policy. And the organization facilitated fourteen meetings to prepare neighborhood groups for the St. Louis empowerment zone.

A key member of SLECP's four-person staff is Lance McCarthy, who seeks out financing to create new jobs in St. Louis. An African-American former salesman and art gallery owner, McCarthy pursues his mission among banks, pension funds, venture capital groups, and all levels of government. He is also exploring the establishment of environmental industrial parks in the inner cities of St. Louis and East St. Louis, Illinois.

Despite this community involvement with SLECP, despite Mary Ann McGivern's roots in St. Louis—she broadcast weekly five-minute radio commentaries on KWMU for years—and despite her status as his former teacher, His Honor the mayor doesn't invite Mc-

Givern to the truly important municipal meetings on economic development. These, she noted, are dominated by corporate CEOs.[23]

Nevertheless, SLECP has been able to engage McDonnell Douglas in discussions about starting a venture capital fund to launch new firms in the region. For McDonnell Douglas, prolonged discussions on this subject may simply be a tactic to prevent the reintroduction of more resolutions by McGivern at future company shareholder meetings. If so, it is evidence of how much McGivern and her allies, representing almost 10 percent of shareholders at recent meetings, nettle the top management.

SLECP intends to continue to press hard for regional planning and expanded light manufacturing in the defense-dependent St. Louis area.

New Currents in a Navy Stronghold

As the Cold War ended, San Diego was home to U.S. Navy ships and planes, Tomahawk and advanced cruise missile plants, naval shipbuilding yards, hundreds of small defense firms, and a heavy concentration of military retirees. Federal expenditures on military contracts, active-duty personnel, and veterans' pensions totaled nearly $10 billion a year, accounting for more than 20 percent of San Diego's annual gross regional product.[24]

Faced with layoffs at defense plants and the Naval Training Center and the shift of Hughes Aircraft's missile operations to Tucson, San Diego had one asset that helped it cope with dislocations: local leadership.

As he had in Tucson, Lloyd Jeffry Dumas of the University of Texas–Dallas started a chain reaction that spawned first grassroots and then political leadership in San Diego. In 1985, Dumas, his former professor, Seymour Melman of Columbia University, and retired Admiral Eugene Carroll of the Center for Defense Information discussed defense conversion at a public meeting in the Navy stronghold. Local residents responded by founding the nonprofit San Diego Economic Conversion Council (SDECC). Marcia Boruta became one of the board members.

Boruta came from a devoutly Catholic Polish-American family in Grand Rapids, Michigan. Both parents were blue-collar workers. Boruta attended the University of Detroit, a Jesuit institution where her awareness of social injustice was sharpened. From her apartment window in Detroit she could see a contrasting urban landscape of mansions and the Twelfth Precinct, site of the city's worst riots.[25]

After dropping out of the university and working in Detroit, Boruta moved to San Diego in 1974. She received a degree in communications from the University of California–San Diego and became interested in a new subject, the transfer of military resources to economic development. In 1989, when the Berlin Wall was about to fall, Boruta was named director of SDECC. Like her counterparts in Tucson, Maine, and St. Louis, she arrived on the doorstep of defense conversion via the peace and justice movement.

Boruta persuaded Congressman Jim Bates (D.–Calif.) to hold a hearing on defense conversion in San Diego. That hearing, attended by City Councilman Bob Filner and Mayor Larry Agran of Irvine, California, a strong advocate of defense conversion, encouraged Filner to take a leading role on the issue. Filner introduced a resolution in the City Council calling for a subcommittee to "plan for the orderly and smooth transition of the San Diego economy to a peace-based economy." The resolution passed in April 1990, while many defense-dependent communities were still denying they had a problem.

A Mix of Backgrounds

Filner named Boruta, defense contractors and other business people, the commander of the naval base, local officials, labor representatives, and academics to an advisory group. They discussed possible conversion measures. A plan emerged in 1991, supported by federal and state grants. These enabled San Diego to set up a high-tech resource center, a technology incubator to assist start-up firms, a technology alliance to aid companies in bidding on federal economic and defense-conversion grants, a world trade center, and a seed capital fund.

Meanwhile, Filner was elected to Congress and San Diego elected a pro-business mayor, Susan Golding. SDECC was conspicuously absent from her advisory groups, which were composed largely of business people. Seeing the need for more, not less, public participation, SDECC called town meetings to "democratize conversion" and encourage San Diegans to hold their new institutions accountable. The organization, with other groups, cosponsored town meetings on such specialized subjects as retraining, military base conversion, and mag-lev trains. A series of SDECC-sponsored business breakfasts grew out of these meetings, bringing together defense-firm CEOs and local officials.

The town meetings were so successful that SDECC was able to win a federally funded subcontract from the city to organize four more in 1995. The purpose of the meetings, held in cooperation with local economic development councils, was to inform the community about existing economic adjustment programs and to solicit input about local needs.

Congressman Duncan Hunter, a Republican hawk, addressed his East County constituents by telephone at the first of these meetings. He spoke of the need for a strong defense and declared in dire tones that "it's a dangerous world out there." Participants told him they were there to discuss defense conversion; no one spoke up to defend Hunter's views.[26]

As SDECC looked ahead in 1995, financially strapped though it was—like other citizens' groups working for defense conversion—it could take pride in helping business, labor, and government cooperate for change. Yet distrust lingers. According to Boruta, businessmen don't trust government officials, Mayor Golding is wary of Congressman Filner and his friends, and "peace people" are skeptical of ties with defense contractors.[27] But looking beyond these obstacles, SDECC keeps expanding its horizons: Can a cooperative economic development project be initiated, it wonders, with neighboring Tijuana across the Mexican border?

Common Threads

Each of the four activist groups described above arrived at a different mechanism to achieve their common goal of defense conversion: hands-on help to small defense firms in Arizona; preparing the ground for new state institutions in Maine; community-based industrial policy in St. Louis, and town meetings in San Diego. Nonetheless, these distinct experiences reveal some common threads.

First, a tiny handful of well-organized citizens succeeded in putting together unlikely coalitions and moving their communities in new directions. Second, local resistance to change and distrust of other groups weakened the efforts to overcome defense dependence. Third, without a modest infusion of federal dollars, the success of these grassroots campaigns would be problematical. Fourth, all the groups recognize that defense conversion requires broad national policies capable of generating economic growth and well-paid jobs.

9 State Governments Take Action

"Our No. 1 strategy is not to diversify the economic base," Connecticut Commissioner of Economic Development Joseph McGee announced in 1992. "It is to make absolutely certain that we're getting our share of defense contracts, as well as nondefense contracts, for Connecticut companies."[1]

This dismissal of economic diversification showed that Independent governor Lowell Weicker's administration, in the nation's most defense-dependent state,[2] was not yet ready to kick the habit of reliance on the Pentagon.

Long before there was a Pentagon, even before there was a United States, Connecticut had been building cannons and warships. Wars hot and cold continually built up the state's defense industry. By the end of the Cold War, New London County—center of submarine building—had the highest per capita Pentagon income in the nation.[3] Change would not be easy.

Governor Weicker's approach to economic development did not help. According to Thomas Moukawsher, former counsel to the state legislature's Commerce Committee and to the president of the Senate, Weicker's policy focused on subsidizing companies that threatened to leave Connecticut and on "capturing" big corporations from other states.[4]

That approach fell far short of the recommendations of a National Governors' Association study in 1992:

> In the final analysis, an effective defense diversification strategy is a good economic development strategy. State economic development policies should support firms' efforts to improve their competitive po-

sition. While defense-dependent firms face unique difficulties in converting to a civilian market, they share with other firms the need to have a well-trained, flexible workforce, to adopt modern management practices, and to continually develop new product and process innovations in order to remain internationally competitive. Policies that support firms' efforts to achieve world-class standards also will help these companies succeed in their diversification efforts.[5]

States with sizable defense industry and installations could choose from a menu of options to meet the challenge of international competition.

Connecticut

Cash, Tech Centers, Casino

In Connecticut, groups worried about big defense layoffs and a painful recession persuaded the state legislature to adopt some measures that could make the economy less dependent on military spending. The legislature took the first step even before Commissioner McGee's scornful reference to diversification.

Connecticut's Defense Diversification Act of 1991 provided funds for grants, loans, and loan guarantees to defense firms. An initial $22.5 million was increased by $10 million in 1994. This infusion of credit helped scores of small firms survive the downturn in military procurement.

Under a longer-term view than Commissioner McGee's, the state also created a number of technology and oceanographic research centers. These will have a more lasting effect on defense dependence than even the ready credit. The state invested, on a matching basis, in institutes at the University of Connecticut that partner with small firms. Defense companies have been linked with the university's Institute for Industrial and Engineering Technology and the state's Science Park in a network designed to promote new business. This program, known as Procurement Technical Assistance Centers, began in 1993 at Seatech, a nonprofit economic development organization that Congressman Sam Gejdenson (D.–Conn.) helped found. The center at Seatech guides clients in identifying and bidding on government contracts and exploring new markets. Seatech offers additional services to start-up firms and provides loans to marine science and fishing enterprises. In time, Connecticut centers will link up with counterparts in Rhode Island and elsewhere.

In addition, the state has invested in a marine science center and an ambitious project called Ocean Quest, both in heavily defense-dependent New London County. Former submarine builders and Navy veterans are constructing a complex there that includes a learning center devoted to undersea activities, a school, a museum, a camp, a hotel, and a conference center.

These projects will generate hundreds of permanent jobs in southeastern Connecticut, where layoffs at Electric Boat and other Navy-related businesses in the early 1990s churned up waves of anxiety.

By 1995, employment in the region had improved, but not chiefly because of actions by governments or local business groups. The Foxwoods Resort Casino, owned by the Mashantucket Pequot tribe, opened in 1992 with 2,300 employees. Three years later, the casino was earning $1 billion a year and employing 11,000 people.[6] It had become the top employer in the area.

When I visited southeastern Connecticut in fall 1994, no one seemed sure what had happened to all the skilled defense workers who had been laid off. It's a good bet that thousands of them have quietly taken jobs at Foxwoods. They aren't making sixteen dollars an hour as they might have at Electric Boat, but the work is steady. The casino offers "the excitement of hundreds of table games," slot machines, a 3,200-seat Bingo Hall, a resort hotel, a 280-room country inn, a theater, a disco, an arcade, and Italian, Chinese, and American delicacies in the dining rooms; "Gaming in its natural state," as one of the Foxwoods brochures exults.

Have we glimpsed the future in Connecticut? Dwindling manufacturing; some of the job loss offset by gambling, a growth industry; tourism and entertainment picking up some of the slack; simultaneously, more sober citizens struggling against the odds for government investment in education, training, and modern infrastructure, and small defense firms trying to penetrate commercial markets. Given the current opposition to public investments to raise living standards, that could indeed be a preview of future trends.

The legislature passed two labor-backed bills in 1994. One required all Connecticut firms with DoD contracts exceeding $1 million that receive state economic development aid to establish alternative use committees. These labor-management units would identify civilian products for future business. The second bill required the state's grant-making agencies to add job creation and retention to its list of goals.

Will Elections Alter the Picture?

John Rowland, a Republican, was elected governor in 1994 along with a GOP legislative majority on a platform of reduced spending and taxes. Will the changed political landscape wipe out earlier economic development measures?

One of these was the creation of Techconn, a private nonprofit corporation. Its mission is to generate manufacturing jobs for displaced defense workers through emerging environmental, energy, transportation, and marine technologies. For example, with federal, state, and private funds and industrial partners, Techconn is attempting to convert municipal sewage sludge into electric power for motor vehicles. Connecticut is also helping fund a joint project in which Techconn and others bring electronic lessons about energy and the environment into school classrooms.

Clifford Neal, Techconn's former president and general manager, found federal funding through TRP to be "disappointing."[7] The amount of money was not the problem; TRP provided over $1 million to Techconn for several projects. Rather, the problem was the requirement that all new technologies have a military as well as civilian use. "The program has been hijacked by the Defense Department," Neal complained. "Dual use is being used to save costs on military research and development, with industry paying half."

"Dual use" was also built into Connecticut's Defense Information and Services Network (DISN), which helps defense firms both secure additional military contracts and identify alternative markets. DISN has used a federal grant to provide field consultants to businesses, to conduct workshops and conferences with federal procurement officials, and to publish a newsletter and a resource guide to key technologies.

Betsy Hunt, special project manager for the Connecticut Department of Economic Development, says that this civilian-military approach is designed to improve Connecticut firms' competitiveness in either sector.[8] She also reported in fall 1995 that the only change made by the Rowland administration as of that time was abandonment of state grants to defense firms. From the outset, however, most financial aid to these firms had been loans and loan guarantees, not grants.[9]

Washington State

Community Involvement

Like Connecticut, Washington State was heavily defense dependent as the Cold War ended. For years the state's aerospace and ship-building industries and military installations had benefited from the unstinting generosity of two powerful Democratic senators: Scoop Jackson (known as "the Senator from Boeing") and Warren Magnuson. In 1990, Washington firms received an estimated $5 billion to $6 billion a year in military contracts.[10] As late as 1993, 5.7 percent of the state's workforce was tied to Defense Department spending.[11] As the state began to cope with the problem at the local level, it found that almost 80 percent of the people on north Whidbey Island, a long, narrow island northwest of Seattle, were economically dependent on the naval air station there.[12]

Unlike Connecticut, however, Washington State planned for the transition with the participation of the people most affected. A Community Diversification Advisory Committee, composed of military-oriented businesses, economic development authorities, labor organizations, state and local agencies, peace activists, and representatives of the military, helped develop the plan. The Northwest Policy Center at the University of Washington assisted the advisory committee.

The 1990 legislation that placed the Department of Community Development in charge of the new program stated:

> It is the intent of the legislature to assist communities in planning for economic change, developing a broader economic base, and preparing for any shift in federal priorities that could cause a reduction in federal expenditures, and assist firms by providing information and technical assistance necessary for them to introduce new products or production processes.[13]

Armed with that broad mandate, the state convened focus groups in six counties and among business and labor representatives. Each focus group was led by an experienced facilitator, using a discussion guide to ensure that each meeting covered comparable topics. The conclusions reached were compiled and published, along with a survey of defense contractors. "Virtually all community, business and labor leaders consulted in this study," the survey concluded, "support the goal of diversifying community economic bases and firms away from high degrees of reliance on military budgets."[14] Democratic participation and real leadership led to a dynamic far different from the one set in motion by the Weicker administration in Connecticut.

Leveraging Fresh Investments

State officials encouraged residents to take local initiatives and provided the money to get things moving. Accordingly, the Community Diversification Program (CDP) used $290,000 in state funds in 1993–1994 to leverage nearly $1.8 million in federal funds and $535,000 in local and private investment.[15] With these funds, the state helped initiate a series of economic development projects in defense-dependent communities and even in whole industries.

The Bremerton area, in Kitsap County, across Puget Sound from Seattle, for example, is home to three naval installations: a shipyard, the Keyport Undersea Warfare Center, and the Bangor Submarine Base. Spurred by layoffs, the community held meetings and decided to pursue diversification. The county hired a diversification director and proceeded to build a technology and business center, create a business incubator that would help get new firms going, provide entrepreneurial training for defense workers, and revitalize Bremerton's downtown.

Independently, the IAM assembled a consortium interested in building passenger ferries, which are in demand in the Pacific Northwest. Unions, Italian and Australian ferry designers, a small private shipyard, and a naval architect signed on, but the Navy yard refused to lease facilities to the group.[16]

On Whidbey Island, federal, state, county, and city funds are being used to diversify the economy of the area surrounding the city of Oak Harbor. The city's contribution is backed by officials who were initially dubious about diversification.[17]

Washington State helped organize "flexible networks" of small defense-dependent firms that pool resources to find markets beyond the reach of a single firm. One such network is the Pacific Manufacturing Group, composed of machining and tooling shops. Acting jointly, the group bids on new contracts, purchases raw materials, and employs a full-time marketing director. "In the past," said Karen West, the research director of the Northwest Policy Center, "these companies were job shops for Boeing. They've been called the 'magically disappearing machine shops.'"[18]

The largest grants for any single program, including $1.5 million from the federal TRP, have gone to the Washington Alliance for Manufacturing (WAM). Intended to "function like an aggressive consulting group providing affordable and critical direct assistance" to aerospace and electronics companies,[19] WAM was seen as part of an expanding network of manufacturing extension centers. During its short life, WAM contended, it "made a real difference in the competitive fortunes" of twenty-seven smaller manufacturers.[20] The political changes of 1994, however, eventually killed the program.

1994 Elections Dampen Prospects

The 1994 elections brought a Republican majority to the Washington State legislature. While Democratic Governor Mike Lowrey was sympathetic to state support of diversification, the GOP-dominated legislature was not. It cut $1.5 million from the state's economic development programs, almost one-tenth of which had been earmarked for diversification. WAM, needing a significant state match for its share of the federal grant, was turned down by the legislators. WAM was dissolved in 1995.

Despite the knockout blow to WAM and the shriveling of state funds for diversification in general, Washington State has managed to keep other projects alive through federal and private grants. The newest projects include the creation of Shipnet and the Washington Aerospace Alliance, parallel efforts to achieve reduced costs and expanded sales through cooperative action. Shipnet, for example, which includes shipyards ranging from giant Todd, a major player on the West Coast, to hundred-worker facilities, is exploring joint purchase of insurance by its affiliates. The Aerospace Alliance, with an emphasis on global markets, plans to hire a salesperson to solicit major aerospace manufacturers and prime contractors worldwide.

Pioneering in Ohio

Former governor Richard Celeste of Ohio was the first state leader to showcase the issue of defense dependence. Celeste, a Democrat, called a high-profile conference in January 1990 that assembled small and medium-sized Ohio defense firms, federal officials, military procurement specialists, union staffers, and even Soviet ambassador Yuri Dubinin.

I went to the conference in Columbus, which was held just as the Cold War was coming to an end, wondering what the company representatives were thinking. The outlook of some was expressed by John MacAulay, the CEO of MacAulay Brown, a Dayton aerospace company. He told the group, "I'm not enthusiastic about abandoning this marketplace before seeing if we can expand our share." Harvey Gordon, director of government relations for Martin Marietta, explained how his company was trying to enlarge its share: by "subcontracting into more areas to expand [its] political constituency."

Nonetheless, Governor Celeste put on display a range of existing state government services available to firms that did want to diversify. Those services and others added after Celeste left office have helped numerous Ohio enterprises through technical and business advice, tax credits, and direct investments. Tax credits and a tax abatement on capital investments enabled one firm, BMY Wheeled Vehicles Division, to switch from production of military vehicles to school buses. BMY, which is spending $6 million on the conversion, is expected to add 427 new jobs over five years.[21]

Head Start in New York

New York State had 2,000 defense-dependent companies and 350,000 defense workers at the Cold War's end.[22] It also had in place the Industrial Effectiveness Program, established under the Omnibus Economic Development Act of 1987. This program, originally designed by Governor Mario Cuomo's administration to improve the productivity of New York manufacturers, was extended to defense firms facing the problems of transition.

The ARO Corporation of Buffalo was one such firm. ARO made oxygen-supply equipment for high-altitude and tactical aircraft. Looking inward, it found its organization "glued to government procurement."[23] With the aid of New York State specialists, ARO set up teams of employees to improve the quality of work, to find commercial products it could make, and to learn marketing. The partnership attained its goal. Work defects were reduced by 40 percent, the company produced a new product for the medical market, and its commercial division grew rapidly.

On Long Island, William Cahill is one of the New York State economic development specialists who provide hands-on advice to troubled defense firms. Cahill is a portly, gregarious man who formerly ran his own business. When I went with him to visit some of the firms, it was obvious that he enjoyed a close rapport with the managers he has counseled. He explained that there were conditions for this collaboration. Management has to agree in advance that the workforce will be involved in the process, and if the company is unionized, the union has to affirm in writing that it is not opposed to the outside consultation. In October 1994, Cahill was proud that the firms he worked with were commercializing effectively. Moreover, he told me, seventy companies had agreed to remain on high-cost Long Island. They pledged to conserve energy while they benefited from a state-sponsored abatement in their electricity rates.[24]

After the 1994 election of a Republican governor and a Republican legislative majority, the budget for New York's economic development agency was cut. The programs in support of defense diversification, however, continued. One program utilized federal funds to help small defense firms upgrade the skills of their employees and thus prevent layoffs.

Late Start in Texas

Texas, site of many military bases, had almost as many defense employees in 1991 as did New York if military personnel and Pentagon civilians are included.[25] That year, military procurement and payrolls brought $17.5 billion to the state.[26] The Dallas–Fort Worth area, a major aircraft center, was particularly dependent on Pentagon spending. Yet when defense downsizing began, Texas, unlike New York, had few services in place to ease the transition.

Governor Ann Richards named an impressive task force to tackle the problem. Composed of public officials and business, labor, academic, military, and public interest representatives, the task force had as vice chair Lloyd Jeffry Dumas of the University of Texas–Dallas, a recognized expert on defense conversion. The group recommended creation of a clearinghouse in the Governor's Office, a series of meetings between the governor and defense firms, a guide to help workers apply for assistance programs, and one-stop centers to deliver services to dislocated workers.[27]

Texas set up a small Office of Economic Transition. The state published a series of guides, sponsored a conference for small defense firms and, most importantly, established Texas-One, a computerized information system designed to improve the competitiveness of

Texas businesses. Established with federal and state funds, Texas-One is mandated, among other missions, to inform defense firms about diversification programs, federal laboratories, technology transfer, and export markets.

Texas received a federal matching grant to create a network that would provide hands-on services to small manufacturers, including defense firms. In this, Texas lagged behind other industrialized states.

When George W. Bush became governor in 1994, he changed the name of the Office of Economic Transition to the Texas Office of Defense Transition Services and transferred it to the Department of Commerce. The advantage of these changes is questionable. Phone calls to the renamed office in September 1995 found employees gathering information and "trying to figure out where to go." Bush also named an advisory council to help develop a coordinated approach to diversification among all levels of government and the private sector. The move gave the appearance of reinventing the wheel.

Closing the Gaps in Maryland

At the end of the Cold War, Maryland had in place a wealth of programs to bolster its manufacturers' competitiveness. When the state government looked at the special needs of Maryland's defense-oriented R&D firms and contractors, however, it found some important gaps. These centered, as elsewhere, on the firms' difficulties in entering the commercial world and their lack of working capital.

With federal support, Maryland undertook to fill the gaps. The Strategic Assistance Fund paid for half the cost of consultants to aid individual companies and groups of companies, especially in identifying new markets. The Defense Adjustment Loan Fund provided $2 million in federal and state funds, with additional funds from the private sector, for loans to firms in defense-impacted areas. As of 1995, it was too early to see the effects of these measures.[28]

Transitional Aid in Massachusetts

A survey of Massachusetts defense firms[29] showed that the most popular state programs were tax credits for R&D expenditures and investment in plant and equipment. That response is consistent with

Republican Governor William Weld's policy: Improve the economy as a whole; don't target aid to the defense sector.[30]

Nevertheless, during a transitional period the Weld administration supports an extensive array of services to defense-dependent companies, workers, and communities. The Industrial Services Program (ISP) provides matching grants to help firms develop and market new products, operates a $2.7 million revolving loan fund ($2 million from the federal government), finances workplace training for nonmanagement employees, and sponsors worker assistance centers for dislocated defense workers.

As of 1994, the ISP had received $7.8 million from the federal government, $800,000 from the state, and $1.6 million from private sources.[31]

A $10-million federal grant enabled the state to establish an industrial extension network to assist smaller firms, 13 percent of which were defense oriented in 1995. The network, based on partnerships among companies in five regions of Massachusetts, received a total of $30 million from all sources in initial funding.[32]

The Strategy of Economic Development

As the National Governors' Association concluded, "An effective defense diversification strategy is a good economic development strategy." To the degree that state governments foster development of the economy as a whole instead of trying to lure businesses away from other states, they help create the conditions that make defense conversion less difficult. This is especially true on the job front, where a growing economy can more easily absorb workers laid off by defense companies.

By using federal matching grants wisely, state governments can help manufacturers in general and defense firms in particular prepare for the competitive global marketplace and can nudge defense-dependent communities toward developing more diversified local economies. Washington State's experience as a catalyst in mobilizing local communities, which are often fearful of change, can serve as a model to other parts of the country.

On the other hand, state governments do defense firms no favor by helping them hold onto military contracts. The defense-industry sector is so different from the modern commercial world, especially in the former's notorious inability to keep costs low, that continued pursuit of Pentagon contracts only delays the necessary shift into new markets. Certainly, the shift cannot be made overnight. But companies, like governments, have limited resources, and the more energy and money spent on preserving comfortable but unsustainable old habits, the less there is to spend on learning the new ways of the future.

10 Pink Slips for Defense Workers

The big losers in the post–Cold War military-industrial complex have been defense workers. After a decade (1977–1987) of rapid expansion, defense employment reached a peak of 3,665,000 jobs before a gradual decline set in.[1] The Bureau of Labor Statistics estimated a drop of over 1.8 million from that peak by fiscal 1997.[2] Between 1990 and mid-1995, some 800,000 defense-industry jobs vanished.[3]

To put these numbers into perspective, we should note that there were *more* defense jobs almost five years after the Cold War ended than in the tense year of 1980: 2,340,000 in fiscal 1995, 1,990,000 in 1980. The overall total of active-duty military personnel, Pentagon civilians, and private defense-industry employees, however, dipped slightly from 4,969,000 to 4,750,000 over those fifteen years after reaching a high of almost 7 million in 1987.[4]

The Human Dimension

As always, statistics tell only a fraction of the story. When Gregory Stone of the *New London Day* visited St. Louis in 1992, the human toll exacted by two rounds of layoffs at McDonnell Douglas was much in evidence.[5] Robert Argent, a production planner there, had been out of work for thirteen months. Other employees had been jobless for two years. Argent told Stone: "The week before I was laid off, my wife said, 'I'll find out I'm pregnant and you'll lose your job.' This happened, and she was blaming herself for saying that." Argent eventually landed a defense job in Georgia.

Many others were not so fortunate. According to a survey in St. Louis County, fewer than half the workers laid off by McDonnell Douglas in 1990 and 1991 had found jobs by 1992; fewer than half of those lucky ones were making within $5,000 of what they had formerly earned.[6]

In focus groups sponsored by the Labor Department, laid-off and at-risk New England defense workers talked about people having to settle for jobs at wages 30–50 percent below their old rates, and frequently with no benefits. The pain this caused was suggested by a worker with thirty years' experience when he observed that extreme loss of income, disruption of his family's standard of living, and the need to start over again were "a lot to put on a person."[7]

A Rand Corporation study of California aerospace workers—older and more highly unionized than the national average—reported that close to 39 percent of those who had left their jobs since 1989 had dropped out of the workforce. Another 27 percent had not found permanent, secure jobs; when they did work, they earned roughly 14 percent less than they had in their former jobs.[8]

This predicament was not confined to displaced defense workers. Their joblessness in the early 1990s lasted approximately as long as that of many other manufacturing workers hit by mass layoffs. And within defense-industry ranks, it was African-American and female workers who were most likely to exhaust their unemployment insurance benefits.[9]

For the first time, many of those who received pink slips from defense firms were white-collar employees, high-skill production workers, engineers, and even managers. Previously, most of those affected by industrial layoffs had held lower-skilled blue-collar jobs.[10] Corporate downsizing in the commercial sector exhibited a similar trend, aggravating the unemployment problem. It was a bewildering, painful experience, especially for those who had not previously lived with the blue-collar worker's job insecurity.

Some civilian employers resisted hiring laid-off defense employees. Out of work for seventeen months, a "retired" California aerospace engineer complained in 1992: "The commercial sector looks at aerospace (workers) as overpaid and overqualified. They think we're the guys who design $600 toilet seats for the Pentagon."[11] A vocational counselor for the laid-off McDonnell Douglas workers agreed: "There's a stigma just to have designed electrical systems for aerospace. Their knowledge base is just too defense-industry bound."[12]

The Winners

While defense jobs were evaporating, shareholders in companies with the big contracts enjoyed the rewards of the stock market. Average stock price increases for the twenty top contractors, tracked by *Defense News*, beat the Dow in 1993–1994.[13] Top management did well, too. The CEOs of General Dynamics, Lockheed, and McDonnell Douglas received total compensation, respectively, of $12,454,000, $2,371,000, and $1,613,000 in 1994.[14]

The contractors did not pressure the Bush administration to help laid-off workers, and the administration resisted congressional efforts on behalf of the unemployed. In 1990 Congress authorized the transfer of $150 million from the Pentagon to a DoL retraining program, plus another $50 million to the Economic Development Administration in the Commerce Department. The administration fought the transfer. Finally, in May 1991, DoL received $50 million, a niggardly amount given the magnitude of the problem.[15]

Of $19.3 billion proposed by President Clinton to promote defense reinvestment and conversion for the 1993–1997 period, just one quarter was earmarked for training and related programs. Former military personnel and Pentagon civilians, not industrial workers, were the primary beneficiaries.[16]

Modest numbers of defense workers took advantage of a variety of services under the Economic Dislocation and Worker Adjustment Act (EDWAA), financed through Title III of the Job Training and Partnership Act. Although more than 85 percent received some form of job-search assistance, only one in five enrolled in training programs.[17] EDWAA services and those provided through the Trade Adjustment Assistance (TAA) program were implemented through state agencies, schools, and private firms.

Poor Prospects

Prospects for jobless defense workers are poor regardless of the support they receive in seeking new employment, according to a study by Elizabeth Mueller of the New School for Social Research. She compared the experience and success rate of laid-off employees of Unisys in rural New Jersey and McDonnell Douglas in St. Louis. The Unisys workers—without benefit of a union, supportive management, cooperative state officials, or a diverse local economy—received an average of only 3.8 weeks of training under TAA. Many of them were surprised to discover they were being trained for entry-level positions at low wages. Mueller reported that schools often lured workers with promises of eventual high wages, but these applied to management positions rather than the lower-level occupations for which the job seekers were actually being trained.[18]

In St. Louis, by contrast, McDonnell Douglas employees benefited from all the support the Unisys workers lacked and also received aid from a variety of federal and state grants. Yet their reemployment rate was not significantly higher than those of their counterparts in New Jersey. "In both cases," Mueller wrote, "workers are facing a job market that will not provide jobs with similar wages even if jobs are the same. In many cases, workers will need to change fields."[19]

The outlook in New England was similarly glum. Laid-off defense workers assembled in focus groups acknowledged that new employment at their level of skill or past earnings was unlikely. Participants in nearly all these focus groups, which included defense workers whose jobs were at risk, expressed no interest in additional training unless that was tied to a field where actual job opportunities existed.[20]

What if There Are No Jobs?

Manufacturing jobs, once the gateway to the middle class for millions of Americans, have been disappearing. Only one person in six is now employed in that sector.[21] Since most defense jobholders worked in manufacturing and are older as a group than other employees, their plight is particularly acute. Pentagon civilians employed on military bases fare somewhat better. They get more advance notice of layoffs, and the surrounding communities tend to receive targeted federal aid.

In the industrial sector, according to Suzanne Teegarden, director of the Massachusetts Industrial Services Program, most workers "must not only move from defense-dependent firms to firms based in the commercial market, they must also move into new industries, new occupations, new forms of work organization and new skills. These workers must rethink their lives and careers in fairly fundamental ways."[22]

Clearly, "stand-alone" training programs, with no connection to existing jobs, are totally inadequate as a bridge to such profound change. Elizabeth Mueller recommends the following steps to cope, at least partially, with this deep-seated problem: greater use of on-the-job training (which she says is underused by EDWAA and TAA); loans to facilitate employee stock-ownership plans; better oversight of training institutions; and technical assistance for retraining management.[23]

Gregory Bischak proposes a broader set of measures, including incentives for prime contractors that involve their workforce in conversion planning, high-tech business incubators, job training specifically linked to job-creation efforts, and a regional economic development role for the twelve Federal Reserve District Banks.[24]

The need for solutions comes at a time when broad economic and technological trends have converged and thereby, in the words of Labor Secretary Robert Reich,

> split the old middle class into three new groups: An underclass largely trapped in central cities, increasingly isolated from the core economy; an overclass of those who are positioned to profitably ride the waves of change; and, in between, the largest group, an anxious class, most of whom hold jobs but who are justifiably uneasy about their own standing and fearful for their children's futures.

There were 8 million jobless Americans when Reich painted that picture in 1994.[25]

George David, the president of United Technologies, a company that eliminated 33,000 U.S. jobs while adding 15,000 jobs in other countries, has painted an even starker picture. Of the 120 million Americans working today, he predicted, as many as 30 million will be at risk: 18 million in administrative support jobs prone to automation, 10 million in manufacturing jobs susceptible to foreign competition, and 2 million additional white-collar jobs "that medium and large companies like ours, under the pressure of competition, will learn to live without."[26]

The entire workforce, not just defense workers, will need added skills and education in the uncertain future. George David has urged the government to stop taxing as income the tuition reimbursements companies like his offer employees who go back to school. But even that would not be enough.

"In the end," the Congressional Budget Office (CBO) concluded in 1993, "the best solution for displaced defense workers, and for others unfortunate enough to lose their jobs, is not more federal or state programs. Rather, it is a growing economy."[27] The CBO calculated that if the U.S. economy gradually returned to full use of its capacity, it would generate 9 million additional new jobs in the 1993–1997 period. This would help "absorb displaced defense workers much more easily than did the relatively stagnant economy of recent years. Even so, however, defense workers may find it difficult to secure new jobs equivalent to those they lost."[28]

Nonfarm employment actually grew by 8.5 million between January 1993 and March 1996, with unemployment rates holding below 6 percent for an extended period.[29] Many of the new jobs were in the service sector, which "includes many low-wage positions, but also many high-wage positions in financial services, hospitals, and computer and accounting services."[30] Yet the older defense workers laid off in manufacturing could not easily secure the better-paid new service jobs.

Despite the brightening employment picture, the ranks of the jobless equaled New York City's entire population in 1996. And the real wages of those with jobs continued to stagnate, although mid-1996 saw a slight upward movement.

New manufacturing jobs are needed to reduce current unemployment, to boost wages, and to reopen the gateway to the middle class for the millions of young Americans who will not attend college in the future.

More Jobs in the Civilian Sector

One way for the U.S. economy to reach full productive capacity, a subject treated at greater length in Chapter 13, is through increased public and private investment in new industries such as advanced transportation and alternative-energy technologies. Such investments are likely to produce more jobs than is military spending, Congress's favorite jobs program.

Two studies by the Congressional Research Service (CRS), a decade apart, concluded that higher levels of employment would be generated by nondefense government expenditures than by military spending. A November 1982 report showed 8.4 percent more jobs would be created by nondefense activities.[31] In 1993, CRS studied the effects of a shift of $3 billion from military spending into a range of state and local government activities. It found that the shift would produce a net addition of 18,762 jobs, or 6,254 jobs per billion dollars.[32]

Economists Robert Solow and Albert Sommers contend that the same amount invested in rapid transit, housing, or fiber-optic networks could have created more jobs and more national wealth than the huge investment in weaponry. Paul Krugman of MIT adds, "It is crazy that we should need to have defense lead the way in public spending."[33]

A New Industry

In California, a unique nonprofit consortium, founded in 1992, is attempting simultaneously to combat the state's high unemployment and smog by creating an advanced transportation industry that could generate jobs and reduce pollution. Dubbed Calstart (see Chapter 13), the consortium's participating companies hope to create new jobs by developing an aluminum electric vehicle (EV) chassis, equipment to charge the vehicles, appropriate batteries, and other features.

Progress, however, has been slow, in good part because the Big Three automakers and the oil industry campaigned successfully against California's tailpipe emissions mandate. The mandate would have required 2 percent of the vehicles offered for sale in California in 1998 to have zero emissions. That requirement would have created a market for an estimated 38,000 EVs in California, New York, and Massachusetts, states that were prepared to implement the 2-percent mandate. It was replaced by agreements with seven U.S. and Japanese automakers to supply a total of only 3,750 EVs by the year 2000. Much of the industry opposition centered on the relative inefficiency of the traditional lead-acid battery.

Yet an efficient new battery, the nickel metal hydride, was already powering EV test vehicles in 1995. Cars powered by these batteries won the annual Tour de Sol race every year from 1994 to 1996, driving 373 miles without recharging in 1996. The developer of nickel metal hydride, the Ovonic Battery Company, a subsidiary of Energy Conversion Devices, was so confident of its product that it planned an advertisement in *Fortune* magazine. The ad was to read: "Ovonic batteries make electric cars practical."[34] But Ovonic was a partner of GM in developing the battery, and GM insisted the ad be pulled. It never appeared. Ironically, within the year GM announced the introduction of an electric car, the "EV1." Ovonic was slated to provide its nickel metal hydride battery to a second generation of the EV1, which debuted with a lead-acid battery.

Industry insiders offered the following analysis, off the record: The oil companies vigorously opposed any alternative vehicles. The automakers' opposition to mandates, however, was partly hostility to government regulation and partly inability to engage in long-range planning. But when GM, faced with Japanese competition, was finally convinced an efficient battery could be produced, it took the critical first step toward an electric vehicle industry. Chrysler and Ford followed.

Another reason for slow progress in launching a new industry, according to Lou Kiefer, the IAM manufacturing conversion coordinator, relates to the EV prototypes developed by Calstart affiliates. The prototypes were "too long-term" to mature smoothly into the production phase, he said.[35]

A new phase began on Labor Day 1995, when President Clinton announced two federal grants via Calstart to Amerigon, one of its main participants. The grants will jump-start creation of an electric-car plant at the former Alameda Naval Air Station in Oakland, California. Amerigon will manufacture EV chassis there, hiring up to a hundred workers by the end of 1996.[36] The site will also house an advanced-transportation business incubator. Meanwhile, Amerigon is not waiting for the Big Three automakers. It is busily selling EV chassis to countries in Asia. Likewise, Ovonic is finding Asian markets for its batteries even before it secures major outlets in the United States. How many jobs in the new worldwide EV market will be American?

A New Approach to Work

The search for new, well-paid jobs has led to a fresh focus on workplace partnerships. In addition to its work with Calstart, the IAM also applied for and received a Labor Department grant for a pilot project to retrain three hundred defense workers and managers for a future in advanced transportation. "Labor and management both need to be educated on how to form a winning partnership in the global marketplace," explained Lou Kiefer.[37]

Kiefer and his colleagues went on to develop "high-performance work organizations" (HPWOs), an outgrowth of the "quality management" movement but with a crucial difference: In the IAM's view, most of the efforts to improve the efficiency of manufacturing firms had avoided worker empowerment. "So," Kiefer said, "we've added several important elements such as workers and management jointly learning how to find markets . . . how to cost a product from prototype to delivery, drafting a joint business plan."[38]

The HPWO approach has been promoted by others as well. Former labor secretary Ray Marshall has identified eight components of high-performance workplaces, one of them being "effective use of all company resources, especially the insights and experience of front-line workers, in order to achieve continuous improvements in productivity."[39] And New York State's Department of Economic Development, in advising defense firms on the shift into commercial markets, offers this insight into HPWOs: "True empowerment means viewing people as the ultimate source of competitive advantage" and "giving employees—at all levels—a real voice in managing their work day-to-day."[40]

High-performance work organizations first took root in civilian soil, on three continents: in Asia with American management expert W. Edwards Deming's influence on Toyota, in Europe with labor-management power sharing in West Germany, and in North America with GM Saturn's applied philosophy of mutual trust. Some American defense contractors adopted the concepts and practices of those industrial pioneers when the Cold War ended.

It is no accident that smaller defense firms that show the greatest promise of success in converting to commercial production have followed an HPWO approach. Among them are Ace Clearwater in California, Seyer Industries in St. Louis, Frisby Airborne and Gull Electronics on Long Island, and M/A-Com in Massachusetts. BIW is the only large defense company, however, to embrace the notion of giving all of its employees a real voice in managing their work. Moreover, BIW made this approach a basic tenet of its labor-management agreement. Large or small, all of these companies have become more efficient and competitive by utilizing the insights of their employees.

The IAM has provided HPWO training to smaller southern California defense firms, including HR Textron. (See Chapter 6.) Lou Kiefer conducted workshops on this approach countrywide, visiting at least one company a week during 1994. Corporate representatives have requested the union's advice on HPWOs, and the Air

Force has encouraged a series of case studies of HPWOs in a number of firms.[41]

As the nation searches for new sources of jobs, an empowered, decision-making workforce should be a top goal for the workplace of the future.

11 Congress, Pork, and Defense Jobs

Democratic senator Dianne Feinstein of California was extolling the virtues of the B-2 stealth bomber in a June 1994 floor debate. "And it can deliver a large payroll,"[1] she assured the Senate. "Payload," she doubtless meant to say, making a military case for supporting the additional twenty B-2s that would double the number on order. But the Freudian slip gave away what was surely uppermost in the senator's mind: jobs for her constituents during a tough election contest.

A year later, the House of Representatives narrowly preserved funding for more B-2s despite vigorous opposition led by Republican John Kasich of Ohio, chairman of the House Budget Committee, and Democrat Ron Dellums of California, former chairman of the House Armed Services Committee. A bipartisan coalition of members who thought their districts stood to gain from more B-2 money had been meeting regularly to plot strategy. Among them were Democrats Jane Harman of California, Norman Dicks of Washington (where Boeing was a major subcontractor), Ike Skelton of Missouri, and Martin Frost of Texas and Republicans Jerry Lewis and "Buck" McKeon of California. Dicks lined up many of the Democrats who voted for the project, which had more than 3,000 subcontractors spread over forty-eight states.[2]

"Enemies come and enemies go, but weapons programs endure forever," Stephen Chapman wrote in the *Chicago Tribune*.[3]

Dipping into the pork barrel is an old story on Capitol Hill. Two factors, however, differentiate military pork from such traditional examples of pork as water projects and roads: the "national security" label and the enormous sums involved. Even the somewhat-reduced post–Cold War military budgets offer a cornucopia for legislators looking to bring home the bacon for their constituents.

"Tip" Ladles It In

"You will read a lot about 'pork barrel' projects being a waste of money," wrote former Speaker of the House Tip O'Neill shortly before he died. "I don't believe it. A good definition of a 'pork' project is one that's not in your area."[4]

Raytheon loomed large as the top employer in Tip O'Neill's Massachusetts district. When company officials came to Washington in the 1970s to complain that the Army, dissatisfied with test results, was threatening to cancel their Patriot missile contract, O'Neill acted quickly. He

> set up a meeting of the Massachusetts delegation with Joe Addabbo, the congressman who was the head of defense appropriations, and had him watch a movie the Raytheon people had made. We were able to convince Joe that with additional trials Raytheon could ultimately achieve a 90 percent success rate. Of course, I was primarily interested in keeping those 8,000 people working at Raytheon.[5]

The Patriot was funded. Years later, it was used against Iraqi Scud missiles in the Gulf War. The initial glowing reports of the Patriot's wartime success were subsequently challenged by defense specialists.[6] But whatever the missile's ultimate performance, Tip O'Neill's goal had been achieved. Eight thousand of his constituents kept their well-paid defense jobs, in the name of national security.

Everybody But the Taxpayers

Everybody gains from this arrangement except the taxpayers. Contractors earn profits. Working people get jobs. Jobs mean votes, so members of Congress boast of their prowess in funneling military dollars into the local economies. Pentagon officials boost their careers through support of big-ticket arms programs. In perennial competition for a heftier slice of the defense pie, the Air Force, Army, Navy, and Marines maneuver to ensure that "their" weapons systems get funded.

Although high levels of military spending during the Cold War were driven mainly by the perception of a serious Communist threat and by faith in a "strong defense," pork barrel considerations often determined which weapons, bases, and facilities were built.

In the 1950s and '60s, the Southern Democrats who chaired the House and Senate Armed Services committees, Representative Carl Vinson and Senator Richard Russell, both from Georgia, steered numerous defense contracts and bases to that state. When Mendel Rivers of South Carolina became chairman of the House committee, he redirected some of the Pentagon's generous spending toward his home state. At a lavish Washington luncheon to honor Rivers in 1970, Vice President Spiro Agnew jokingly said he wanted "to lay to rest the ugly, vicious, dastardly rumors" that Rivers "is trying to move the Pentagon piecemeal to South Carolina."[7]

In 1960, Senator Robert Kerr of Oklahoma, powerful Democratic chairman of the Finance Committee, was visited by a delegation from North American Aviation. The delegation pitched the merits of the B-70, a strategic bomber the company wanted to build to replace the B-52. Kerr responded sympathetically, then added: "But there's one thing missing." "What's that, Senator?" a North American engineer asked. Kerr paused for dramatic effect, then replied with a wide smile, "You haven't told me what's in this for Oklahoma!"[8]

Subcontractors: Lobbying Support

What's in this for most of the states was spelled out in the Air Force lobbying campaign for the B-1 bomber in 1975. Rockwell was the prime contractor, with subcontractors in forty-eight states. "Rockwell and Air Force lobbyists," chronicler Nick Kotz reported, "armed themselves with meticulous lists of every B-1 subcontract location, cross-referenced by state, town and congressional district. The studies, prepared by both Rockwell and the Air Force comptroller's office, showed how many dollars of B-1 money flowed into a congressional district each month."[9] Members of Congress took notice. Those dollars added up to a lot of jobs.

The lobbying campaign went all-out: unstinting hospitality for members of Congress at Rockwell's fishing complex, hunting lodges, and resort; letter writing by Rockwell and subcontractor employees; lobbying assignments for government officials, generals, and members of the Air Force Association; solicitation of support from veterans' organizations; contractor-generated films, ads, and editorials.[10]

The barrage finally paid off in 1981 with President Reagan's decision to build a hundred B-1B bombers. Three crashed during test flights. Because of technical problems, the remaining planes were not flown in the Gulf War despite Air Force claims that they could be converted to carry conventional bombs. (Their original mission was to drop H-bombs on the Soviet Union.) With a $35 billion price tag in 1995 dollars,[11] the B-1 has been a costly make-work program. But it did produce jobs and profits, if not more military strength.

The Air Force used similar techniques in the early 1980s when it teamed up with a different contractor, Lockheed, to sell Congress on buying an updated version of the C-5 cargo plane despite the fact that the original C-5A had been plagued with cost overruns, mechanical failures, and a bad maintenance record. The campaign utilized subcontractors for heavy lobbying that emphasized jobs, and it even made special approaches to members of the Congressional Black Caucus.[12]

Undeterred by revelations in the press of the lobbying plan, the House approved the C-5B by a whopping 289–127 vote. The GAO investigated the lobbying for the cargo plane and concluded that use of federal money to organize such grassroots legislative pressure was prohibited. Its report went to the Reagan Justice Department, which decided not to prosecute.[13]

Anchors Aweigh!

The Air Force and its contractors held no monopoly on selling arms to a willing Congress. The Navy too perfected the jobs argument in its campaigns for more aircraft carriers. In 1987, the Virginia delegation to the House spearheaded a campaign to build two new carriers at Newport News. Tenneco Shipbuilding & Dry Dock Company, the biggest private employer in Virginia, would do the work.

The Navy already had fourteen carriers, enabling it to project U.S. power to literally every corner of the earth. Representative Lynn Martin (R.–Ill.), who later became secretary of labor, tried to eliminate both carriers. She complained that the Navy had distributed to members' offices projected carrier-related job gains, listed by congressional district. "I do not fault the Virginia delegation," she said on the House floor, "for trying to protect for its state some of the most incredible jobs, and, frankly, pork of the century. Were it my district, I would do the same. But our obligation is a different one. It is to make sure this nation is ready, and that the nation's security will not be impaired, even to the benefit of one, two or three states."[14] Nevertheless, the House funded the carriers.

Seven years later, even though the Cold War had ended, the Navy, Tenneco, and the Virginia delegation were back for more. In a closed hearing on May 5, 1994, the House Armed Services Acquisitions Subcommittee had just voted for a new nuclear-powered carrier, CVN-76. Representative Norman Sisisky (D.–Va.), who represents Newport News, asked chairman Ron Dellums for "a 30-second break." Dellums asked why. "I have 50 people waiting outside who want to hear this," Sisisky replied. Dellums agreed, and Sisisky left the room. "You could hear cheering from the corridor," a staff member told me.[15]

Reporting on the full House Armed Services Committee session the next day, the Associated Press wrote: "Lobbyists representing the Navy, the shipyard and the United Steelworkers pressed committee members for support. According to a Navy estimate, the carrier project affects 120,000 jobs in 40 states."[16] Aircraft carriers make waves on land as well as at sea.

With the purchase of CVN-76, to be commissioned in 2002, the Navy will be able to maintain a twelve-carrier fleet well into the next century. In order to make way for the new carriers, six old ones are being retired prematurely—nine to nineteen years before the end of their anticipated life-spans. American central cities, bridges, and sewer systems may decay, but up-to-date nuclear-powered aircraft carriers will continue to serve as the U.S. Navy's "forward presence" around the world.

Carriers don't sail the seas alone. They move in battle groups. Not counting supply ships, a battle group includes one carrier, two cruisers, four destroyers, helicopters, planes, submarines, and an oiler. The cost in 1994 dollars: $18 billion a year for procurement, plus $740 million a year to operate[17]—all this with barely a word to explain why the United States needs so many warships in a world where most of the wars are bloody internal clashes among contending ethnic groups.

Aligned with Contractors

With the disintegration of Soviet military power, those who seek to keep military spending near Cold War levels have trouble finding foreign threats to justify such expenditures. The Clinton administration based its Bottom-Up Review on the need to counter two regional threats, in the Middle East and the Korean peninsula. Yet Iraq and North Korea combined don't quite measure up to the old threat from Soviet missiles and land armies. There also is sincere talk about maintaining military "readiness" and the "defense-industrial base." But what majorities in Congress really believe is that military spending is the best defense against unemployment. The Soviet Union is gone, but joblessness back home is a clear and present danger.

Senator David Pryor (D.–Ark.) said as much in April 1994 as he described a meeting that morning with a group of Democratic senators. "They were saying we can't cut military spending any more," he told me. "They don't admit it, but it's about jobs. I wish we would call it a jobs program instead of defense. We've been at it for 40 or 50 years. It's a huge spigot that's been flowing too long."[18]

The spigot was much in evidence that year during House debate over McDonnell Douglas's C-17 transport plane. Designed to carry tanks and armored vehicles to Third World landing fields, the C-17 had a history of cost overruns, delays, and technical problems. The House Armed Services Committee had cut from six to four the number of C-17s to be authorized in 1995. The savings were to be used to explore alternative aircraft, including the conversion of civilian wide-bodied planes. Democrat Jane Harman and Republican Steve Horn, both from southern California, led the efforts in the House to restore the two C-17s.

The easiest way to keep track of the debate, an Air Force official involved in the lobbying told the *Washington Post*,

> is by knowing which member of Congress is aligned with which military contractor. House Majority Leader Richard A. Gephardt (D.–Mo.), for example, is counted on as a C-17 supporter because he represents St. Louis, where McDonnell Douglas is headquartered. [Norman] Dicks, by contrast, is generally a C-17 skeptic; Boeing, which would benefit if the C-17 program is kept small, is headquartered in Washington [State]. Still other members are known as 'Lockheed types,' since that company builds the C-5, and also could benefit from the C-17's demise.[19]

This close, bipartisan alignment with the big defense contractors back home turns members of Congress into the companies' sales force on Capitol Hill. Occasionally the competition is hot, but the customer is eager. On the C-17 issue, the House voted 330–100 to restore the two cargo planes.

The Case of Jane Harman

Representative Jane Harman provides an illuminating case study in the dynamics of defense politics. Her Los Angeles–area district contains a mix of aerospace workers and affluent constituents and almost an equal number of Democrats and Republicans. In the campaign leading to her first election in 1992, she called for continued military cuts, coupled with efforts to retrain workers and reorient defense contractors.[20] In her freshman term, however, she was a leader of the fight for the C-17.

When I interviewed her in 1994, Harman spoke of assessing foreign threats first, then "we may stress something because of jobs."[21] She cited regional threats, nuclear proliferation, and terrorism as reasons for needing a "strong defense," although how more military power can combat the latter two is not always clear. Harman had already joined Democrats for a Strong Defense, a House group that opposed further military reductions.

She had three possible motives for promoting the C-17: First, thousands of workers, many of them constituents, built the plane very close to her district. Second, more-senior members of the Armed Services Committee hesitated to step forward because of the C-17's poor reputation. Third, McDonnell Douglas was beginning to overcome production problems. The first reason was undoubtedly most compelling.

There was no comparable reason for Harman to help lead the 1995 fight for more B-2s and to urge White House chief of staff Leon Panetta to back the bomber.[22] Potential job gains in her district were minimal. There were many other bombers on airfields and under construction. But Harman, a former corporate lawyer married to the owner of a consumer electronics company, is socially close to the top executive of Northrop Grumman, manufacturer of the B-2. Observers report that she is very comfortable in settings where company executives are present. Harman's social milieu may have contributed, at least indirectly, to her embrace of big weapons programs.

So did the 1994 election, which she won by only 812 votes. Frightened by near-defeat, Harman appears to have increased her dependence on defense contractors and employees. Like many other legislators, Jane Harman worries about her constituents' jobs—and her own. By 1996, she was advocating production of the F-18E/F fighter, which the GAO had advised against. Northrop Grumman's plant that is the main subcontractor for the plane is in Harman's district.

Northrop Grumman will be there for Jane Harman. During the first seven months of 1995, the company's political action committee (PAC) gave $230,950 to congressional candidates. Nearly a third of this total was distributed in the weeks following a key B-2 House vote, almost all to lawmakers who voted to fund the bomber. The $5,000 gift to Harman was the biggest Northrop Grumman gave in that period to any House member.[23] This was in addition to the $86,050 Harman received from defense-firm PACs in 1993–1994, $10,000 of which came from Northrop.[24]

Does Money Prevail?

The 219 House members who voted for the B-2 in June 1995 received, on average, $3,285 from Northrop Grumman and major subcontractors' PACs in 1993–1994, compared to $1,305 for those who voted against it.[25]

What role did money play in the outcome? No member of Congress will admit that campaign contributions affect his or her votes. But contributions are only one source of pressure among many that defense corporations can apply. Northrop Grumman, for example, spent over $1 million in print advertising during a one-month period of its B-2 campaign.[26] Prime contractors often hire high-priced Washington lobbying firms to bolster their own staffs in campaigning for weapons programs. The mobilization of subcontractors, perhaps the most potent source of pressure, also costs money. It's hard to pretend money has no influence.

Against that backdrop, let's look at who gives and who gets campaign contributions. Defense PAC contributions rose a steep 784 percent during the decade ending 1988, comparable to the increase among all corporate PACs.[27] Although defense PACs no longer disburse as much money as do those from some other sectors, they still contributed a sizable $7.5 million to members of Congress in 1994.[28] In that election year, Lockheed and Martin Marietta, before their merger, contributed a total of $1.1 million. Northrop and Grumman, before their merger, gave a total of almost half a million dollars. General Dynamics, still campaigning for the Seawolf submarine, provided $385,112.[29]

Defense contractors contribute primarily to incumbent members of the Armed Services and Defense Appropriations committees. Kenneth Mayer, who teaches political science at the University of Wisconsin, wrote in 1991 that "defense PAC money is split two to one in favor of hawks."[30]

The PACs' largesse favors the majority party, which controls the chairmanships. Before the 1994 elections, Democrats were favored. Following the Republican congressional victory, defense PACs quickly switched their attentions from Democrats to Republicans, the latter receiving almost three times as much money as the beleaguered Democrats in the first six months of 1995.[31]

Congressman John Murtha (D.-Pa.) has been the longtime favorite of the defense PACs. As the veteran chairman of the House Defense Appropriations Subcommittee until the GOP takeover of the House, Murtha rarely met a military program he didn't like. A true believer in both military and legislative power, Murtha single-mindedly used his post to boost projects in his home state: steel subcontracts for new aircraft carriers; overhaul of a carrier in the Philadelphia Naval Shipyard; the V-22, a helicopter made in Pennsylvania and Texas that the Bush administration had tried, unsuccessfully, to kill; and an armored ammunition carrier to be built in York, Pennsylvania.[32] Defense PACs gave him $208,325 in 1993–1994. Charles Wilson (D.-Tex.) and Norman Dicks (D.-Wash.) were runners-up among House members.[33]

In the Senate, Dan Coats (R.-Ind.), a member of the Armed Services Committee, leads in the defense-money race—he received about $350,000 in the 1989–1994 period—followed by Ted Stevens (R.-Alaska), Bennett Johnston (D.-La.), Arlen Specter (R.-Pa.), and Phil Gramm (R.-Tex.).[34]

Kenneth Mayer contends that defense PACs may as well save their money. Contributions to influential members of the relevant committees, he wrote, "do not purchase votes; careful analysis shows that nearly all defense contractor PAC money flows to members who are predisposed to support defense programs—their voting behavior would have been the same even if contributions had stopped."[35]

Norman Ornstein of the American Enterprise Institute, one of the country's most astute observers of congressional affairs, thinks the technique of spreading defense subcontracts into many congressional districts "speaks 100 times louder" than campaign contributions. The impact of local spending by the Pentagon and the potential of gaining or holding defense jobs, he asserts, are a powerful force on Capitol Hill.[36]

Why, then, do defense firms continue to contribute to congressional incumbents? Because, says former congressman Tom Downey (D.–N.Y.), now a lobbyist, "PACs are organized just so the companies can be in the game. Everybody else is in it."[37] And given the expense of congressional campaigns, generous contributions can help keep friends in office.

The influence of defense companies may be measured not only by the campaign contributions they give members of Congress (and the $210,000 in "soft"—unregulated—money they sent to the Republican National Committee in the first two months of 1995).[38] Their employees, subcontractors and suppliers, lobbyists, recreational facilities, and advertising budgets—all have been repeatedly mobilized to keep the contracts coming; just another cost of doing business with the government, paid for by the taxpayers.

Not All Succumb

Not all members of Congress succumb to these pressures. In the House, the late Stewart McKinney (R.–Conn.) voted his conscience rather than going along with the narrow interests of local defense firms. Jim McDermott (D.–Wash.) opposes the B-2 despite Boeing's towering presence. Pete Stark (D.–Calif.) has bucked Lawrence Livermore, which is located in his district. Barney Frank (D.–Mass.) has led numerous struggles to reduce military spending in the face of a sizable group of defense-dependent constituents. Tom Andrews (D.–Maine) was a leader in opposing conventional arms exports even though BIW exerted heavy pressure on the other side.

In the Senate, John McCain (R.–Ariz.), who spent five and a half years as a prisoner of war in North Vietnam, has led a sometimes lonely crusade against military pork. In a phone call from Phoenix in 1994, he described as "obscene" all the money for pork. "It's a total corruption of democracy," he said heatedly.[39] McCain is particularly incensed at the practice, perfected by John Murtha and his former Senate counterpart, Daniel Inouye (D.–Hawaii), of injecting projects that have little to do with defense into defense appropriations bills. This usually takes place behind closed doors in House-Senate conferences, where the differences in the separate bills are ironed out.

McCain is a stalwart supporter of the military and was the recipient of a sizable $142,000 from defense PACs in the 1989–1994 period. That, however, did not deter him from reciting a list of unneeded, big-ticket weapons systems, all duly authorized by congressional committees, none sneaked in through the back door: the B-2; the upgrade of the troubled B-1; the submarine-launched Trident II missile, whose target vanished along with the Soviet Union; the MILSTAR satellite communications system, originally devised to fight a six-month nuclear war; and LHD amphibious assault ships. McCain further declared construction of barracks and bases "a big pork barrel."[40] McCain, joined by Senator John Warner (R.–Va.), later expanded the list to include the Seawolf submarine, C-130 cargo planes, and additional equipment for the National Guard and Reserve forces.[41]

Did a GOP Majority Change the System?

The new Republican majorities roared into Congress five years after the Cold War ended. Particularly in the House, they brandished the Contract with America, whose Item 6 called for more military spending, a missile defense system, and no U.S. troops under UN or foreign command in NATO.

The bottom line was made clear in the opening days of the session. Floyd Spence (R.–S.C.) and C. W. Bill Young (R.–Fla.), respectively the chairmen of the renamed House National Security Committee and the House Appropriations Subcommittee on National Security, wrote, "Even after the Clinton defense budget is 'scrubbed' for internal savings, a commitment of substantial additional resources to the defense budget will be required."[42]

It did not take long for the new leaders to resort to the old tricks. Speaker Newt Gingrich urged Defense Secretary Perry to spend much of the $501 million appropriated for military reserve aircraft on C-130 planes made near Gingrich's district.[43] Senate Majority Leader Bob Dole, on a campaign swing through New England, switched from opposition to support of the third Seawolf submarine,[44] thus following the example set by candidate Bill Clinton in 1992.

It was the work of the defense committees, however, that provided the true test of whether pork would continue to drive military spending in a period of budget austerity. By July 1995, the report card was ready.

The Senate Armed Services Committee added a net $4.7 billion to the fiscal 1996 defense authorization bill. Four-fifths of the increase would go to states represented by members of the armed services or defense appropriations committees. The Council for a Livable World, which released this study of "pork business as usual," dubbed Trent Lott (R.–Miss.) "champion" for securing almost $2 billion in business for Mississippi contractors.[45] John Isaacs, president of the council, said that because of congressional cuts in domestic spending, "the inconsistency and hypocrisy are more blatant than in the past."[46]

The House National Security Committee's military-construction budget contained $500 million in add-ons, and more than 80 percent of those extras were earmarked for projects in committee members' states. The projects included new squash courts at the Puget Sound Naval Shipyard and renovation of an Air Force band's recording studio. When *Newsweek* learned these facts, it asked Chairman Floyd Spence for a comment. Spence replied that every new project passed a "rigorous, self-imposed screening process."[47]

And in the House Appropriations Committee, efforts by Representative David Obey (D.–Wis.) to cut funding for the F-22 fighter and missile defense were defeated by a 4–1 ratio, with numerous Democrats joining Republicans: a tribute, wrote Dan Morgan of the *Washington Post*, "to the support that even some liberals are willing to give to a project that will provide thousands of jobs nationwide."[48]

The GOP-dominated Congress, contrary to normal routine, passed a military appropriations bill before the authorization bill that spells out policy. The appropriation was $7 billion higher than President Clinton's proposed budget, $5 billion of which was for weapons. He let it become law without his signature in order to pay for the operation in Bosnia. But when Congress passed the authorization bill, Clinton vetoed it. He objected to its support for a missile defense that could upend the ABM Treaty and for new restrictions on the president's power to deploy troops on peacekeeping and humanitarian missions.

In the Senate, respected defense specialist Sam Nunn (D.–Ga.) cast his first vote against a military bill in twenty-three years. He objected to the antimissile measure and to "earmarks" specifying particular shipyards to build ships authorized by the bill. The yards are in the states and districts of key committee members: Senators William Cohen and Trent Lott and Representatives Bob Livingston, Duncan Hunter, and Curt Weldon—all Republicans.[49] The Senate passed the bill by a largely party-line vote, 51–43. John McCain and Mark Hatfield were the only Republicans to vote against it. Four Democrats voted in favor.

In 1996, the second year of Republican congressional control, Senator Charles Grassley (R.–Iowa) bucked his party's drive for increased military spending. He moved to cut $8 billion from the military authorization. The move was defeated, 57–42. Only a handful of Grassley's GOP colleagues backed him. Ten Democrats, including both senators from Connecticut and from Louisiana, voted against his proposal. The Senate then gave the military $13 billion more than President Clinton had requested. On the House side, 75 Democrats joined 197 Republicans in passing a bill that exceeded the Clinton administration's request by $12 billion. The full Congress agreed to a military authorization that was $11 billion above the president's request.

That inflated authorization bill, amounting to almost $266 billion in taxpayers' money, corresponded roughly to the Republicans' federal budget-reduction plan, which encompassed reductions in almost everything except "defense." Meanwhile, an informal, bipartisan White House–congressional coalition kept military spending "off the table" in budget negotiations.

By preserving the military budget as a sacred cow while chopping civilian programs, this coalition sapped the nation's international as well as domestic strength. The State Department's international-relations budget—addressing such key issues as nuclear proliferation, access to foreign markets, the flow of refugees, and terrorism—was at 49 percent of its Cold War high in 1996. Combined military and intelligence expenditures were at 80 percent.[50] Moreover, Congress slashed the funds to implement the hard-won U.S.–North Korean nuclear agreement.

Ironically, those who believe military issues should be decided for military, not economic, reasons made their best showing in two narrow House votes for additional B-2 bombers, which even the Pentagon did not support. Pork in the form of the B-2s survived, but in this case 40 percent of Republican freshmen voted against the B-2, compared to 30 percent of the rest of the Republican conference.[51] One of the opponents, Frank Riggs (R.–Calif.), talked about the pressures that had been exerted by Northrop Grumman and members of the California delegation. The latter, he said, "look at the B-2 in the context of a parochial program for California, a jobs program."[52]

It is understandable that members of Congress should want more jobs for their constituents, especially as manufacturing employment becomes more uncertain. But in dipping shamelessly into the military pork barrel to reach that goal, they distort the country's priorities, block fresh approaches to military policy, and undermine the search for new, well-paid, long-term jobs in the civilian economy. Congress embodies defense addiction at its worst.

12 The Clinton Administration and Dual Use

In an article that appeared in *Think*, the IBM magazine, back in 1960, Senator Hubert Humphrey quoted some advice from Federal Reserve Board chairman William McChesney Martin, Jr. Martin was concerned about federal preparation for the day when Cold War clouds would disappear. "Much as I believe in the market process and the desirability of private enterprise," he said, "I think that government would have to assume a role in that sort of transition similar to the work that the Defense Mobilization Board is presently doing for mobilizing our resources in case of the opposite situation."[1]

As one who helped draft that article, I've been watching since then to see whether the government would indeed do contingency planning for transition to a post–Cold War economy. It has been a long wait.

Neither the Eisenhower nor the Kennedy administrations created anything resembling a *Disarmament* Mobilization Board. But on August 2, 1963, Senator George McGovern vigorously raised the issue in a Senate speech. He attacked military overspending and proposed standby plans for the conversion of defense industry to civilian production. McGovern was a freshman Democrat from South Dakota who was impressed with the ideas on defense conversion of Seymour Melman, professor of industrial engineering at Columbia University.

By then, Humphrey, McGovern's neighbor in suburban Maryland, was Senate Majority Leader. McGovern had sent him an advance copy of the speech. I accompanied McGovern from his office on his way to speak on the Senate floor. We encountered Humphrey in the Capitol. He told McGovern, "That's a great speech, George. But hold off. It's too risky." Humphrey's admonition was prompted by the Senate ratification debate on the Limited Nuclear Test Ban Treaty. When this controversial first U.S.-Soviet arms-control agreement came up, a distinctly Cold War atmosphere prevailed in the Senate. In urging McGovern to "hold off," Humphrey ignored the political value of having a forward-thinking ally break ground for a cautious leadership.

McGovern went ahead and delivered the speech. In October, he introduced the National Economic Conversion Act. It would have created a commission to study nonmilitary market opportunities and obliged defense firms to do their own planning. Although the bill attracted thirty-one cosponsors, the Vietnam War buried it.

In 1970, a Senate Government Operations Subcommittee chaired by Abraham Ribicoff circulated a questionnaire to industrial leaders that asked their opinion on whether the government should establish an interagency conversion commission. His survey report complained of "the lack of initiative" by private industry and urged "a strong federal role in conversion and in the use of industry resources for public programs."[2]

Representative Ted Weiss (D.–N.Y.), also influenced by Seymour Melman, subsequently introduced bill after bill incorporating a strong federal role. His measures would have mandated "alternative use committees" made up of representatives of defense management and labor, and including nonvoting members from local government, to plan for commercial production. These bills garnered liberal Democratic support but went nowhere.

Thirty Years of Inaction

It took no less than the end of the Cold War in 1990 plus a recession to nudge the government into some kind of action. And Congress, not the executive branch, stirred first.

Congress, as already noted, funded the modest worker-retraining programs whose implementation the Bush administration significantly delayed. A task force named by Senate Democrats came up with recommendations for assistance to laid-off Pentagon civilians and military personnel, to the defense industry, and to defense-dependent communities. These recommendations, with others, were enacted into law in the fiscal 1993 Defense Authorization Act. The Pentagon was given the primary responsibility for carrying them out, but there was no overall plan to smooth the transition.

The 1993 law, however, did direct the secretary of defense to prepare regulations requiring defense contractors to plan for diversification. The Defense Department failed to comply.[3]

While Congress was debating the defense bill, Bill Clinton was running for president. He had a plan, or at least the outline of one. A campaign document, "Clinton/Gore on Defense Conversion," listed the following program commitments under the rubric of targeting defense cuts to infrastructure investments: "Transportation: renovate our country's roads, bridges and railroads; create more American jobs by developing a high-speed rail network to link our major cities and commercial hubs; invest in 'smart' highway technology to expand the capacity, speed and efficiency of our major roadways; and develop high-tech short-haul aircraft."[4]

The Democratic candidate also promised to create a national information network (the "information superhighway"), to increase investment in civilian high-tech applied R&D, and to "reinvest every dollar that would otherwise be cut from defense R&D and technology industries into federal civilian R&D and generic technology programs."[5] A promise to establish a civilian advanced technology agency modeled after the Pentagon's Defense Advanced Research Projects Agency (DARPA) made no mention of dual use—the development of technologies that serve both military and commercial purposes. Yet dual use would dominate the Clinton administration's efforts in the transition away from a Cold War economy.

For the first time, U.S. political leaders announced a broad defense-conversion strategy that envisaged public-private investments in cutting-edge industries and infrastructure. These investments were meant to raise living standards and create new jobs in the civilian sector. Would the leadership deliver?

Clinton's Choices as President

At a Westinghouse plant near Baltimore in 1993, President Clinton announced a program called "Defense Reinvestment and Economic Growth Initiatives." The program, at a cost of almost $20 billion over five years, would affect both the military and civilian sectors. It included nearly $5 billion for dual use technologies, $5 billion for helping displaced personnel, and almost $10 billion to be allocated among nonmilitary R&D partnerships between industry and government, certain civilian manufacturing projects, and advanced-technology projects.[6]

Clinton seemed most interested in the dual use segment. He announced a toll-free number, 1-800-DUAL-USE, to receive proposals from corporations willing to set up industry consortia. These would work with the Advanced Research Projects Agency (ARPA) in the Defense Department.

The Technology Reinvestment Project was created as an interagency body to implement the dual use approach to R&D. It operated under the wing of ARPA. That agency, in its earlier existence as the Defense Advanced Research Projects Agency (DARPA), had helped subsidize Sematech, the semiconductor industry's consortium. ARPA was experienced in working with high-tech industry and tapping into its technologies for military uses. Not surprisingly, a sharp tilt toward the military emerged at TRP, although not all at once.

At the outset, Clinton clearly hoped that TRP would serve a broader purpose. In April 1993, he said it "will play a vital role in helping defense companies adjust and compete [in the civilian sector]. I've given it another name—Operation Restore Jobs—to expand employment opportunities and enhance demonstrably our nation's competitiveness."[7]

Under Attack, TRP Bent

Roughly a quarter of early TRP grants went to large defense companies. Lesser shares went to large civilian companies, small civilian companies, and colleges and universities.[8] Few small defense firms participated. Some of these grants helped a few defense companies, such as BIW, explore new commercial possibilities. But as TRP came under conservative attack as some wild "industrial policy" that would divert Pentagon dollars into defense conversion, the emphasis became unabashedly military. A 1995 TRP report stated: "The TRP's basic strategy is to leverage commercial market size, technological know-how and investments for military benefit by entering into cost-shared investments with private organizations."[9] If that wasn't explicit enough, the report added: "Over the past year, the

TRP has made a concerted effort to increase the number of militarily relevant proposals it receives."[10]

As for Operation Restore Jobs, in December 1995 TRP director Lee Buchanan stated emphatically, "I don't care" about jobs.[11] For Buchanan, the agency's purpose was to redirect defense managers toward a lower-cost, more commercially oriented defense-industry base. By then the GOP-led Congress was defunding TRP out of existence—but dual use would live on. The promise to expand employment opportunities in civilian industry went the way of empty political rhetoric.

Military industry would certainly benefit from exposure to commercial mores. For several decades, defense industry has been less efficient than the commercial sector. Raymond Kammer, deputy director of the National Institute of Standards and Technology (NIST), told me flatly, "military technology is inferior."[12] He pointed to thirteen-to-fifteen-year procurement cycles for defense, compared to procurement cycles of eighteen months in commercial electronics and eight months in the software industry. "We've induced military industry to dumb down," Kammer observed.

"Today," Jacques Gansler writes, "the defense industry is what the economists term a 'sick' industry, and it is getting worse. The current congressional and executive bailouts—through extension of old, unneeded production—and the simultaneous increase of government regulation and oversight are only making the inevitable changes more difficult."[13] The White House has admitted that many commercial firms refuse to do business with the Defense Department.[14]

Piggybacking

When he was deputy secretary of defense, John Deutch was frank about how to overcome the problem: "We have to benefit from economies of scale and keep up with leading-edge technologies. That means we must piggyback on commercial production."[15] What Deutch called "piggybacking" is commonly termed dual use.

Kenneth Flamm of the Brookings Institution, who worked for Deutch in the Pentagon, cites these reasons for dual use: (1) It can speed up long-term, leading-edge R&D for the military; (2) if this development can be hastened, it can spin out military technology into commercial areas; and (3) it can insert commercial technology into weapons systems. The military could then buy some components off the shelf, thus lowering costs.[16]

It sounds good, but it may not happen. If the ultimate goal is to lower costs to the Pentagon and to taxpayers, the savings won't show up for years. Meanwhile, decreased competition in the defense industry, due to merger mania, may lead to higher, not lower, costs.

Nor is it clear that dual use will benefit the commercial sector. First, most firms that sell components off the shelf to the military are unlikely to increase their business significantly. Second, in "defense-unique" production areas (such as production of tanks, fighter jets, missile seekers, or submarine reactors), commercialization is not relevant. Third, corporations that operate in military markets are generally organized very differently from those that operate in commercial markets. Companies with a foot in each market often erect walls to prevent the practices of the defense side from contaminating their commercial business. Raymond Kammer mentions Motorola as an example of a company that has built such internal walls.[17] The administration hopes to break down these barriers, but it won't be easy.

The Economic Roundtable in Los Angeles expressed its skepticism about dual use by asserting that it resembles "trickle-down economics" in its expectation that technological benefits will flow from military to commercial markets.[18]

In addition, the Clinton administration's pursuit of future dual use technologies does little for those defense-dependent firms that seek to enter commercial markets now. Their chief needs are information and capital. In focus groups composed of defense-sector representatives in seven cities from California to Maine, researchers for the Northeast-Midwest Institute found widespread demand for government information on markets, marketing, and conversion success stories, and for access to existing military technologies. "In essence, they asked for one-time help to make the transition," the researchers reported; "they do not seek ongoing subsidization, just a bridge over the chasm."[19]

In emphasizing military needs, the administration's dual use policy ignores manufacturing sectors, such as steel and textiles, that suffer from a lack of R&D funding. As administered, the policy is also largely oblivious to areas of major national need—including advanced transportation and renewable energy[20]—despite a dual use project to develop technology applicable to both fighter planes and school buses.

Procurement Reform

Hand in hand with dual use, the Clinton Pentagon has undertaken reform of its bizarre procurement system. That reform, since it addresses the differences between commercial and military industry, may be valuable, but it is hardly a substitute for defense conversion.

Over the years, the Defense Department and Congress have developed a heavy-handed system of regulation and oversight for the purchase of weapons and supplies. A Pentagon document characterized it as "an extremely complex system spanning acquisition needs from nuclear weapons to chocolate chip cookies."[21] Some 31,000 mil specs have been imposed on contractors,[22] raising production costs. The military pays $10 for computer chips that are virtually the same as ones being sold commercially for $1, according to a White House report. "The $9 difference is due to contractor overhead and other costs of DoD's special but often unnecessary requirements."[23]

A history of contractor abuse was a major reason for the heavy-handedness. "The need to protect against contracting abuses," said a report prepared for DoD in 1994, "must be balanced by a concern for the cost of this oversight. However, while horror stories about over-priced toilet seats are very visible . . . the costs of regulatory compliance are difficult to identify."[24]

In order to cut these costs and streamline its buying practices, DoD has decided to replace mil specs wherever practical with commercial and performance standards. Certain components of larger weapons systems would be bought off the shelf. The revamped system, announced in June 1994, began with new contracts and was later extended to existing contracts. Top officials predicted eventual savings of several hundred million dollars a year.[25]

The Pull of the Market

Growing markets drive technology, not the other way around. For that reason, the Electronic Industries Association (EIA) concluded in 1994 that "any conversion approach which emphasizes technology as a driver, not an enabler, is doomed to failure." EIA declared that government leadership might be helpful and that government funding was "essential" in stimulating markets based on major national needs. Among those needs: information superhighways, telecommunications systems, intelligent highway systems, air transport, and protection against crime and fraud.[26]

The electronics industry and the 1992 Clinton/Gore campaign both sketched out a range of investments in high-tech infrastructure that could link expanding markets to national needs. With that potential in mind, let us see how the Clinton administration and Congress actually spent money on defense conversion understood in its broadest sense.

The private National Commission for Economic Conversion and Disarmament has tallied these expenditures for fiscal 1993–1996, the final year's figures confined to the budget request. The total came to $17.3 billion, not far from the figure President Clinton proposed in 1993 for a five-year period.[27] The largest single slice, $6.145 billion, went for dual use initiatives. Another $5.641 billion was spent on aid to defense-dependent employees and communities, the lion's share going to military personnel entering civilian life. The third largest segment, $4.167 billion, was invested in such high-tech programs as information highways, intelligent vehicles, and environmental technology.

Modest efforts by two civilian agencies accounted for the balance of the expenditure. NIST ran the Advanced Technology Program (ATP). It sought to improve U.S. industrial competitiveness through cooperative agreements on high-risk R&D projects, many of them in biotechnology and materials. The Republican Congress moved to end this program, and succeeded in cutting its budget in half. NIST also operates the Manufacturing Extension Partnership, which sends engineers out to work at regional centers with private enterprises seeking technical advice. Maritech, the second agency, helped defense firms find technologies that could be applied in commercial shipbuilding. Together, NIST and Maritech received $1.3 billion for work that could be judged conversion related.

As for civilian R&D, there was no dollar-for-dollar transfer from military programs. Rather, there was Clinton's high priority for industrial technology, much of it geared to the armed services. The Pentagon's share of federal R&D spending dipped slightly from 58 percent in 1993 to 53 percent in 1996.[28]

Underfunding Investments

The greatest weakness in Clinton administration policies on defense conversion was overemphasis on dual use and underfunding of investments in advanced transportation, energy alternatives, and the environment. Even when NIST and Maritech programs are added to the funding of high-tech initiatives, the four-year total reaches only half of the $10 billion promised in 1993.

When Clinton dropped most of his 1993 "stimulus" package under pressure from those championing deficit reduction, he provided an early clue to his reluctance to fight for goals he had staked out during the election campaign. An example of that retreat: Even before Republican majorities took over Congress, the Clinton administration decided it could not afford even the token appropriation to study mag-lev trains that originated under President Bush. "It's very unfortunate," said Ken Van Dillen, the chairman of the High Speed Rail Association's mag-lev task force, "that the U.S. has not moved out on mag-lev the way Germany and Japan have."[29]

Intelligent highway R&D was decently funded, but there was no renovation of railroads, roads, and bridges. The Republican Congress even slashed operating funds for Amtrak. All of this left the United States without a national railroad system worthy of the name, much less a comprehensive transportation system linking airports, trains, highways, and regional mass transit.

Through spending cuts, House Republicans also sought to end the various government-industry partnerships that, they feared, were helping Clinton build bridges to business.[30] TRP was phased out and ATP was attacked. More important, single-mindedness on budget reduction and GOP hostility to government investments effectively buried any hope that Clinton would keep his 1992 promises to invest in the future.

In its near-term programs to help the defense-dependent, the administration fell short in retraining workers and helping companies identify commercial markets and find new sources of capital. DoD's Office of Economic Adjustment (OEA) and the Commerce Department's Economic Development Administration (EDA) did a generally good job aiding in the reuse of closed military bases. OEA's grants proved invaluable in helping some small defense firms convert. EDA's work in communities facing defense-contract cuts, however, was somewhat uneven. The Office of Economic Conversion Information, housed in EDA, answered 4,000 requests a month from the public in 1995.[31] But it wasn't quite a one-stop-shop for all the government's scattershot conversion programs.

The Other Side of the Street

Two policies of the Clinton administration negated the modest achievements of its conversion programs. First, the administration kept military spending higher than the international situation warranted. Second, in the name of the "defense-industrial base," it bought costly weapons systems the military didn't need.

Early in his term Clinton proposed spending $120 billion less on the military in 1994–1999 than President Bush had, a difference of a scant 1 percent a year. Then Clinton added another $36 billion for 1995–1996. In 1995, Lawrence Korb, reviewing figures he had previously used, calculated that the United States already spent over four times as much on defense as any other nation, almost twice as much as the other fifteen NATO nations combined, and more than all the rest of the major nations in the world combined.[32]

By the time Senate and House Republicans reached agreement in 1995 on balancing the budget in seven years, their plan called for *increasing* the military budget by $58 billion while *cutting* so-called discretionary domestic programs by $190 billion and entitlement programs such as Medicare and Medicaid, plus debt service, by another $766 billion.[33] Half or more of all discretionary spending—the part of the budget that Congress can control—was devoted to the military during fiscal 1993–1997.

Clinton, for his part, made no effort to make the Pentagon take its proportionate share of budget cuts. Both before and after the Republican takeover of Congress, military spending was effectively off the budget-balancing table. Nor did Clinton reduce the Pentagon's expensive secret programs. An estimated $14 billion was lavished on secret R&D for new weapons in 1996, not counting "undiscoverable billions spent for operations, support and construction projects."[34]

In the absence of any major military threat, what explains this generosity toward the Pentagon during a period of austere budgets? On the surface, the answer is the Pentagon's Bottom-Up Review, which assumes a need to fight two regional wars almost simultaneously and without allies. This would require U.S. forces costing about a quarter of a trillion dollars a year into the next century. But the real answer is jobs and pork.

One existing military factory in the hand is thought to be worth ten potential high-speed rail plants in the bush. As we have seen, members of Congress scramble to land military contracts for the factories and shipyards back home because contracts mean jobs and jobs mean votes. For Clinton, it was no doubt easier to go with the flow of pork to military industry as a jobs program than to make the case for future public investments.

Furthermore, because of charges that he evaded the draft during the Vietnam War, Clinton felt too politically vulnerable to challenge military leaders in their own domain.

Unneeded Weapons

There is a case to be made for keeping military production lines "warm," not allowing a big gap in orders to cause layoffs and loss of skills. There is an equally logical case to be made for limiting the so-called defense-industrial base to that needed to meet real-world military threats. Bill Clinton chose the former over the latter.

Candidate Clinton's embrace of Electric Boat's Seawolf submarine during the 1992 election campaign was a transparent attempt to woo voters. As a Democrat, he would have been unlikely to carry Virginia, home of Electric Boat's competitor in Newport News. But he had to carry New England, and there the Seawolf was the ticket to thousands of votes. Three years later, Bob Dole's political situation was different, but he embraced the Seawolf for essentially the same reason.

As president, Clinton fully backed the Connecticut legislators' campaign to buy three Seawolfs from Electric Boat, thus tiding over the company until the next generation of attack subs could be built. Yet the builders of the Seawolf, which was designed to destroy its Soviet undersea counterparts, had to look for new missions for their costly product after the USSR dissolved. Even if a plausible military mission had been found, the work could have been shifted to Newport News, probably at less cost. That, however, would have destroyed the sub's real reason for being: jobs and votes in Connecticut and Rhode Island.

The Seawolf is a clear case of an unneeded post–Cold War weapons system. The addition of B-2 bombers is another. While the administration did not support more money for the B-2, it was unable to dissuade Congress. Funding passed by only three votes in the House. Congress repealed the twenty-plane cap on B-2s and added $493 million to the 1996 defense bill Clinton signed. The president then ordered aides to take "a fresh look" at buying more bombers.

House Budget Committee Chairman John Kasich commented, "The Pentagon has already done a thorough and complete review and concluded it doesn't want any more B-2s. I get the sneaking suspicion that California politics is behind this latest move."[35] Finally, with Defense Secretary Perry and the Joint Chiefs of Staff opposed to more spending on B-2s, Clinton decided against adding money—beyond the $493 million.

Excessive Pentagon spending has repercussions well beyond electoral politics. It conveys a dangerous message to defense-dependent companies and communities: Don't prepare for change; the status quo will keep you safe. It also makes balancing the federal budget more difficult, perhaps forcing deeper cuts in domestic spending. For the price of a single B-2 bomber, for example, the nation could pay the annual health-care expenses of 1.3 million Americans.[36] If Congress refused to buy unneeded bombers, it would have more flexibility in funding popular domestic programs such as Medicare.

By opting for defense jobs in key states, Clinton flabbily accepted the notion that military spending had been cut enough—from the grotesquely high mid-1980s levels of the Reagan administration. In so doing, he helped starve his own domestic programs and provided ammunition to those who say government can do little right beyond maintaining strong armed forces.

In the competition for scarce tax dollars, military spending should be treated neither as a sacred cow nor as a pork barrel—rather, it should be treated as one important government responsibility among many.

13 The Bigger Picture

Americans are approaching the millennium in an anxious mood. Despite socioeconomic conditions that people elsewhere envy, including low inflation and interest rates, booming sales of consumer electronics, and a rising proportion of college graduates, many Americans are haunted by insecurity. They worry about jobs and income, about their children's future.

As 1996 began, AT&T announced plans to eliminate 40,000 jobs. Staggering as the number was, it had already been surpassed by IBM (63,000) and Sears (50,000).[1] Big corporations have chosen downsizing as the way to cut costs and meet global competition. Wall Street seems to love downsizing. AT&T stock jumped $2.50 the day of the announcement. But elsewhere the announcement spread gloom, aggravated by a steady erosion of real wages and the wider use of temporary employees in a workforce where fewer than one in seven are unionized and drawing union wages.[2]

Global competition now arrives with a relatively new twist: Many manufactured goods are no longer made in a single country. Secretary of Labor Robert Reich once described a sports car that had been financed in Japan, designed in Italy, and assembled in Indiana, Mexico, and France, containing advanced electronic components invented in New Jersey and fabricated in Japan.[3] A few years later, Reich could have cited Boeing's most modern passenger plane, the 777, whose parts are manufactured on four continents. This global dispersion of labor drives down costs—and reduces the number of manufacturing jobs in the United States. On the other hand, foreign-owned corporations add some manufacturing jobs by investing in plants in the United States.

Job losses add to problems trailing in the Cold War's wake. The first five post–Cold War years brought little change to the witches' brew of inner-city joblessness, poverty, crime, drugs, racial divisions, and crumbling infrastructure. If the majority of Americans are now employed and living in reasonable comfort despite anxiety about the future, that is small consolation to the many who live trapped in near–Third World conditions—but with TV sets.

In some ways the defense industry parallels the larger economy. Rising stock prices and solid profits accompany massive layoffs. Defense firms, too, see a shrunken workforce as the most direct path to reduced costs. But firms in the defense sector, unlike firms in the commercial market, cannot survive without the direct support of the federal government.

How, then, do we as a nation climb out of our post–Cold War predicament? How can we reduce defense dependence while building a peacetime economy that provides opportunity to all Americans? If there is a simple answer, I don't know it. But I can suggest new directions and a first step.

The first step requires a coolheaded reassessment of what truly threatens us. For two generations Americans were more or less unified by a perceived threat from armed communism. That threat has dissolved. Today the threats are both global and domestic, but they are not primarily military. As we examine them, it becomes evident that we must broaden our view of security.

A Survey of the Threats

The world's population has doubled since 1950. So has per capita income.[4] More people and more intensive use of resources have taken a toll of the earth's fisheries, forests, aquifers, and soils. Fish and other seafood stocks are being depleted, and 30 percent of the world's cropland is losing productivity because of soil erosion.[5]

Topsoil loss, deforestation, and, in Africa, the spread of deserts have driven millions into cities. Shantytowns fester from Guatemala to Brazil, from West Africa to India. Travel to scores of Third World countries has convinced Robert D. Kaplan that conditions in Lagos, Nigeria, are the prototype of "the coming anarchy": overcrowding, urban crime, pollution, disease, and social breakdown.[6]

These conditions prevail where population growth is highest, governments are incapable of coping or indifferent to suffering, or both, and armed bands often rule the countryside. "A large number of people on this planet," writes Kaplan, "to whom the comfort and stability of a middle-class life is utterly unknown, find war and a barracks existence a step up rather than a step down."[7]

Seeking food and fleeing war, millions have become cross-border refugees, in the process making immigration a hot political issue. In the future, environmental and demographic stress and widespread lawlessness will produce still more refugees, while wealthier nations will increasingly be called on to fight famines, wars, and disease.

One huge problem that does not respect borders threatens the world's rich and poor alike: global warming. Carbon emissions from fossil fuels, the chief offender, increased from 1.6 billion to 5.9 billion tons between 1950 and 1994.[8] The Intergovernmental Panel on Climate Change forecast in 1995 that if these emissions continue to increase, Earth's temperature could go up four degrees Fahrenheit by 2100. As a result, the next century could see droughts, destructive storms, and rising sea levels.

Bangladesh and Egypt would be most exposed to flooding; other coastlines, including those on both sides of the Atlantic, would be threatened as well. To avert such climate change, global emissions would have to fall sharply. But despite international agreements limiting emissions, many countries lack the political will for restraint. In the United States and other developed countries, the oil and coal industries lobby to curtail limits on fuels that produce the warming gases, while Third World countries claim rights the First World has already exercised in order to raise their peoples' living standards.

Action to introduce alternative energy sources is urgently needed. Insurance companies and bankers have increasingly become advocates for solar energy as the costs of massive storm damage threaten them with bankruptcy.

After experiencing the blizzard and frigid temperatures of 1996, some Americans scoff at the notion of global warming. They are not aware that climate change does not abolish winter; rather, it adds moisture and energy to the atmosphere. According to James Hansen, director of NASA's Goddard Institute for Space Studies, "Global warming has made the Atlantic an even greater source of moisture."[9] And more moisture has already produced punishing storms from Panama and Massachusetts to France, India, and Korea.

As the earth warms, other changes will occur. Tropical diseases will move into the temperate zone, exposing its inhabitants to maladies such as malaria and dengue.[10]

Stuck in the Military Rut

The Clinton White House, however, discerned other specters: "Instead of a potential confrontation with a global nuclear power, we find ourselves facing challenges that are different but no less complex: the spread of nuclear weapons and other weapons of mass destruction; major regional, ethnic and religious conflicts; and opposition to democratic reform in the former Warsaw Pact and the Third World."[11] Top officials saw these as demanding Cold War levels of military force and spending.

The spread of nuclear weapons is an implausible rationale for the fast, mobile military forces the White House seeks to maintain—unless it is preparing to invade the closet nuclear states of India and Pakistan. The two most hostile near-nuclear countries, Iraq and North Korea, are severely constrained by internal and external pressures. The former was badly wounded by U.S. forces in the Gulf War, subjected to economic embargo, and forced to accept intrusive international monitoring, although Saddam still holds power. And North Korea, many of whose citizens were going hungry in 1995–1996, has signed an agreement with the United States to limit its nuclear program to civilian purposes.

Terrorists with a suitcase bomb might become a more realistic future threat than Iraqi or North Korean weapons, but military forces would probably be irrelevant in that scenario.

Opposition to democratic reform is an even flimsier pretext for current U.S. force levels. Do we send in the Marines as recycled Communists win elections in Eastern Europe? Do we invade Mobutu's fiefdom of Zaire? Saudi Arabia? Nigeria? If the president ever discussed the specifics of this argument in public, he would be laughed off the podium.

That leaves regional and civil wars, at the heart of the Pentagon's current strategy. Among the most common of post–Cold War conflicts, regional wars would indeed require fast, mobile forces if the United States decided to intervene. But in the highest-profile regional war, two U.S. administrations took almost four years to send U.S. troops to Bosnia, and then they were sent only after the warring parties had signed a peace treaty and other countries made the operation multinational. The American public is wary of unilateral military interventions, and if asked would not have supported a strategy based on two simultaneous regional wars—without allies.

Alternatively, the United States could, without undue risk, prepare to fight one regional conflict while keeping some forces on standby for use in international peacekeeping. Colonel Daniel Smith and Marcus Corbin of the Center for Defense Information have calculated that smaller armed forces that included beefed-up reserves could implement such a strategy at an annual cost of $175 billion. This would save $185 billion over three years by comparison with Clinton administration projections.[12] U.S. armed forces, backed by nuclear weapons, would remain the most powerful in the world.

Home-Front Weaknesses

On the domestic scene, long-festering problems have produced rifts similar to the stark gaps we see between rich nations and poor. Deep divides separate employed from unemployed, educated from ill-educated, skilled from unskilled, top management from ordinary workers, whites from minorities, native-born from immigrants, men from women.

These divisions, most visible in our growing segregation by income, sap our ability to resolve complex problems. The top fifth of American households, which earned 49 percent of all income in 1994,[13] tend to wall themselves off from their fellow citizens. Twenty million affluent Americans live in private, gated communities that are in many cases policed by armed guards.[14] Segregation by income, combined with the effects of dwindling federal reimbursement of state and local government spending, has led to unequal public services.

The public schools most clearly reflect this inequality. Teachers in the affluent Boston suburb of Belmont, for example, earn almost a third more than those in poverty-stricken Chelsea, where children bring a host of problems to school with them every day.[15] Wouldn't the other way around make more sense?

New Directions

Economic development and environmental protection should form the keystone of foreign and domestic policies, bolstered by international cooperation abroad and cooperation among government, business, and labor at home. Smaller, less-costly U.S. defense forces and strengthened UN peacekeeping should deal with the military dimension of security.

To employ the millions of Americans, including those laid off by defense industry, looking for reasonably secure and well-paid jobs, the United States needs new productive enterprises, new products, and new environmentally clean industries as engines of growth. While the private sector will have to steer the engine, government will have to help fuel it. The private sector alone cannot provide the building blocks of healthy expansion, namely, an upgraded infrastructure, a trained and literate workforce, and civilian R&D that addresses national needs. Together, these building blocks can raise productivity through public as well as private investment.

Upgraded Infrastructure

Infrastructure absorbed over 6 percent of the nation's nonmilitary federal budget every year in the 1950s; by the 1980s, that share of the budget had dropped to only 1.2 percent. In 1989, the DoT estimated that to repair 240,000 bridges would cost $50 billion. Repairs to highways would require $315 billion.[16] Two years later a French government economist remarked to Jacques Gansler, "I can't understand your country putting billions into placing a man in orbit when your highways and railroads don't work."[17] The wealthiest country in the world limps toward the twenty-first century transporting people and goods on crumbling highways, shaky bridges, slow trains, and overcrowded airports.

Assessing national needs in physical capital—highways, transit, aviation, rail, and water and sewage—the Economic Policy Institute estimated that federal investments should be roughly $55 billion annually to overcome a growing public investment deficit. Some of the investments would have to last for years.[18] Looking more broadly at 1994 investment needs in new equipment, upgraded transportation and communications systems, public education, and worker retraining, C. Fred Bergsten of the Institute for International Economics put the figure at $300 billion a year from both public and private sources.[19] Here, too, investments would have to continue over the long term. The alternative is a nation in decline.

A Trained, Literate Workforce

As I visited defense firms in ten states while gathering material for this book, I heard tales of workers—not all of them immigrants—who didn't know English well enough to read directions. Apparently this deficiency exists across the American industrial landscape, at a time when modern factories demand communication and math skills.

Clearly, our education system has to do a better job preparing youngsters for a fast-changing future. Better-qualified teachers, smaller classes, computers, and a longer school year, should be only the starting point. For the three-quarters of students who don't go on to college, especially as the demand for lower-skilled workers decreases, an apprenticeship system comparable to those of Europe should be set up. For laid-off workers as well as employees, educational loans or on-the-job training should be offered to upgrade existing skills and to teach new ones. Training should be oriented toward job openings or promising fields.

Training, however, should go beyond learning better ways to shape metal or plastic. It should also deal with workplace organization. The smaller defense firms I visited that show the most promise of converting to commercial production have switched from top-down management to participation by the entire workforce in decisionmaking. Throughout the economy, adaptive, flexible companies have organized cross-functional work teams that decide how to improve quality and cut costs. Ideally, everyone works toward a clear, measurable set of goals.

About one worker in ten was organized in teams in 1995. Industrial psychologist Richard Wellins estimates that 30–50 percent will be working in teams by 2000.[20] But changing the work culture is hard. Managers and workers alike need to be trained for it. This is a job for the private sector, guided by outside consultants.

Civilian R&D

A civilian R&D program geared to national needs faces a serious hurdle: the continuing dependence of many scientists and engineers on Pentagon money. Military spending and an estimated half of space spending accounted for 60 percent of federal R&D funding between 1974 and 1984. This meant a large majority of research scientists and engineers depended on subsidies from the Pentagon and NASA.[21] Of the $19 billion the aerospace industry spent on R&D in 1989, almost $16 billion came from the government.[22] The level of dependence has declined somewhat since then, but the Pentagon continues to dominate federal high-tech R&D.

Meanwhile, our competitors, especially Japan and Germany, invest relatively more of their resources in civilian R&D.[23] The public-private investments in consumer electronics by Japan, for example, helped that country steal the march on American industry. "If the brightest engineers in Japan are designing video recorders and the brightest engineers in the United States are designing MX missiles," MIT economist Lester Thurow said as the Cold War ended, "then we shouldn't find it surprising that they conquer the video recorder market."[24]

Many civilian markets remain to be conquered. To prepare the way, federal R&D funding has to be redirected into civilian areas and imbued with a heightened environmental consciousness. Gary Chapman and Joel Yudken urge building the principles of sustainable development into all R&D programs. They define sustainable development as economic development that does not curtail opportunities for future generations because of environmental damage or resource depletion. The application of this principle can take many forms: pollution prevention, recycling, development of renewable energy sources, conservation, and development of new production processes.[25]

Achieving a Consensus

Advocates of eliminating the federal budget deficit make the valid point that the burden of debt should be lifted from our children and grandchildren. By the same token, we should also be investing in those things that will enable present and future generations to lead a decent life.

At a time of tight budgets, a balance should be struck between deficit reduction and long-term investment. The most democratic way to reach this balance would be for the political leaders we choose to sponsor a serious public debate on broad national priorities rather than simply on the role of government. Is deficit reduction more important than repairing the infrastructure? Education more important than a tax cut? Renewable energy more or less important than retraining? Where does health care figure in the overall picture?

The president and legislative leaders could formulate the questions, urge private groups and the media to discuss them in many forums over several months, and invite individual responses from the public. Once the public has been heard from, the government—the executive branch and Congress—could shape new spending priorities with some confidence that real choices had been aired and a broad consensus achieved.

Partnerships

Just as the private sector, by itself, cannot repair our infrastructure, improve the skills of our workforce, and fund civilian R&D, neither can the federal government. Public-private collaboration is needed to carry out this immense task.

Some collaboration is so common that we take it for granted. Private firms, for example, repair roads and bridges under federal and state contracts and provide innumerable services to government agencies. Other less-traditional forms of cooperation are still evolving. The agreements between private companies on the one hand and the national labs and federal research programs on the other could serve as prototypes for joint R&D projects.

Rob Stein, former chief of staff to the secretary of commerce, is of the opinion that individual government agencies by themselves no longer have the capacity to make things happen in our complex society or in the global economy. Stein favors strategic alliances of agencies working on common problems.[26] Likewise, individual private firms may not have the resources to take on high-risk R&D projects. Strategic alliances of businesses, labor, and federal agencies should work on these projects, particularly through consortia in which costs and risks are shared. In the recent past, consortia have included few smaller firms, and labor has been virtually invisible. Efforts are needed to bring in both.

The case for including labor is based on the conviction, held by several unions, that jobs can and should be created through the introduction of new products with worldwide appeal—electric cars, for example. These unions also believe that labor and management should be partners in developing products and designing production processes. This approach could accelerate the pace of research projects and keep the goal of job creation in plain view.

Consortia can also be launched at the state and regional levels. Calstart in California, for example, has become a significant model. Organized to promote advanced transportation and thus help clean California's polluted air and create jobs, Calstart brings together defense and aerospace firms, high-tech companies, vehicle manufacturers, electric and natural gas utilities, universities, national labs, public agencies, and labor and environmental organizations. The DoT and ARPA are working with Calstart on electric, natural gas, and hybrid vehicles.

By sharing information and development costs, participants have been able to enter a new industrial frontier at reduced risk. Among the achievements of this cooperative venture as of mid-1995 were development of a showcase EV applying twenty technologies from seventeen companies, an electric school bus, hybrid school buses powered by compressed natural gas, a light-weight chassis for EVs, and a range of other technologies. In a survey of Calstart's participants, forty firms predicted they would create a total of 12,000 new jobs by 1999.[27]

If government agencies, including the Pentagon, purchase fleets of EVs, if California and other states maintain at least minimal incentives for emission-free vehicles on their roads despite industry pressures, and if automakers proceed with the manufacture of electric cars, economies of scale will reduce the price of this nonpolluting transportation. Thus, a new industry bringing good jobs will burst on the American scene. In the process, we will reduce our dependence on foreign oil and on the ruling groups of Persian Gulf countries. Solar-powered vehicles could be next—if the federal and state governments help create the market.

But Isn't This (Gasp) Industrial Policy?

Isn't the collaboration between government and business that I am proposing just another example of the "industrial policy" that has provoked such fervent denunciation? Call it what you will. Industrial policy is probably as good a name as any, but there are real differences between what I am proposing and what has been called "industrial policy" in the past. What I am proposing would bring existing policy out of the closet, reorient it, and include labor as a participant.

Since World War II, the U.S. government has had an unavowed policy of lavishly subsidizing the big defense and space contractors. Ann Markusen and Joel Yudken have described this closet industrial policy as one that targets particular sectors as growth leaders, provides capital, determines the number of competitors, guarantees a government market, and provides generous support for R&D. Initially the government targeted the aircraft industry; later on, computers, space, and communications.[28]

Federal support for these industries eventually spun off a number of civilian byproducts in addition to computers: jet engines, transistors, nuclear power plants, space satellites, lasers, polymers.[29] As a result, there is lingering popular support for the proposition that military spending ultimately provides useful products to consumers. That, however, becomes increasingly untenable as military technology falls further behind its commercial counterparts.

Instead of waiting for civilian products to trickle down from costly military programs, the government should drop dual use R&D and let the Pentagon sponsor military research. At the same time, civilian agencies should pursue civilian R&D linked to national needs and share risks and costs with those that stand to benefit from resulting products: private enterprises.

In working with business and labor, the federal government need not provide the package of benefits and inducements offered to defense and space contractors. But Washington can make an important contribution by helping open new civilian markets. A story told by Peter diCicco of the AFL-CIO Industrial Union Department illustrates the point. A few years ago, union representatives urged Jack Welch, chairman of GE, to start manufacturing rail cars in a plant scheduled for major layoffs. As diCicco tells it, "Welch said he would be quite happy to make rail cars as soon as the federal government established a national transportation policy."[30]

Imagine how manufacturers would react if the government adopted—and fully funded—policies favoring high-speed trains, solar and wind energy, and even good old-fashioned bridge maintenance and repair!

Who Should Underwrite Investments?

The money for expanded public investments could come from cuts in military spending, an environmentally friendly tax code, and a variety of other sources—if the will is there. There are ways to produce an effective military at lower cost. Before he became secretary of defense, William Perry helped devise one that conformed to the realities of the post–Cold War world and would save many billions of dollars. Working as a private citizen with colleagues from universities and think tanks, Perry embraced the concept of "cooperative security."

This approach encompasses (1) strict controls on nuclear forces; (2) defense conversion; (3) international treaties to restrict military forces to defensive capabilities; (4) multilateral military intervention, and that only as a last resort; and (5) open access as the basis for verification of international agreements, including those on the spread of advanced technologies.[31]

Perry wrote:

> A fundamental principle of a cooperative security regime is that each member agrees to limit its military forces to what is necessary for defense of its territory. However, a small number of nations, including the United States, must maintain certain elements of their armed forces beyond that required for territorial defense and make these elements available to multinational forces when needed. The objective of limiting national military forces to a defense capability is to create a situation in which aggression cannot succeed, and therefore is not likely to occur.[32]

Regrettably, Perry didn't try to introduce this concept when he became secretary of defense. But cooperative security remains a constructive, less-costly strategy despite some unanswered questions. Among them: How could governments be assured that such a strategy would be practical and safe? What would happen if some governments accepted it while others rejected it? What would be a feasible and useful U.S. contribution to multinational forces?

The last question is easiest to answer. Assuming an international effort to strengthen the UN's capability to repel aggression, prevent mass slaughter and widespread starvation, and monitor armistice agreements, the United States should place specified airlift and sealift units on standby for possible use by the UN should the Security Council vote for a military response. The United States has the unique capability of enabling multinational operations to respond rapidly anywhere in the world. Other countries should provide ground troops, also on standby: the unsung veterans of UN peacekeeping from Canada, Scandinavia, Fiji, Ireland, and Austria; the untested modern armies of Japan and Germany; and the powerful forces of Great Britain, France, India, and Pakistan.

The tougher questions about cooperative security can best be answered through the sustained exercise of American leadership. Since no nation has a monopoly on brains or cash and many nations are increasingly bound together by a web of trade and investments, it is wise to address security problems multinationally. Without American leadership, however, multinational efforts often languish.

Leadership can draw upon an array of resources, ranging from the power of example to various forms of aid and diplomatic pressures. In pursuit of cooperative security, the United States could further reduce its excessive nuclear arsenal as it insists that other governments forgo the nuclear option. It could curb its own foreign arms sales before asking others to follow suit. It could push to scale back the military forces of all UN members to defensive status and press U.S. allies to place some ground forces on standby for UN military action, with transport to be supplied by American planes and ships.

Beyond military measures, the United States could also help strengthen multinational efforts on a number of civilian fronts. It could overcome its unenviable status as biggest deadbeat at the UN and pay its back dues. It could encourage expansion of UN fact-finding and mediation services, programs to share new farming and irrigation techniques, and assistance to family planning. We might note that the entire world community now spends a total of $5 billion on family planning,[33] equal to the amount Congress added to the 1996 defense bill for weapons that the Pentagon did not request. In addition, the United States could work to speed up implementation of agreements to reduce greenhouse gases and promote an open trading system that mandates environmental and labor standards.

A cooperative strategy of that nature would cost far less than a foreign policy largely dependent on a far-flung network of military alliances, troops, and bases—with no real enemies in sight. William Kaufmann, who worked with the team that wrote *Global Engagement*, made some cost estimates in 1992, using President Bush's projections in his calculations. He estimated that powerful but scaled-back U.S. forces could be fielded at savings of $623 billion over ten years.[34]

Three top physicists, Philip Morrison, Kosta Tsipis, and Jerome Wiesner, one of whom had served as President Kennedy's science adviser, presented their own plan in 1994. They proposed armed forces including but not limited to six active Army and Marine divisions, six Reserve divisions, five carrier groups, and eight hundred nuclear warheads. The savings came to $670 billion in 1994 dollars by the end of the decade, based on President Clinton's projections.[35]

Savings of that magnitude could finance a lot of infrastructure.

As could a more environmentally aware use of the tax code. Today the federal government subsidizes the fossil fuels most responsible for global warming and pollution. The oil companies, for example, have been receiving a depletion allowance for decades, along with other tax breaks. International oil companies are allowed to write off substantial profits earned abroad. Coal and gas companies are similarly favored, as are mining and timber interests that deplete our resources.

Instead of encouraging environmentally harmful activities, we should provide tax breaks to companies that produce electricity through solar and wind power. Subsidies to producers of polluting fuels should be phased out. Coal, oil, and gas could be taxed at the source, both to limit pollution and to bring in more revenue.[36]

Additional investment funds can be found, provided the political leadership is willing to take on entrenched interests. Prime candidates are a revamped tax structure, Medicare reforms, corrected Social Security indexing, and termination of subsidies to corporate agriculture and tobacco. An end to the tobacco subsidy would also contribute to lowering the nation's medical bills.

Which Way Public Opinion?

Is the public ready for major change? Americans are certainly eager to improve their own economic situation, however much they differ over specifics. As far as military and foreign policy are concerned, polls show that a majority favor cuts in military spending and the principle of UN peacekeeping.

A 1995 poll by the University of Maryland's Program on International Policy Attitudes found that a modest majority backed significant cuts in the military budget and putting military spending "on the table" in efforts to balance the budget. In another survey, approximately two out of three favored contributing U.S. troops to UN peacekeeping and paying UN peacekeeping dues in full. An overwhelming 89 percent embraced the position that "when there is a problem in the world that requires the use of military force, it is generally better for the U.S. to address the problem together with other nations, working through the UN, rather than going it alone."[37] Right-wing nationalists may make more noise, but most ordinary Americans appear open to a strategy of cooperative security.

Bucking Conventional Wisdom

Some of the ideas presented here run counter to the conventional wisdom and today's public cynicism. The conventional wisdom, however, is not always wise. It ignores major problems: job insecurity, the widening gap between the most affluent and the poorest Americans, conditions in our inner cities. When the conventional wisdom prevails, it often results in bad decisions. Thus, even though the United States accounts for fully 37 percent of the world's annual military spending and defense appropriations consume half of discretionary federal spending,[38] a bipartisan consensus allows the Pentagon's budget to rise.

Public cynicism is even more damaging than bad decisions. It distances voters and taxpayers from civic and political involvement. Yet such involvement would be the most direct means of changing the country's direction.

Conclusion

At its core, America's defense addiction is largely economic, a pursuit of jobs, careers, and profits. Since the excesses of the defense sector drain treasure, natural resources, skills, and brainpower from the nation's efforts at renewal, the cure also resides in the economic domain.

Virtually unchallenged, the U.S. military establishment is now assured of annual budgets exceeding a quarter of a trillion dollars into the next millennium. Its 800,000 civilian employees form the single biggest slice of the federal bureaucracy.[1] Nuclear weapons installations and military bases continue to harbor the costly accumulated pollution of decades of Cold War. The Pentagon's arsenal, from H-bombs to rifles, far exceeds military requirements in today's troubled but relatively safer world. Before leaving the Pentagon, retired Air Force Chief of Staff Merrill McPeak observed that the U.S. Air Force is the world's largest and the U.S. Navy's air wing ranks third, after China's air force. McPeak, incidentally, favors a one-regional-war strategy with a downsized armed force of 1 million members.[2]

Pentagon spending levels feed defense addiction, and defense addiction keeps Pentagon spending at levels disconnected from global realities. Meanwhile, the public has been robbed of any "peace dividend."

This cycle won't be broken until defense-dependent Americans admit they have a problem, and this they are unlikely to do until they clearly see economic alternatives. Practical alternatives won't surface until political parties, opinion leaders, academics, and the media take seriously the urgency of educating the public about realistic choices in today's world.

Hard-headed public education must start at a very elementary level. Only 24 percent of Americans could name both of their senators in a January 1996 survey. Only 34 percent knew that Bob Dole was Senate Majority Leader even as he ran for president a third time; nearly half didn't know Newt Gingrich was Speaker of the House. They believed the government was spending more on foreign aid (actually less than 2 percent of the federal budget) than on Medicare (13 percent).[3] With the Cold War over, much of the public didn't even see any real reduction in the possibility of a third world war.[4]

Good News and Bad

Within the defense-industry sector, there have been some encouraging developments along with additional bad news.

The really good news is that many smaller defense firms are successfully navigating the passage into commercial markets. Their flexibility and commitment to the transition provide a worthy model for the whole industry. Moreover, one prime contractor, Hughes Electronics, is steadily expanding its commercial business, while GE, Westinghouse, and others have essentially quit the defense field.

More modestly, several defense companies have parlayed their long experience with commercial products into profit-making diversification. Raytheon and TRW, for example, are selling to both civilian government agencies and individual consumers while maintaining their military business. Even some of the top military contractors have a few commercial lines. And the Defense Department is promoting reform of the convoluted military procurement system.

There are three pieces of bad news. First, most of DoD's reforms are "smoke and mirrors," in the words of one defense-company CEO. Second, the big defense corporations that are sticking to their guns in the military-industrial complex have grown even bigger through mergers. Finally and most significantly, the military-industrial complex retains its powerful influence in American life.

The CEO, speaking anonymously, observed that basic change in the defense industry is not possible so long as the sole buyer of weapons (the Pentagon) and the sellers (defense firms) necessarily deal only with each other. This closed system, dominated by the Pentagon and manipulated by the contractors and their political allies, is light-years away from a free market. No amount of buying minor items off the shelf at Circuit City will alter the limited scope of defense competition, the clout of big contractors, or the eagerness of powerful members of Congress to dip into the military pork barrel.

As to corporate giantism, it translates into enhanced political clout. Now the Maryland headquarters of Lockheed Martin, largest of the defense conglomerates, can quickly mobilize the support of its own employees—plus the subcontractors to the three formerly separate major companies (Lockheed, Martin Marietta, and Loral) spread strategically across the country. Northrop Grumman can do almost as well. As we have seen, subcontractors have long played a critical role in lining up congressional backing for major weapons programs, including some military leaders did not request.

Having amassed ample assets through long-term public largesse, the big defense firms should now fend for themselves without special treatment from the government. They are able to vie with each other for military contracts and to try to expand into civilian work. Either way, the coddling should end. Federal and state programs to facilitate the conversion of defense companies should be limited to small and medium-sized firms, whose needs are primarily technical assistance and credit.

Norman Augustine and Kenneth Adelman made an interesting proposal for defense conversion in 1992, their "substitution model." It would provide

> government assistance and incentives to small start-up entrepreneurial enterprises that then selectively hire away the employees of the existing defense firms and, in some cases, even buy or rent parts of existing defense factories. This approach helps assure that the existing management and culture are left behind eventually to wither away, residues of excessive government-imposed bureaucratic oversight attuned to a different era. Under this model technology is transferred the way it has always been transferred—although seldom recognized as such—in the minds and skills of the workers.[5]

The authors' proposal was addressed to the ex-Communist countries. Why limit it to them?

To be sure, the military-industrial complex has undergone some changes since President Eisenhower warned about its unwarranted influence. Its place in the economy is relatively smaller, it is made up of fewer defense contractors, and it employs fewer workers, scientists, and engineers. But the complex continues to roll on, escaping close scrutiny as it shapes national priorities and military policy.

Elected decisionmakers—the president and Congress—are still theoretically in charge. Unfortunately, they abdicated their responsibility well before the noisy arrival of seventy-three Republican freshmen in the House in 1995 made their task even more difficult. Spiritual heirs of Ronald Reagan, largely unschooled in military matters beyond their reflexive support for Star Wars and a "strong defense," the freshmen's fiscal conservatism did not always extend to the military establishment. With GOP majorities in both houses, Republicans replaced Democrats at the military pork barrel, for which they were generously rewarded by defense PACs, less concerned with party labels than with the ability to deliver.

One Republican, Chairman John Kasich of the House Budget Committee, stood out as a consistent, across-the-board budget cutter. But when Kasich moved to reduce Pentagon spending, the chairman of the House National Security Committee, Floyd Spence, accused him of "siding with people who want to destroy the nation's defense."[6]

Economic Development

It may be impossible to satisfy such accusers, but in fact economic development is today's key to constructive change *and* national security. I obviously do not mean development that offers inducements to polluting industries, sports stadiums, and gambling casinos. We need development that will raise living standards and create jobs— particularly in the country's most neglected and underdeveloped areas—while sparing air, soil, and water from pollution.

Such development includes but goes beyond the public infrastructure, R&D, and training discussed in Chapter 13. As Ann Markusen and Joel Yudken have pointed out, a governmental economic development strategy is not just a spending program; it aims at leveraging spending from the private sector[7] and, through private investment, achieving economic growth.

The benefits of economic development must percolate down to localities and areas of greatest need if the strategy is to succeed. As one small example, municipally owned electric buses, bought from private companies but manufactured to meet government standards, could link particular residential areas with industrial parks. This by no means uncommon scenario would bring together nonpolluting mass transit, private investment, and access to the workplace for workers who need jobs.

Tackling one of the biggest obstacles to local development, economist Martin Melkonian of Hofstra University has proposed a way to provide credit to needy areas: a revolving fund at the Federal Reserve for interest-free loans to state and local governments.[8] Under a 1970 law, the Federal Reserve had earlier taken a little-known step to encourage community development: It had permitted bank holding companies to invest in community development corporations that assist low- and moderate-income people. In a deteriorating Chicago neighborhood, the South Shore Bank showed what could be accomplished through that mechanism.[9]

The bank received authorization to become a community development corporation. Bank officials went to neighborhood meetings to tell residents they wanted to invest in the community. They sought depositors nationwide to amass the capital needed for renovating unlivable apartments. The bank put together financing from private, city, state, and federal sources to build 446 subsidized apartments. It made dozens of loans to first-time entrepreneurs, most of them African-American couples and Croatian janitors, to help them buy and rehabilitate their own buildings. That, too, is economic development.

But a national policy of economic development that reaches down to the communities won't come without a coalition effort. Who would join? Potentially, a mix of interests: business executives restructuring their companies to improve quality, cut costs, and stand up to tough competition; entrepreneurs; scientists and engineers leaving weapons work; environmentalists; economic development officials; organized labor; unorganized white-collar and blue-collar employees worried about the future; the unemployed and underemployed; some city, county, and state government leaders.

To put together such a coalition would require massive public education and organizing. But unless Americans have quite lost their resourcefulness and drive, that's hardly beyond their talents.

A Can-Do People

Americans have been a practical and problem-solving people. Endowed with abundant natural resources, enriched by the work ethic and the contributions of successive waves of immigrants, strengthened by the efforts of legions of volunteer groups, Americans have created a democratic, relatively prosperous society that, for all its shortcomings, still serves as a magnet to the world.

So what's holding us back? Shifting economic and social currents have recently shaken our belief in the future. This has happened before, as it did in the far grimmer 1930s. But to be capable of renewal, a society must look to the future with confidence.

A new vision of peacetime development and a cooperative spirit can unleash a lot of energy and restore that confidence. Once we start pulling together, animated by that vision, we may find that our defense addiction has been reduced to a post–Cold War hangover. Americans can deal with that.

NOTES

Introduction

1. *1995 CDI Military Almanac* (Washington, D.C.: Center for Defense Information, 1995), p. 17.
2. Gregory D. Foster, *In Search of a Post–Cold War Security Structure* (Washington, D.C.: National Defense University Institute for National Strategic Studies, 1994), p. 23.
3. Gary Lee, "Radiation Tests Were Widespread," *Washington Post*, October 22, 1994, p. A1; Paul Hoversten, "Radiation Test Report: 16,000 Were Subjects," *USA TODAY*, August 18–20, 1995, p. A1.
4. Wallace Peterson, "The Silent Depression," *Challenge,* July–August 1991, pp. 30–31.
5. Robert Heilbroner, "Lifting the Silent Depression," *New York Review of Books*, October 24, 1991.
6. *Economic Report of the President* (Washington, D.C.: Council of Economic Advisers, February 1995), p. 312.
7. Andrew Hacker, *Two Nations: Black and White, Separate, Hostile, Unequal* (New York: Scribner's, 1992), p. 103.
8. "Poverty in the United States" (Washington, D.C.: Bureau of the Census, August, 1991), p. 24.
9. Keith Schneider, "Toxic Messes: Easier Made Than Undone," *New York Times*, October 2, 1994, p. E5.
10. Martin Calhoun, "Nuclear Threat at Home: The Cold War's Lethal Leftovers," *Defense Monitor* 23, no. 2 (1994):1.
11. *Closing the Circle on the Splitting of the Atom* (Washington, D.C.: Department of Energy, Office of Environmental Management, January 1995), p. 90.
12. Lawrence J. Korb, statement before House Committee on Armed Services, Subcommittee on Oversight and Investigations, July 27, 1994, copy provided to the author by Lawrence Korb.
13. Quoted in Brian McCartan, "No Business Like War Business," *Defense Monitor* 16, no. 3 (1987):6.
14. Ibid., p. 6.
15. Karl Vick, "It's Closing Time for Base Commission," *Washington Post*, December 29, 1995, p. A21.

16. Lawrence J. Korb, "The Readiness Gap: What Gap?" *New York Times Magazine*, February 26, 1995, p. 40.

17. Dana Priest, "Defense Gives Its Accounting System a '3'," *Washington Post*, November 15, 1995, p. A7.

18. *Congressional Record*–Senate, February 16, 1961, p. 2210.

19. Richard A. Stubbing, with Richard A. Mendel, *The Defense Game: An Insider Explores the Astonishing Realities of America's Defense Establishment* (New York: Harper & Row, 1986), p. xii.

20. A. Ernest Fitzgerald, *The High Priests of Waste* (New York: Norton, 1972), p. 56.

21. Ibid., p. 59.

22. Ibid., p. 61.

23. Ibid., pp. 62–63.

24. Quoted in George C. Wilson and Peter Carlson, "Stealth Albatross," *Washington Post Magazine*, October 29, 1995, p. 15.

25. Ibid., p. 12.

26. Fitzgerald, *The High Priests of Waste*, p. 204.

27. Jacques S. Gansler, *The Defense Industry* (Cambridge, Mass.: MIT Press, 1980), p. 75.

28. Eli Catran, interview by author, November 5, 1994.

29. Ibid.

30. Stubbing and Mendel, *The Defense Game*, p. 185.

31. Franklin C. Spinney, "Look What $2 Trillion Didn't Buy for Defense," *Washington Post*, October 30, 1988, p. C4.

32. Eleanor Chelimsky, "The U. S. Nuclear Triad: GAO's Evaluation of the Strategic Modernization Program," statement before the Senate Governmental Affairs Committee, June 10, 1993 (Washington, D.C.: Senate Governmental Affairs Committee), pp. 10, 6.

33. Stephen I. Schwartz, "Atomic Audit: What the U.S. Nuclear Arsenal Has Cost," *The Brookings Review*, Fall 1995, p. 14.

34. National Defense Budget Estimate for FY 1995 (Washington, D.C.: Office of the Comptroller, Department of Defense, March 1994), p. 139.

35. Les Daly, "But Can They Make Cars? Defense Contractors Learned Well How to Please Uncle Sam—and Not to Compete," *New York Times Magazine*, January 30, 1994, p. 26.

36. Ibid., pp. 26–27.

Chapter 1

1. William A. Anders, "Rationalizing America's Defense Industry," keynote address to *Defense Week*'s twelfth annual conference, 30 October 1991, p. 13.

2. Ibid., p. 4.

3. Ibid., p. 13.

4. W. R. "Ray" Lewis, staff vice president, investor relations, General Dynamics, interview by author, August 26, 1994.

5. General Dynamics, 1993 Shareholder Report, p. 2. Shareholder reports are available to the public from any office of public corporations.

6. John Mintz, "Muscular or Moribund: It's a Matter of Opinion When It Comes to the Fate of General Dynamics," *Washington Post,* Washington Business, December 26, 1994, p. 10.

7. "Executive Pay," *Wall Street Journal,* April 13, 1994, p. R19.

8. W. R. "Ray" Lewis, phone interview by author, March 27, 1995.

9. General Dynamics, First Quarter 1994 Shareholder Report, p. 2.

10. General Dynamics, 1991 Shareholder Report, p. 5.

11. *Selected Acquisition Reports (SARs) as of September 30, 1994* (Washington, D.C.: Department of Defense), p. 4. As calculated in 1990 dollars, three Seawolf submarines cost $12 billion, hence $4 billion each. The total cost increases to $12.9 billion by 1994 if calculated in then-year dollars for each of the intervening years.

12. Jerry Ray, interview by author, April 26, 1994.

13. Ibid.; Dana Priest and John Mintz, "Sub Has More Friends Than Enemies: Building Navy's Third Seawolf Will Shoot Defense Dollars at Many States," *Washington Post,* October 13, 1995, p. A4.

14. Neil Ruenzel, interview by author, October 3, 1994.

15. Ibid.

16. "The Seawolf and Our Cities," *America's Defense Monitor,* August 16, 1992.

17. John Isaacs, phone interview by author, April 3, 1995.

18. Defense Economic Adjustment and Conversion Program (Newport, R.I.), hearing before the House Armed Services Investigations Subcommittee, December 16, 1991 (Washington, D.C.: House Armed Services Investigations Subcommittee), p. 5.

19. "A Region That Built Nautilus Can Renew Its Industrial Base," *New London Day,* November 12, 1992, p. 1.

20. Ray, interview.

21. Eric Rosenberg, "Seawolf Battle Fought with Charts and Greenbacks," *Defense Week,* May 26, 1992, p. 9.

22. Ruenzel, interview.

23. Ibid.

24. "A Region That Built Nautilus."

25. "Wanted: Nuclear Submarine Builder. Only One Company Need Apply," Newport News Shipbuilding ad, *Washington Post,* May 15, 1995, p. A13.

26. "What do 55 members of the submarine industrial base know about competition that the U.S. Government doesn't?" Newport News Shipbuilding ad, *Washington Post*, June 27, 1995, p. A13.

27. John Mintz, "Torpedoing a $100 Million Favor," *Washington Post*, August 26, 1995, p. C1.

Chapter 2

1. Norman Augustine, interview by author, October 13, 1994.

2. Martin Marietta Corporation, 1993 Annual Report, p. 63.

3. Richard M. Weintraub, "Augustine's Imperative: To Martin Marietta's CEO, Merging with Lockheed Is a Matter of Defense Survival," *Washington Post*, September 4, 1994, p. H1.

4. Ibid.

5. John Mintz, "Lockheed Martin Will Pare 19,000 Workers," *Washington Post*, June 27, 1995, p. D1.

6. Jeff Cole, "Merger of Lockheed and Martin Marietta Pushes Industry Trend," *Wall Street Journal*, August 30, 1994. p. A1.

7. Phillip S. Giaramita, vice president, public affairs, Martin Marietta, phone interview with author, October 18, 1994.

8. "100 Companies Receiving the Largest Dollar Volume of Prime Contract Awards, FY 1993" (Washington, D.C.: Department of Defense, Directorate for Information, Operations and Reports).

9. Joseph W. Stout, manager of public affairs, Lockheed Fort Worth Company, interview by author, November 29, 1994.

10. Ibid.

11. Ibid.

12. Lockheed Corporation, 1993 Annual Report, p. 2.

13. John Mintz, "Arms Race with an Altitude? Lockheed Missile's Impact on ABM Treaty Worries Critics on Left and Right," *Washington Post*, October 18, 1994, p. C1.

14. Carlton Caldwell, manager, marketing communications, Lockheed Martin Information Systems Co., phone interview by author, April 20, 1995.

15. Craig Duncan, phone interview by author, April 18, 1995.

16. Mike Mills, "Lockheed Martin Finds a New Niche: Firm Gains Right to Launch Satellite for Asian Wireless Phone System," *Washington Post*, May 13, 1995; "Lockheed Martin, AT&T Plan Satellite Services," *Washington Post*, October 5, 1995, p. B13.

17. "Lockheed Martin Astronautics and Rose Health Care System Form New Company to Bring Defense Technology to the Fight Against Breast

Cancer," Lockheed Martin press release, Bethesda, Maryland, April 20, 1995.

18. Augustine, interview.

19. "Lockheed Martin Consolidation Plan to Yield $1.8 Billion in Annual Cost Savings," Lockheed Martin press release, Bethesda, Maryland, June 26, 1995.

20. John Mintz, "At Lockheed, a Political Pilgrimage to Plead for Jobs," *Washington Post*, June 27, 1995, p. D1.

21. Augustine, interview.

22. Ibid.

23. Norman R. Augustine, chairman and chief executive officer, and A. Thomas Young, president and chief operating officer, Martin Marietta Corp., testimony to House Armed Services Oversight and Investigations Subcommittee, July 27, 1994 (Washington, D.C.: House Armed Services Oversight and Investigations Subcommittee), p. 3.

24. Patrick J. Sloyan, "Pentagon's Sweet Deal: Top Brass Gave Breaks to Ex-Employer," *Newsday*, June 30, 1994, p. A3.

25. Ibid.

26. Lawrence J. Korb, statement before the House Armed Services Subcommittee on Oversight and Investigations, July 27, 1994, copy provided to the author by Lawrence Korb, p. 4.

27. A. Ernest Fitzgerald, *The High Priests of Waste* (New York: Norton, 1972), p. 310.

28. Phillip S. Giaramita, phone interview by author, April 17, 1995.

29. Response to query, DoD Directorate for Defense Information, January 16, 1996.

30. William Gould, defense aide to Representative Bernie Sanders, phone interview by author, January 29, 1996.

31. Nick Kotz, "Mission Impossible," *The Washingtonian*, December 1995, p. 138.

32. Patrick J. Sloyan, "Pentagon Waives Ethics Rule Allowing New Officials to Deal with Ex-Clients," *Newsday*, December 4, 1994, p. A10.

33. Philip J. Simon, *Top Guns* (Washington, D.C.: Common Cause, 1987), pp. 21–22.

34. Quoted in ibid., p. 23.

35. John Mintz, "Alexander Due Payout in Merger," *Washington Post*, March 29, 1995, p. F3.

36. Ibid.

37. Augustine, interview.

38. John Mintz, "Going Great Guns," *Washington Post*, October 22, 1995, p. H1.

39. Tom Downey, former representative (D.–N.Y.), interview by author, January 29, 1994.

40. Larry Hamilton, director, public affairs, Washington Office, Northrop Grumman, interview by author, April 20, 1995.

41. Steven Pearlstein, "On a Wing and a Prayer: Northrop's Fate in Balance as Congress Nears Decision on B-2 Bomber," *Washington Post*, September 22, 1991, p. H1.

42. Ibid.

43. Northrop Corporation, Annual Report, 1993, p. 4.

44. Bradley Graham, "Pentagon Defends B-2 Performance but Continues to Oppose Ordering More," *Washington Post*, July 18, p. A16.

45. Mintz, "Going Great Guns."

46. John Mintz, "Another Addition to the Loral Corral: Its Winning Bid for Unisys's McLean Division Makes It Fastest-Growing Defense Firm," *Washington Post*, March 22, 1995, p. F1.

47. Loral, Annual Report, 1994, p. 4.

48. John Mintz, "Maverick CEO Guides Loral's Leap Forward: Schwartz Makes IBM's Local Unit Latest in a String of Acquisitions," *Washington Post*, March 6, 1994, p. H1.

Chapter 3

1. McDonnell Douglas, 1991 Annual Report, Letter from the Chairman, p. 2.

2. Andy Pasztor, "Pentagon Set Bailout Plan for McDonnell," *Wall Street Journal*, March 25, 1992, p. 4.

3. "McDonnell Douglas Bailout: No Chrysler. Corporate-Welfare Requests Must Get Public Scrutiny," *Los Angeles Times* (Washington Edition), March 24, 1992, p. 10.

4. Margaret Gilleo, "Analysis of St. Louis' Participation in the Arms Trade," paper prepared for the St. Louis Economic Conversion Project, December 7, 1992, pp. 4, 7.

5. McDonnell Douglas, 1991 Annual Report, p. 4.

6. Quoted in *Aerospace Daily*, July 10, 1992, p. 63.

7. *Arms Sales Monitor*, a publication of the Federation of American Scientists Fund, mid-June–July, 1992, p. 1.

8. "Arms Sales to Saudi Arabia and Taiwan," *America's Defense Monitor*, November 28, 1993.

9. "F-15s Made in America," undated McDonnell Douglas promotional brochure.

10. "F-15s Made in America," annotated by the Federation of American Scientists and the National Commission for Economic Conversion and Disarmament, May 1992.

11. Ibid.

12. Ibid.

13. *Arms Sales Monitor*, February 15, 1995, p. 2.

14. Daniel Smith, "A U.S. Conventional Arms Transfer Policy," *Defense Monitor* 23, no. 7 (1994):1.

15. Michael Klare, "The Arms Overstock," *Harper's*, November 1979, p. 24.

16. Ibid.

17. Hubert Humphrey, in commentary by Edward P. Morgan, *In the Public Interest* radio broadcast, January 12, 1976.

18. Anthony Sampson, *The Arms Bazaar: The Companies, the Dealers, the Bribes. From Vickers to Lockheed* (London: Coronet Books, 1978), p. 117.

19. Ibid., pp. 118–139.

20. William D. Hartung, *And Weapons for All: How America's Multibillion-Dollar Arms Trade Warps Our Foreign Policy and Subverts Democracy at Home* (New York: HarperCollins, 1995), p. 39.

21. John Mintz, "Volleying for Big Positions at Lockheed Martin," *Washington Post,* Washington Business, May 8, 1995, p. 5.

22. David B. Ottaway, "Saudi Court Case Raises Question of Wide Corruption by Leadership," *Washington Post*, January 2, 1996, p. A1.

23. Caryle Murphy, "Exiled Saudi Dissidents Launch Media Campaign," *Washington Post*, June 1, 1994, p. A24.

24. John Mintz, "Official's Asylum Request Could Complicate Saudi-U.S. Diplomacy," *Washington Post*, July 8, 1994, p. A11.

25. Steve Coll and John Mintz, "Saudi Aid to Iraqi A-Bomb Effort Alleged," *Washington Post*, July 25, 1994, p. A12.

26. Richard F. Grimmett, *Conventional Arms Transfers to the Third World, 1986–93*, Congressional Research Service Report for Congress, July 29, 1994, p. 58.

27. Dana Priest and John Mintz, "Attack Puts Spotlight on American Presence," *Washington Post*, November 14, 1995, p. 15.

28. John Lancaster, "Five Americans Killed by Car Bomb at Military Building in Saudi Capital," *Washington Post*, November 14, 1995, p. 1.

29. John A. Richards, deputy assistant secretary, Industrial Resource Administration, Department of Commerce, interview by author, May 25, 1995.

30. Hartung, *And Weapons for All*, pp. 148–154.

31. Ibid., p. 151.

32. *Congressional Record*, January 24, 1992, p. E67ff.; *Congressional Record*, April 21, 1993, p. E971ff.

33. Hartung, *And Weapons for All*, p. 287.

34. *Arms Sales Monitor*, March 20, 1995, p. 3.

35. Ibid.

36. Grimmett, *Congressional Arms Transfers to the Third World, 1986–93,* p. 58.

37. *Arms Sales Monitor,* March 20, 1995, p. 3.

38. William D. Hartung, *U.S. Weapons at War: United States Arms Deliveries to Regions of Conflict* (New York: World Policy Institute, May 1995), p. 2.

39. Lora Lumpe, phone interview by author, May 4, 1995.

40. Hartung, *U.S. Weapons at War,* pp. 37–40.

41. McDonnell Douglas, 1994 Annual Report, p. 54.

42. Fred Whiteford, phone interview by author, December 8, 1994.

43. McDonnell Douglas, 1994 Annual Report, p. 54.

44. John Mintz, "Going Great Guns," *Washington Post,* October 22, 1995, p. H12.

45. Report of the Presidential Advisory Board on Arms Proliferation Policy (Washington, D.C., 1996), p. 16. Available from the Rand Corporation, Santa Monica, Calif.

46. Ibid., pp. 15–16, 19.

47. Ibid., p. 25.

Chapter 4

1. Lockheed Martin ad, *Washington Post,* July 10, 1995, p. A7.

2. John Pike, space expert of the Federation of American Scientists, phone interview by author, July 7, 1995.

3. Sarah Harding, U.S. Postal Service, phone interview by author, Washington, D.C., June 15, 1995.

4. Gary W. Euler and H. Douglas Robertson, eds., *National ITS Program Plan: Intelligent Transportation Systems (Synopsis)* (Washington, D.C.: ITS America, March 1995), p. 4.

5. Pearl M. Kamer and Martin Melkonian, *Long Island's Sustainability Industries* (Garden City, N.Y.: Long Island Alliance for Peaceful Alternatives, March 1995), p. 13.

6. Euler and Robertson, *National ITS Program Plan,* p. 4.

7. Gerald M. Bastarache, manager, media relations, Intelligent Transportation Society of America, phone interview by author, June 26, 1995.

8. Walter Faulconer, phone interview by author, June 13, 1995.

9. Quoted in Joseph C. Anselmo, "Aerospace Firms Stake a Claim in 'Smart Highway' Business," *Aerospace Daily FOCUS,* January 21, 1994, p. 103.

10. Robert Vaage, program manager, Lockheed Martin Systems Engineering and Integration Contract, phone interview by author, June 6, 1995.

11. Mike Connor, director of safety and technology, National Air Traffic Controllers Association, phone interview by author, July 27, 1995.

12. Roger Martino, phone interview by author, August 10, 1995.

13. John Mintz, "Panel Issues Findings on Air Traffic Control Outages," *Washington Post,* January 20, 1996, p. D1.

14. BDM International, 1994 Annual Report, p. 3.

15. Ibid., p. 4.

16. Todd Stottlemyer, senior vice president, BDM International, phone interview by author, June 20, 1995.

17. Ed Gund, phone interview by author, June 15, 1995.

18. Lockheed Martin's 1993 Annual Report quotes "government sources" as estimating uncollected child support in the United States at $34 billion (p. 24); *Washington Post* reporter Peter Baker used the $5.8 billion figure in his article "States to Wield New Child-Support Weapon," July 1, 1995, p. 1.

19. Randy Doblar, director of business development, Advanced Technology Center, Alliant Techsystems, phone interview by author, June 5, 1995.

20. "Military Technology Can Improve Nation's Transit System Capacity," Hughes press release, May 19, 1994.

21. Stephen J. Gluck, Richard Tauber, Bradford Schupp, and J. Edward Anderson, "Design and Commercialization of the PRT 2000 Personal Rapid Transit System," internal paper, available to the public. Raytheon Company, Sudbury, Mass., November 3, 1994, p. 3.

22. "$2.3 B. Tender Offer to Buy E-Systems Ends Successfully," *Raytheon News,* May 1995, p. 1.

Chapter 5

1. Robert Dankanyin, interview by author, May 27, 1993.

2. Hughes Electronics Corporation, 1995 Annual Report, p. 37.

3. Lynn Hill, DirecTV, phone interview by author, January 9, 1995.

4. Tom Shales, "The Future Is Now. And It Isn't on Cable," *Washington Post,* December 21, 1994, p. C1.

5. Estimate from Jan Lachenmaier, Delco Electronics, June 12, 1996.

6. Howard G. Wilson, interview by author, November 4, 1994.

7. Joan Didion, "Letter from California: Trouble in Lakewood," *New Yorker,* July 26, 1993, p. 60.

8. Robert Walkup, interview by author, December 2, 1994.

9. Ibid.

10. Ibid.

11. GM Hughes Electronics Corporation, 1993 Annual Report, p. 1.

12. Jessica Mathews, "Foot-Dragging on the Future," *Washington Post,* January 9, 1995, p. A17.

13. Wilson, interview.

14. Duane "Buzz" Fitzgerald, interview by author, September 26, 1994.

15. Stoney Dionne, interview by author, September 26, 1994.

16. Stoney Dionne, phone interview by author, October 26, 1994.

17. Fitzgerald, interview, September 26.

18. Ibid.

19. George Kourpias, phone interview by author, October 12, 1994.

20. Ibid.

21. Ibid.

22. Chris Black, "Bath's Common Cause: Viable Shipyard," *Boston Globe*, December 26, 1994, p. 1.

23. Fitzgerald, interview, September 26.

24. Buzz Fitzgerald, phone interview by author, February 1, 1996.

25. Buzz Fitzgerald, phone interview by author, October 16, 1995.

26. Fitzgerald, interview, September 26.

Chapter 6

1. John Hoops, director, Bay State Center for Applied Technology, "Defense Economic Adjustment and Conversion Program (Newport, R.I.)," testimony at hearing before House Armed Services Subcommittee on Investigations, December 16, 1991 (Washington, D.C: House Armed Services Subcommittee on Investigations).

2. *Defense Conversion: Capital Conditions Have Improved for Small- and Medium-Sized Firms* (Washington, D.C.: General Accounting Office, July 1994), p. 7.

3. Quoted in Gregory N. Stone, "Smaller Defense Contractors Must Adapt to Changing Demands," *New London Day*, November 2, 1992, p. 1.

4. Greg Frisby, phone interview by author, May 24, 1995.

5. "The Frisby Success Story," *America's Defense Monitor*, July 8, 1990.

6. Ibid.

7. Ibid.

8. Greg Frisby, "Defense Conversion in Small and Medium-Sized Businesses," testimony to House Armed Services Research and Technology Subcommittee, March 1, 1994 (Washington, D.C: House Armed Services Research and Technology Subcommittee), p. 65.

9. James Fallon, manager, business development and strategic initiatives, M/A-Com Microelectronics Division, interview by author, September 30, 1994.

10. Ibid.

11. Ibid.

12. John Stadelmann, vice president/general manager, Gull Electronic Systems Division, interview by author, October 21, 1994.

13. Ibid.

14. Kellie Dodson, Gary Johnson, and King Lum, Ace Clearwater Enterprises, interview by author, November 7, 1994; and King Lum, phone interview by author, August 1, 1995.

15. Joan Didion, "Letter from California: Trouble in Lakewood," *New Yorker*, July 26, 1993, p. 60.

16. The New Economy Project, Final Report, New Vision Business Council of Southern California (Los Angeles, September 16, 1994), p. ES1.

17. Governor's Budget Summary, 1995–96, State of California (Sacramento, February 1995), pp. 7–8.

18. Don Nakamoto, research director/organizer/editor, IAM District Lodge 725, interview by author, November 3, 1994.

19. Mark Wiesel, manager, defense conversion programs, HR Textron, interview by author, November 3, 1994.

20. Don Nakamoto, phone interview by author, July 18, 1995.

21. Wiesel, interview.

22. Daniel Flaming and Mark Drayse, *Technology and Jobs: Defense Conversion in the Los Angeles Region* (Los Angeles: Economic Roundtable, February 8, 1994), pp. 10–11.

23. Greg Frisby, phone interview by author, August 14, 1993.

24. Frisby, testimony, p. 65.

25. Peter Marks, "Hard-Hit Military Contractors Plead for Loans," *New York Times*, June 4, 1993, p. B5.

26. Frisby, phone interview, May 24.

27. Eric Pages, "Defense Technology, Reinvestment and Conversion Issues," testimony to hearings before the House Armed Services Research and Technology Subcommittee, March 1, 1994 (Washington, D.C: House Armed Services Research and Technology Subcommittee), p. 45.

28. Cited in Christine Evans-Klock and Greg Bischak, "Financing Conversion: Touted Studies Questioned," *The New Economy* (Washington, D.C.: National Commission for Economic Conversion and Disarmament), Summer 1994, p. 6.

29. Jon Kutler, "Defense Technology, Reinvestment and Conversion Issues," testimony to hearings before the House Armed Services Research and Technology Subcommittee, March 1, 1994 (Washington, D.C: House Armed Services Research and Technology Subcommittee), p. 85.

30. Ibid., p. 83.

31. Jon Kutler, interview by author, July 19, 1995.

32. Pages, testimony, p. 50.

33. Greg Dierks, program manager, Defense Loan and Technical Assistance, SBA, phone interview by author, August 10, 1995.

34. Jonathan Katkin, "Small Firms Wrangle with Defense Cuts," *Medina County (Ohio) Gazette*, July 17, 1990, p. C1.

35. Frank Sharpf, AM General, phone interview by author, August 2, 1995.

36. Andrew Franzone, interview by author, October 21, 1994.

37. Ibid.

38. William Smith, "How a Prescient Pentagon Contractor Entered Civilian Life," *New York Times*, April 12, 1992, p. F9.

39. Robert Constantino, executive vice president, LAU Technologies, interview by author, September 29, 1994.

Chapter 7

1. Summary of Declassified Nuclear Stockpile Information (Washington, D.C.: Departments of Defense and Energy, undated), p. 173: 56,474 nuclear warheads built and retired as of 1986; "DoD to Slow Pace of Modernization, Cut Strategic Nuclear Arsenal While Maintaining Essential Forces" (Washington, D.C.: Office of Assistant Secretary of Defense, Public Affairs, January 29, 1992): 21,000 nuclear warheads deployed as of September 1990.

2. Betty G. Lall and John Tepper Marlin, *Building a Peace Economy: Opportunities and Problems of Post–Cold War Defense Cuts* (Boulder, Colo.: Westview Press, 1992), p. 39.

3. Ibid.

4. Alexander MacLachlan, interview by author, June 7, 1995.

5. Gilbert Marguth, manager, licensing and regional economic development, Sandia National Laboratory, interview by author, November 8, 1994.

6. MacLachlan, interview.

7. Robert DeGrasse, Jr., director, DoE Office of Worker and Community Transition, interview by author, April 24, 1995.

8. Quoted in John Burgess, "Bombs into Bulldozers," *Washington Post*, August 23, 1992, p. H1.

9. "Lawrence Livermore Assists California Company to Develop New Precision Machine System," Lawrence Livermore National Laboratory press release, September 23, 1992.

10. W. R. Nielsen, phone interview by author, August 7, 1995.

11. Gilbert M. Gaul and Susan Q. Stranahan, "The Price of Keeping Labs Busy," *Philadelphia Inquirer*, June 5, 1995, p. A1.

12. Nuno Vaz, program manager, General Motors Government Partnerships Department, phone interview by author, August 10, 1995.

13. Donald Rej, section leader, Plasma Processing, Los Alamos National Laboratory, interview by author, December 6, 1994.

14. Vaz, interview.

15. Dean Peterson, center leader, Superconductivity Technology, Los Alamos National Laboratory, interview by author, December 5, 1995.

16. Alexander MacLachlan, testimony before the House Energy and Water Development Subcommittee, March 9, 1995 (Washington, D.C: House Energy and Water Development Subcommittee), Charts 5 and 6.

17. MacLachlan, interview.

18. MacLachlan, testimony, p. 7.

19. Pete Lyons, phone interview by author, December 16, 1994.

20. *Alternative Futures for the Department of Energy National Laboratories*, prepared by the Secretary of Energy Advisory Board Task Force on Alternative Futures for the Department of Energy National Laboratories (Washington, D.C.: Department of Energy, February 1995), pp. 4–7.

21. Ibid., p. 7.

22. Ibid., p. 9.

23. Ibid., p. 20.

24. Ibid., pp. 55–56.

25. William Weida and Ann Markusen, "An Alternative to the Galvin Report on Futures for the DoE Nuclear Weapons Laboratories," February 1, 1995, unpublished, unnumbered pages.

26. Kevin Murphy, manager, regional economic development, Technology Transfer & Commercialization Center, Sandia National Laboratories, interview by author, December 6, 1994.

27. James Bridgman and Gregory Bischak, "DOE's Galvin Report: A Critical Assessment," *The New Economy* (Washington, D.C.: National Commission for Economic Conversion and Disarmament, Winter 1995), pp. 4–5.

28. Richard E. Sclove, "Democratizing Technology," *Chronicle of Higher Education*, January 12, 1994, p. B1.

29. Keith Jones, phone interview by author, September 29, 1995; and Buddy Scotto, board chairman, Gowanus Canal Community Development Corp., phone interview by author, October 3, 1995.

30. "Restoring Our Urban Communities: A Model for an Empowered America," brochure (Chicago: Bethel New Life, Inc., and Argonne National Laboratory, undated); Norman Peterson, special assistant to Strategic Planning Group, Argonne National Laboratory, phone interview by author, October 20, 1995.

31. Jim McKenney, director of economic development, American Association of Community Colleges, phone interview by author, October 4, 1995.

32. Kathy Sawyer, "Experts Agree Humans Have 'Discernible' Effect on Climate," *Washington Post*, December 1, 1995, p. A2.

Chapter 8

1. Rosalyn Boxer, phone interview by author, October 12, 1994.

2. Roderick Gary, "Shrinking Military Market Spells Opportunity," *Arizona Daily Star*, June 29, 1992, p. D11.

3. Rosalyn Boxer, interview by author, December 3, 1994.

4. Ibid.

5. "Evaluation of the Defense Conversion Adjustment Demonstration: Interim Report on Implementation" (Washington, D.C.: Department of Labor, 1994), pp. 2/28–2/29.

6. Ibid., pp. 2/32–2/33.

7. Terry Peterson, phone interview by author, October 2, 1995.

8. Rosalyn Boxer, phone interview by author, October 2, 1995.

9. Rosalyn Boxer, phone interview by author, November 15, 1995.

10. Boxer, interview, October 2.

11. Ibid.

12. Gregory N. Stone, "In Tucson, the Community Helps Encourage Conversion Efforts," *New London Day*, November 1, 1992, p. A6.

13. Frank Barton, Office of Economic Adjustment, phone interview by author, October 3, 1995.

14. Susie Schweppe, interview by author, September 26, 1994.

15. Ibid.

16. "Defense Dependency: Impacts and Conversion Efforts in Maine," Maine Economic Conversion Project, June 1994, p. 1.

17. Susie Schweppe, letter announcing termination of MECP, January 15, 1996.

18. Jim Baker, business representative, IAM District 837, interview by author, December 8, 1994.

19. Christopher Seyer, interview by author, December 7, 1994.

20. Ibid.

21. "Progress Report Year II," paper published by the St. Louis Economic Conversion Project, 1994, p. 3.

22. "Industrial Policy," a draft working paper, St. Louis Economic Conversion Project, 1994.

23. Mary Ann McGivern, phone interview by author, October 23, 1995.

24. San Diego City Council resolution adopted April 23, 1990.

25. Marcia Boruta, interview by author, November 2, 1994.

26. Marcia Boruta, phone interview by author, November 6, 1995.

27. Boruta, interview, November 6.

Chapter 9

1. Quoted in W. Joseph Campbell, "State to Stay Focused on Military Contracts," *Hartford Courant*, March 5, 1992, p. D1.

2. *Adjusting to the Drawdown*, U.S. Defense Conversion Commission, December 1992, Annex F, p. 3–3.

3. William Moore, president, Southeastern Connecticut Chamber of Commerce, interview by author, October 3, 1994.

4. Thomas Moukawsher, interview by author, October 5, 1994.

5. Marianne K. Clarke, *A Governor's Guide to Economic Conversion* (Washington, D.C.: National Governors' Association, 1992), p. 41.

6. Thomas Moukawsher, phone interview by author, August 25, 1995.

7. Clifford Neal, interview by author, October 4, 1994.

8. Betsy Hunt, special project manager, Connecticut Department of Economic Development, phone interview by author, September 25, 1995.

9. Ibid.

10. *Diversification: Strategies for Military-Dependent Communities, Firms, and Workers in Washington State* (Olympia, Wash.: Department of Community Development, 1991), p. 2.

11. *Washington State Community Diversification Program Report, January 1993–May 1994* (Olympia, Wash.: Department of Community, Trade, and Economic Development, May 1994), p. 1.

12. Ibid., p. 4.

13. *Diversification*, p. 45.

14. Ibid., p. 31.

15. Paul Knox, "Making It Work on the Ground . . . and Washington," *The New Economy* (Washington, D.C.: National Commission for Economic Conversion and Disarmament, Fall 1994), p. 9; Paul Knox, program manager, Community Development Program, phone interview by author, August 29, 1995.

16. Bill Patz, project coordinator, IAM District 160 Conversion Project, phone interview by author, August 29, 1995.

17. Knox, phone interview.

18. Karen West, "Cooperative Competitors," *Seattle Post-Intelligencer*, July 12, 1993, p. B1.

19. *Washington State Community Diversification Program Report*, p. 6.

20. *Washington Alliance for Manufacturing Final Report* (Olympia, Wash.: Washington Alliance for Manufacturing, August 1995), p. 6.

21. *State Initiatives in Defense Conversion and Diversification* (Washington, D.C.: National Governors' Association, 1994), p. 5.

22. *The New York State Defense Industry Diversification Assistance Program* (Albany, N.Y.: Department of Economic Development, undated), p. 1.

23. Richard Demmings, general manager, statement at New York State briefing on Capitol Hill, March 12, 1992.

24. William Cahill, interview by author, October 21, 1994.

25. *The Defense Drawdown in Texas: The Economic Impact of Defense Spending & Strategies for Defense Industry Diversification* (Austin, Tex.: Department of Commerce, December 31, 1994), p. 6.

26. *Defense Transition: Economic Promise for Texas*, A Report from the Governor's Task Force on Economic Transition (Austin, Tex.: Office of the Governor, February 1993), p. 16.

27. Ibid., pp. 100–103.

28. Marsha Schachtel, director, technology development, Maryland Department of Business and Economic Development, phone interview by author, September 13, 1995.

29. David Keto, undersecretary, Massachusetts Executive Office of Economic Affairs, phone interview by author, September 27, 1995.

30. Ibid.

31. *Massachusetts Industrial Services Program* (Boston, Mass.: Massachusetts Industrial Services Program, April 1994), p. 3.

32. Keto, phone interview.

Chapter 10

1. National Defense Budget Estimates for FY 1995 (Washington, D.C.: Department of Defense, Office of the Comptroller, March 1995).

2. Ronald E. Kutscher, associate commissioner, BLS, testimony before Defense Base Closure and Realignment Commission, April 12, 1993, p. 3, copy provided to the author by Ronald Kutscher; John Mintz, "For Employees, the Ordeal of the Pink Slips Isn't Over Yet," *Washington Post*, October 22, 1995, p. H6.

3. "1990s: 800,000 Defense Industry Jobs Lost So Far," news analysis (Washington, D.C.: National Commission for Economic Conversion and Disarmament, undated), p. 1.

4. National Defense Budget Estimates for FY 1995.

5. Gregory N. Stone, "A Changing World Has Crippling Effect in St. Louis," *New London Day*, October 30, 1992, p. 1.

6. Ibid., p. 6.

7. *Worker Perspectives on Defense Conversion: Results of Ten Focus Groups of New England Workers*, New England Defense Conversion Planning and Technical Assistance Project (Bucksport, Maine: Training and Development Corporation, July 1994), p. 4.

8. Quoted in Michael Oden et al., *Post Cold-War Frontiers: Defense Downsizing and Conversion in Los Angeles* (New Brunswick, N.J.: Rutgers University, 1996), p. 90.

9. *Reemploying Defense Workers: Current Experiences and Policy Alternatives* (Washington, D.C.: Congressional Budget Office, August 1993), p. 25.

10. Robert Lewis and Russell Signorino, "Layoffs of High Skilled Defense Workers and the Response of Impacted Communities," in *Best Practices in Defense Conversion*, Karl F. Seidman and Eva Klein, eds. (Washington, D.C.: National Council for Urban Economic Development, 1995), p. 86.

11. Quoted in Laurent Belsie and Daniel B. Wood, "Builders of Bombers Find Job Market Turbulent," *Christian Science Monitor*, January 14, 1992, p. 7.

12. Quoted in Stone, "A Changing World," p. 6.

13. Christine Evans-Klock, *National Defense Industry Layoffs, 1994 and Mid-Year 1995* (Washington, D.C.: National Commission for Economic Conversion and Disarmament, July 1995), p. 8.

14. Ibid.

15. James Raffel, "Economic Conversion Legislation: Past Approaches and the Search for a New Framework," in *The Socio-Economics of Conversion from War to Peace*, Lloyd J. Dumas, ed. (Armonk, N.Y.: Sharpe, 1995), p. 207.

16. *Reemploying Defense Workers*, pp. xi–xii.

17. Ibid., p. 9.

18. Elizabeth Mueller, "Retraining for What? Displaced Defense Workers and Federal Programs in Two Regions," in Dumas, *The Socio-Economics of Conversion from War to Peace*, pp. 102–109.

19. Ibid., pp. 115, 119.

20. *Worker Perspectives on Defense Conversion*, p. 4.

21. *Reemploying Defense Workers*, p. 20.

22. Suzanne Teegarden, "Responding to the Impacts of Defense Cutbacks on Workers," in Seidman and Klein, *Best Practices in Defense Conversion*, p. 81.

23. Mueller, pp. 121–123.

24. Gregory A. Bischak, "Building Job Bridges for Defense Industrial Conversion," in Dumas, *The Socio-Economics of Conversion from War to Peace*, pp. 176–189.

25. Robert B. Reich, Secretary of Labor, "The State of the American Workforce 1994: The Over, the Under, and the Anxious," speech, August 31, 1994 (Washington, D.C.: Department of Labor), pp. 2, 3.

26. Quoted in David S. Broder, "As Workers Become Weaker," *Washington Post*, February 14, 1996, p. 21.

27. *Reemploying Defense Workers*, p. xiii.

28. Ibid.

29. *Job Creation and Employment Opportunities: The United States Labor Market, 1993–1996*, report by the Council of Economic Advisers with the U.S. Department of Labor (Washington D.C.: U.S. Department of Labor, Office of the Chief Economist, April 23, 1996), p. 1.

30. Ibid., p. 3.

31. Carolyn Kay Brancato and Linda LeGrande, *The Impact of Defense Spending on Employment*, Congressional Research Service, November 4, 1982, p. 4.

32. Linda Levine, *The Employment Effects of Shifting Three Billion Dollars from Defense to State and Local Government-Related Activities*, Congressional Research Service, February 1, 1993, p. 3.

33. Quoted in Louis Uchitelle, "Cuts in Arms Spending: No Help for the Economy," *New York Times*, August 12, 1992, p. D2.

34. "Carmakers' Anti-EV Campaign in High Gear," *The Calstart Connection* (Burbank, Calif.: Calstart, June–July 1995), p. 3.

35. Lou Kiefer, phone interview by author, November 29, 1995.

36. Miriam Pemberton, "Electric Cars to Roll at Converted Base," *The New Economy* (Washington, D.C.: National Commission for Economic Conversion and Disarmament, Summer 1995), p. 14.

37. Quoted in "Manufacturing the Future," *Positive Alternatives* (Mountain View, Calif.: Center for Economic Conversion, Winter 1995), p. 8.

38. Ibid.

39. Ray Marshall, keynote address to AFL-CIO Human Resources Development Institute Conference on High Performance Work and Learning Systems, September 26–27, 1991, Washington, D.C.

40. "Understanding Empowerment," undated fact sheet, New York State Department of Economic Development, Long Island Regional Office.

41. "Manufacturing the Future," p. 14.

Chapter 11

1. *Congressional Record*—Senate, June 30, 1994, p. S.8066.

2. Bradley Graham, "Divided House Votes to Fund B-2 Components," *Washington Post*, September 8, 1995, p. A6.

3. Stephen Chapman, "No Defense: Buying More B-2 Bombers a Pointless Extravagance," *Chicago Tribune*, July 30, 1995, Section 4, p. 3.

4. Tip O'Neill with Gary Hymel, *All Politics Is Local: And Other Rules of the Game* (New York: Times Books/Random House, 1994), p. 101.

5. Ibid., pp. 101–102.

6. George N. Lewis and Theodore A. Postol, "Video Evidence on the Effectiveness of Patriot During the 1991 Gulf War," *Science and Global Security* 4 (1993):1–63.

7. Quoted in Sanford Gottlieb, "State Within a State," in *The Seventies: Problems and Proposals*, Irving Howe and Michael Harrington, eds. (New York: Harper & Row, 1972), p. 185.

8. Quoted in Nick Kotz, *Wild Blue Yonder: Money, Politics, and the B-1 Bomber* (Princeton, N.J.: Princeton University Press, 1988), p. 49.

9. Ibid., p. 129.

10. Ibid., pp. 130–136.

11. *1995 CDI Military Almanac* (Washington, D.C.: Center for Defense Information, 1995), p. 7.

12. Dina Rasor, *The Pentagon Underground* (New York: Times Books, 1985), pp. 237–250.

13. Ibid., pp. 257–260.

14. *Congressional Record*—House, May 7, 1987, p. H3281.

15. Interview by the author, May 19, 1994.

16. "House Subcommittee Backs $264 Billion Defense Budget," *Washington Post*, May 7, 1994, p. 2.

17. Ronald O'Rourke, *The Cost of a U.S. Navy Aircraft Carrier Battle Group*, Congressional Research Service, June 26, 1987. Dollar figures updated by Center for Defense Information.

18. David Pryor, interview by author, April 13, 1994.

19. John F. Harris, "Military Budget as a Matter of Jobs," *Washington Post*, May 22, 1994, p. 16.

20. *Politics in America 1994* (Washington, D.C.: Congressional Quarterly Press, 1993), p. 208.

21. Jane Harman, interview by the author, April 25, 1994.

22. Bradley Graham and John F. Harris, "White House May Beef Up Order for B-2 Bombers," *Washington Post*, February 4, 1996, p. A8.

23. "PAC Profile: Northrop Grumman," *Money in Politics Alert* (Washington, D.C.: Center for Responsive Politics, September 5, 1995), p. 2.

24. Nancy Watzman and Sheila Krumholz, *The Best Defense: Will Campaign Contributions Protect the Industry?* (Washington, D.C.: Center for Responsive Politics, July 12, 1995), pp. 12, 41.

25. Watzman and Krumholz, *The Best Defense*, p. 5.

26. "Cost of B-2 Advertising Campaign," National Security News Service press release, June 27, 1995.

27. Kenneth R. Mayer, *The Political Economy of Defense Contracting* (New Haven, Conn., and London: Yale University Press, 1991), p. 77.

28. Larry Makinson, *The Price of Admission: Campaign Spending in the 1994 Elections* (Washington, D.C.: Center for Responsive Politics, August 1995), p. 218.

29. Ibid., p. 219.

30. Kenneth Mayer, *The Political Economy of Defense Contracting*, p. 86.

31. "1995 PAC Dollars," *Capital Eye* (Washington, D.C.: Center for Responsive Politics, November 1, 1995), p. 4.

32. *Politics in America 1994*, pp. 1319–1322.

33. Watzman and Krumholz, *The Best Defense*, pp. 14, 37–47.

34. Ibid., pp. 47–50.

35. Kenneth Mayer, *The Political Economy of Defense Contracting*, pp. 8–9.

36. Norman Ornstein, interview by the author, April 25, 1994.

37. Tom Downey, interview by the author, January 29, 1994.

38. Common Cause study, cited in R. H. Melton, "Corporate Contributions Pour into the RNC," *Washington Post*, April 6, 1995, p. A19.

39. John McCain, phone interview by the author, February 16, 1994.

40. Ibid.

41. John McCain and John Warner, "Dear Colleague" letter, December 5, 1995, p. 3, copy provided to the author by McCain and Warner.

42. Floyd Spence and C. W. Bill Young, letter to Chairman John Kasich, House Budget Committee, January 17, 1995, copy provided to the author by Spence and Young.

43. Bradley Graham, "Military Reserve Force a Repository for Pork," *Washington Post,* June 25, 1995, p. A1.

44. Dana Priest and John Mintz, "Sub Has More Friends Than Enemies: Building Navy's Third Seawolf Will Shoot Defense Dollars at Many States," *Washington Post,* October 13, 1995, p. A4.

45. "Senate Armed Services' Fiscal 1996 DoD Authorization Bill: Senators as Eager as Representatives to Seek Projects for Home," Council for a Livable World press release, July 31, 1995.

46. John Isaacs, phone interview by the author, December 6, 1995.

47. "Defense Pork," *Newsweek,* August 7, 1995, p. 6.

48. Dan Morgan, "Defense, Energy Projects Fare Well in Hill Panels," *Washington Post,* July 26, 1995, p. A4.

49. Helen Dewar, "Senate Backs Missile Defense Despite Threatened Clinton Veto," *Washington Post,* December 20, 1995, p. 18.

50. William C. Harrop and Robert J. McCloskey, "Diplomacy on the Cheap," *Washington Post,* June 18, 1996, p. A13.

51. David Maraniss and Michael Weisskopf, "In Test of Strength, Stealth Survives," *Washington Post,* September 24, 1995, p. A1.

52. Quoted in ibid.

Chapter 12

1. Hubert H. Humphrey, "After Disarmament—What?" *Think* Magazine, January 1960, p. 3.

2. James Raffel, "Economic Conversion Legislation: Past Approaches and the Search for a New Framework," in *The Socio-Economics of Conversion from War to Peace,* Lloyd J. Dumas, ed. (Armonk, N.Y.: Sharpe, 1995), pp. 198–199.

3. Ibid., p. 213.

4. Clinton/Gore '92 Committee, "Clinton/Gore on Defense Conversion: Revitalizing Our Commercial Economy," copy in the author's possession.

5. Ibid.

6. Remarks by the president to Westinghouse employees, White House press release, March 11, 1993.

7. White House press release, April 12, 1993, quoted in Michael Oden, Gregory Bischak, Christine Evans-Klock, *The Technology Reinvestment Project: The Limits of Dual-Use Technology Policy* (Washington, D.C.:

National Commission for Economic Conversion and Disarmament, July 1995), p. 5.

8. Oden, Bischak, and Evans-Klock, *The Technology Reinvestment Project*, p. 15.

9. *The Technology Reinvestment Project: Dual-Use Innovation for a Stronger Defense* (Arlington, Va.: Technology Reinvestment Project, 1995), p. 9.

10. Ibid., p. 17.

11. Lee Buchanan, interview by the author, December 13, 1995.

12. Raymond Kammer, interview by the author, June 1, 1995.

13. Jacques S. Gansler, *Defense Conversion: Transforming the Arsenal of Democracy* (Cambridge, Mass., and London: MIT Press/Twentieth Century Fund, 1995), p. 27.

14. *Second to None: Preserving America's Military Advantage Through Dual-Use Technology* (Washington, D.C.: National Economic Council/National Security Council/Office of Science and Technology Policy, February 1995), p. 1.

15. John M. Deutch, "A Problem the Pentagon Will Solve," *Washington Post*, June 21, 1994, p. A17.

16. Kenneth Flamm, interview by author, January 3, 1996.

17. Kammer, interview.

18. Daniel Flaming and Mark Drayse, *Technology and Jobs: Defense Conversion in the Los Angeles Region* (Los Angeles: Economic Roundtable, February 8, 1994), p. 39.

19. Charles Bartsch, Paula Duggan, and Matt Kane, *Defense Adjustment and Conversion: Lessons from Seven Sites,* prepared for U.S. Economic Development Administration (Washington, D.C.: Northeast-Midwest Institute, June 1993), p. 7.

20. Ann Markusen and Joel Yudken, "Building a New Economic Order," *Technology Review*, April 1992, p. 26.

21. *Report of the Process Action Team on Military Specifications and Standards* (Washington, D.C.: Office of the Under Secretary of Defense for Acquisition & Technology, April 1994), p. 1.

22. "Perry Releases Plan to Streamline DoD Purchasing Practices," Office of Assistant Secretary of Defense (Public Affairs) press release, June 29, 1994, p. 1.

23. *Second to None*, p. 1.

24. *The DoD Regulatory Cost Premium: A Quantitative Assessment,* report prepared for Defense Secretary William Perry by Coopers & Lybrand and TASC, Washington, D.C., December 1994, p. 1.

25. DoD news briefing, Secretary of Defense William J. Perry (joined by Paul Kaminski, undersecretary of defense for Acquisition & Technology), December 8, 1995, p. 6.

26. *White Paper on Defense Conversion Programs* (Washington, D.C.: Electronic Industries Association, March 1994), p. 3.

27. *The Technology Reinvestment Project: The Limits of Dual-Use Technology Policy*, p. 41, with fiscal 1995 rescissions added by the author.

28. Budget of the U.S. Government: Supplement FY 1997 (Washington, D.C.: Government Printing Office, 1996), p. 97.

29. Ken Van Dillen, phone interview by author, January 2, 1996; *Budget of the U.S. Government, FY 1996* (Washington, D.C.: Government Printing Office, 1995), p. 727 of Appendix.

30. David Rogers, "General Newt: GOP's Rare Year Owes Much to How Gingrich Disciplined the House," *Wall Street Journal*, December 18, 1995, p. A8.

31. Erik Pages, director, Office of Economic Conversion Information, interview by author, September 26, 1995.

32. Lawrence J. Korb, "Who's in Charge Here? National Security and the Contract with America," *Brookings Review*, Fall 1995, p. 6.

33. "Balancing the Budget," chart, *Washington Post*, June 24, 1995, p. A6.

34. Bill Sweetman, "The Budget You Can't See," *Washington Post Outlook*, July 7, 1996, p. C3.

35. Quoted in Bradley Graham and John F. Harris, "White House May Beef Up Order for B-2 Bombers," *Washington Post*, February 4, 1996, p. A8.

36. Martin Calhoun, "Balanced Budget, Unbalanced Priorities?" *Defense Monitor* 24, no. 7 (1995):7.

Chapter 13

1. William Raspberry, "Business Is Great—You're Fired," *Washington Post*, January 4, 1996, p. A25.

2. AFL-CIO Research Department, January 5, 1996, phone conversation.

3. Robert B. Reich, *The Work of Nations: Preparing Ourselves for 21st Century Capitalism* (New York: Knopf, 1991), p. 112.

4. Lester R. Brown, Nicholas Lenssen, and Hal Kane, *Vital Signs 1995* (Washington, D.C.: Worldwatch Institute, 1995), p. 15.

5. Ibid., p. 20.

6. Robert D. Kaplan, "The Coming Anarchy," *Atlantic Monthly*, February 1994, pp. 44ff.

7. Ibid., p. 72.

8. Brown, Lenssen, and Kane, *Vital Signs 1995*, p. 66.

9. Quoted in Sharon Begley, "He's Not Full of Hot Air," *Newsweek*, January 22, 1996, p. 27.

10. David Brown, "Infectious Disease May Rise as the World Gets Warmer," *Washington Post*, January 17, 1996, p. 2.

11. *Second to None: Preserving America's Military Advantage Through Dual-Use Technology* (Washington, D.C.: National Economic Council/National Security Council/Office of Science and Technology Policy, February 1995), p. 1.

12. Daniel Smith and Marcus Corbin, "A Post–Cold War Military Force," *Defense Monitor* 24, no. 3 (1995):1–12.

13. Steven Pearlstein, "Reshaped Economy Exacts Tough Toll," *Washington Post*, November 12, 1995, p. 14.

14. Michael Walzer, "What's Going On? Notes on the Right Turn," *Dissent*, Winter 1996, pp. 9–10.

15. Reich, *The Work of Nations*, pp. 272–276.

16. Ibid., p. 254.

17. Jacques S. Gansler, *Defense Conversion: Transforming the Arsenal of Democracy* (Cambridge, Mass., and London: MIT Press/Twentieth Century Fund, 1995), p. 170.

18. Jeff Faux and Todd Schafer, *Increasing Public Investment* (Washington, D.C.: Economic Policy Institute, undated), pp. 15–16.

19. Steven Pearlstein, "Study: U.S. Competitive Ills Persist," *Washington Post*, July 11, 1994, p. A6.

20. Quoted in Jay Mathews, "Odd Jobs," *Washington Post*, August 13, 1995, p. H5.

21. Lloyd J. Dumas, *The Overburdened Economy* (Berkeley and Los Angeles: University of California Press, 1986), p. 210.

22. Ann Markusen and Joel Yudken, *Dismantling the Cold War Economy* (New York: Basic Books, 1992), p. 53.

23. Gansler, *Defense Conversion*, p. 172.

24. Quoted in Tom Redburn, "Unwinding the Cold War Could Crank Up Economy," *Los Angeles Times*, January 8, 1990, p. 1.

25. Gary Chapman and Joel Yudken, *Setting a New Course for Science and Technology Policy* (Palo Alto, Calif.: Computer Professionals for Social Responsibility, July 1993), pp. 14–15.

26. Rob Stein, interview by the author, April 19, 1995.

27. *1995 Update: Jobs and Industry Growth* (Burbank, Calif.: Calstart, 1995).

28. Markusen and Yudken, *Dismantling the Cold War Economy*, pp. 51–53.

29. Gansler, *Defense Conversion*, pp. 26–27, 36, 172.

30. Quoted in Sandra I. Meadows, "Viable Defense Skills Base Object of Labor Campaign," *National Defense*, November 1993, p. 34.

31. *Global Engagement: Cooperation and Security in the 21st Century*, Janne E. Nolan, ed. (Washington, D.C.: Brookings Institution, 1994), p. 10.

32. William Perry, "Military Action: When to Use It and How to Ensure Its Effectiveness," in ibid., p. 235.

33. Joel Cohen, Rockefeller University biologist, interview on *Fresh Air*, National Public Radio, January 22, 1996.

34. William W. Kaufmann, *Assessing the Base Force: How Much Is Too Much?* (Washington, D.C.: Brookings Institution, 1992), p. 91.

35. Philip Morrison, Kosta Tsipis, and Jerome Wiesner, "The Future of American Defense," *Scientific American*, February 1994, pp. 38–45.

36. Brent Blackwelder, director, Friends of the Earth, phone interview by author, January 24, 1996.

37. Program on International Policy Attitudes, University of Maryland, "Americans on Defense Spending," December 19, 1995, p. 1; Program on International Policy Attitudes, University of Maryland, "Americans on UN Peacekeeping," April 27, 1995, p. 1.

38. Anthony Lewis, "The Defense Anomaly," *New York Times*, January 22, 1996, p. A15.

Conclusion

1. National Defense Budget Estimates for FY 1996 (Washington, D.C.: Office of the Under Secretary of Defense, Comptroller, March 1995), p. 165.

2. Mark Thompson, "Why the Pentagon Gets a Free Ride," *Time*, June 5, 1995, p. 26.

3. Richard Morin, "Who's in Control? Many Don't Know or Care," *Washington Post*, January 29, 1996, p. A1.

4. Thomas B. Edsall, "Public Grows More Receptive to Anti-Government Message," *Washington Post*, January 31, 1996, p. A5.

5. Kenneth L. Adelman and Norman R. Augustine, "Defense Conversion," *Foreign Affairs*, Spring 1992, p. 43.

6. Thompson, "Why the Pentagon Gets a Free Ride," p. 27.

7. Ann Markusen and Joel Yudken, *Dismantling the Cold War Economy* (New York: Basic Books, 1992), p. 252.

8. Martin Melkonian, "Monetary Policy," in *Conference on Jobs, Conversion, and Sustainability* (Washington, D.C.: National Commission for Economic Conversion and Disarmament, June 1995), p. 67.

9. Ronald Grzywinski, "The New Old-Fashioned Banking," *Harvard Business Review*, May–June 1991, p. 231.

ABOUT THE BOOK AND AUTHOR

Whatever happened to the post–Cold War "peace dividend"? Why does military spending continue to escape federal budget reductions? Why, despite the nearly universal desire to reduce government waste and budget deficits, is the United States still saddled with a costly, bloated military-industrial complex? The answer, says Sanford Gottlieb, is the debilitating dependence of a key sector of the American economy on defense jobs and profits.

Defense Addiction is based on hundreds of interviews with defense contractors, union representatives, members of Congress, state and federal officials, lobbyists, economic development professionals, and local activists. Gottlieb explains how these groups and individuals cope with defense dependence, competition for federal funds, and budget and job cuts—painting a sobering picture of how this addiction hampers the nation's ability to deal effectively with a host of domestic and global problems.

Gottlieb's engaging and jargon-free volume points to civilian public investments, reduced military spending, strengthened international peacekeeping, and other measures that could help our country kick the defense habit. His book also provides guidance to companies and communities struggling to break free in the face of inadequate government policies.

Sanford Gottlieb has thirty-four years of experience in military-related activities. He joined the U.S. Navy during World War II and later served as executive director for the National Committee for a Sane Nuclear Policy (SANE), New Directions, and United Campuses to Prevent Nuclear War. For seven years he was senior producer of *America's Defense Monitor*, a weekly television program of the Center for Defense Information. He has written and spoken widely on defense and foreign policy issues.

INDEX

Ace Clearwater Enterprises, 71–72, 121

Addabbo, Joe, 124

Adelman, Kenneth, 167

Advanced Research Projects Agency (ARPA), 140. *See also* Defense Advanced Research Projects Agency (DARPA)

Aegis destroyers, 61, 63

Aerospace and Defense Diversification Alliance in Peacetime Transition (ADDAPT), 75

Aerospace industry, 8, 72, 105, 107, 108, 114, 129

Aerospace Technologies, 66

Afghanistan, 37, 42

African Americans, 2, 86, 97, 114, 169
  young black men, 3

Africa, West, 150

Agnew, Spiro, 125

Agran, Larry, 99

Aircraft carriers, 2, 126–127, 131
  battle groups, 127
  CVN-76, 127

Air Force Association, 125

Air Force, U.S., 6, 8, 21, 29, 30, 33, 35, 121, 124, 126, 134
  lobbying, 125–126
  procurement practices, 5–6

Airlift, 160

Air traffic control, 48–49, 54

Alabama, 6, 14, 50

Alexander, Lamar, 28

Alliant Techsystems, 52, 54

Allied Signal, 73

Alternative use committees, 103, 138

Amazon basin, 53–54, 70

American Automar, 63

American Enterprise Institute, 131

Amerigon, 83, 120

AM General, 75

Anders, William, 11–12, 17

Andrews, Tom, 132

Angola, 37

Anti-Ballistic Missile (ABM) Treaty, 22, 134

Anxious class, 117

Apache helicopters, 39, 40

Argent, Robert, 113

Argonne National Laboratory, 86

Arizona, 58, 90, 91, 94, 100
  Legislature, 91
  Phoenix, 49, 132
  Pima County, 90, 91
  Tucson, 58, 59, 89, 90, 91, 98, 99
  University of, 58

Arizona Council for Economic Conversion (ACEC), 90–92

Arkansas, 14

Armed forces, 4, 8
  and arms sales, 37
  branches, 33
  mobile, 152
  smaller, 153, 161

Arms Control and Disarmament
    Agency, 44
Arms sales, 8, 33–44
    Code of Conduct, 41
    Foreign Military Sales program,
        41
Armstrong, C. Michael, 56, 64
Army Corps of Engineers, 86
Army, U.S., 124, 161
ARO Corporation, 108
Asia, 120, 121
Aspin, Les, 24, 27
Associated Press, 127
Atlantic Ocean, 151
Atomic Energy Commission, 2
AT&T, 55, 149
Augustine, Norman, 19, 23, 24,
    26–27, 28, 167
Austria, 160
Automakers, 119, 120
    Chrysler, 59, 82, 120
    Ford, 30, 59, 77, 82, 120
    Japanese, 119, 121
    See also General Motors

Bangladesh, 151
Banks, 73, 74, 77, 92, 93, 97, 151
Barre, Siad, 37
Barton, Frank, 92
Bates, Jim, 99
Bath Iron Works (BIW), 18, 60–64,
    93, 121, 132, 140
Bay Area Rapid Transit (BART), 52
BDM International, 50–51
Belarus, 54
Bergsten, C. Fred, 154
Berlin Wall, 99
Berman, Howard, 72
Bethlehem Steel, 83
Bischak, Gregory, 86, 117
BMY Wheeled Vehicles Division,
    108
Bodenhamer, Howard, 27

Boeing, 20, 67, 69, 106, 123, 132
    and the C-17, 128
    747s, 43
    777s, 149
Bombers, 2, 72
    A-12, 6, 33, 76
    B-1, 125–126, 133
    B-2, 29, 55, 123, 129, 132, 133,
        135, 136, 147–148
    B-52, 125
    B-70, 125
Bonus/profit-sharing, 67, 71
Boruta, Marcia, 98–100
Bosnia, 134, 152
Boston Globe, 14
Bottom-Up Review, 4, 127, 146
Boxer, Rosalyn, 89–92, 94
Branch Davidian, 59
Brazil, 53, 70, 150
Breast cancer, 23, 82
Brennan, Joseph, 93
Bridgman, James, 86
Brookhaven National Laboratory,
    86, 87
Brookings Institution, 44, 141
Brooklyn, 31, 86
Brown, Ron, 39
Buchanan, Lee, 141
Bureau of the Budget/Office of
    Management and Budget, 5
Bureau of Labor Statistics, 113
Bush administration, 2, 3, 13, 16,
    33, 35, 39, 40, 41, 115, 131,
    138
Bush, George, 28, 34, 40, 46, 145,
    146
Bush, George W., 110
Business Executives for National
    Security (BENS), 74, 75
Cahill, William, 108–109
Caldwell, James, 35
California, 24, 47, 48, 52, 58, 59,
    60, 71, 72, 79, 80, 81, 85, 99,
    114, 119, 120, 121, 123, 128,
    135, 142, 157, 158
    California State University, 73
    Glendale Community College, 73
    Irvine, 99

politics, 148
San Francisco, 52
University of California–San
  Diego, 99
See also Los Angeles and San
  Diego
Calstart, 119, 120, 157–158
Canada, 46, 54, 70, 160
  Ontario, 46
  Toronto, 54
Cargo planes
  C-5, 6, 126
  C-17, 8, 33, 43, 128, 129
  C-130, 133
  cost overruns, 128
Carroll, Eugene, 98
Carter, Bud, 14
Carter, Jimmy, 14
Catholics, 86, 95, 98
Catran, Eli, 7
Celeste, Richard, 107–108
Center for Defense Information, 98,
  153
Central America, 42
Central Intelligence Agency (CIA),
  42
Chain, John Jr., 29
Chapman, Gary, 156
Chapman, Mary Ann, 90
Chapman, Stephen, 123
Chelimsky, Eleanor, 8
Cheney, Dick, 6–7
Chesley, Larry, 91
Chicago, 48, 53, 86, 169
  South Shore Bank, 168
Chicago Tribune, 123
China, 40, 53, 54
Chronicle of Higher Education, 86
Cletronics, 75, 76
Clinton administration, 16, 24, 33,
  35, 41, 49, 54, 127, 139–148,
  153
  and exports, 39

Clinton, Bill, 4, 5, 13, 39, 40, 43,
  85, 115, 120, 133, 134, 139,
  145–148
Clinton/Gore campaign, 144
Coats, Dan, 131
Cohen, William, 93, 135
Cold War, 1–4, 7, 13, 16, 17, 33,
  45, 61, 64, 77, 88, 89, 98,
  101, 105, 108, 110, 121, 123,
  124, 127, 138, 139, 156, 165
  post–Cold War era, 4, 8, 19, 24,
  33, 42, 55, 63, 113, 133, 135,
  137, 147, 149, 150, 152, 159,
  166, 170
Colorado College, 85
Columbia University, 98
Combat aircraft, 11, 19, 33, 35, 43,
  60, 69, 108
Communism/Communists, 2, 64,
  124, 150, 152, 167
Computers
  chips, 143
  classroom, 155
  DoD boost to, 97
  network, 92
  software, 49, 59, 141
Congress, 8, 16, 17, 18, 30, 34, 41,
  48, 75, 80, 88, 93, 96, 99,
  115, 118, 138, 139, 141, 144,
  147–148, 168
  Appropriations Committees, 131,
  134
  Armed Services Committees, 29,
  125, 131, 134
  and arms trade, 42
  Budget Committee (House), 123,
  148
  Congressional Black Caucus, 126
  and defense jobs, 123–136
  Democrats, 123, 125, 128, 129,
  134, 135, 138, 168
  "Earmarks," 134
  Finance Committee (Senate), 125

House Armed Services, 123, 127, 128, 129
House Defense Subcommittee, 17, 29, 124, 131
House National Security (renamed), 133, 134, 168
House National Security Subcommittee (renamed), 133
House of Representatives, 15, 16, 97, 123, 129, 147, 168
International Relations Committee (House), 41
members of, 4, 9, 15, 30, 124, 125, 126, 130, 146, 166
military pork, 123–136
pork barrel, 123
Republicans, 41, 83, 96, 133, 134, 135, 141, 145, 146, 168
Sales force for contractors, 127–128
Senate, 15, 41, 123, 134, 135, 138
Senate Armed Services, 18, 131, 134
Congressional Budget Office (CBO), 117–118
Congressional Research Service (CRS), 118–119
Connecticut, 13, 14, 15, 16, 18, 82, 92, 101–104, 105, 106, 135, 147
Legislature, 101, 103
New London, 13, 101, 103
Seatech, 102
Techconn, 104
University of, 102
Connor, Mike, 49
Control Knobs, Inc., 76
Conventional weapons, 35–36, 40, 43–44
Cooperation, 153, 157, 170
Cooperative Research and Development Agreements (CRADAs), 80–84, 88

Cooperative Security, 159–161
Corbin, Marcus, 153
Council for a Livable World, 15, 134
Council on Foreign Relations, 59
Crime, 2–3, 143, 149
Cuomo, Mario, 108
Czech Republic, 54

Daly, Les, 8
D'Amato, Alphonse, 24
Dankanyin, Robert, 56
David, George, 117
Defense Acquisition Board, 43
Defense Advanced Research Projects Agency (DARPA), 139
Defense Base Closure and Realignment Commission, 4
Defense contractors, 3, 8, 19, 33, 45, 52, 64, 69, 99, 105, 115, 117, 121, 124, 129, 139, 143
abuses and bribes by, 29, 37
boards of directors, 27–28
campaign contributions, 4
contract nourishment, 7
cost overruns, 6
executive compensation, 4, 12, 28, 115
hiring DoD employees, 27
lobbying, 125–128, 131
mergers, 8, 19–31, 43, 142, 166
profits, 4, 124, 150
shareholders, 12, 28, 115
stock, 12, 28, 30, 115, 150
subcontractors, 3, 8, 14, 18, 30, 64, 70, 73, 74, 123, 125, 126, 130
Defense conversion and diversification, 62, 89, 95, 96, 100, 101, 106, 107, 108, 109, 110, 111, 115, 121, 137, 138, 139, 140, 142, 143, 144, 146, 167

Defense dependence, 9, 60, 65, 72, 73, 91, 98, 99, 100, 105, 107, 108, 111, 116, 132, 138–139, 142, 144, 145, 148, 150, 165
Defense Finance and Accounting Service, 5
Defense-industrial base, 12, 128, 146, 147
Defense industry, 19, 31, 33, 73, 93, 111, 114, 138, 141, 143, 166
and arms exports, 40, 42, 43–44
Defense Mobilization Board, 137
Defense News, 115
Defense Reinvestment and Economic Growth Initiatives, 139
Defense Week, 11
Defense workers, 8, 103, 113–122
Dellums, Ron, 123, 127
Deming, W. Edwards, 121
Democratic Leadership Council, 40
Denver, 23, 47, 82, 83
Department of Commerce, 35, 39, 115
Economic Development Administration, 115, 145
Department of Defense, 20, 24, 25, 28, 34, 74, 75, 91, 92, 104, 139, 141, 142, 166
and arms sales, 39
civilian employees, 8, 27, 109, 113, 115, 116, 138, 165
contracts, 101, 103, 111–112, 146–147
"cost-plus," 11
and jobs argument, 8
and NASA, 45
Office of Economic Adjustment, 145
overstating threats, 8
political engineering, 7–8
procurement system, 143

progress payments, 25, 65, 67, 74
rescuing defense firms, 7
restructuring payments, 24–26
See also Pentagon
Department of Energy (DoE), 2, 3, 45, 80–85, 87, 88
Department of Housing and Urban Development, 45
Department of Justice, 29, 45, 51, 59, 126
Department of Labor, 50, 73, 76, 90, 91, 114, 115, 120
Department of State, 38, 135
and arms sales, 39, 40, 41
Department of Transportation (DoT), 47, 50
Department of the Treasury, 37, 51
Detroit, 59, 98, 99
Deutch, John, 24, 25, 26–27, 141
DiCicco, Peter, 159
Dicks, Norman, 123, 128, 131
Dionne, John "Stoney," 61, 64
Dixon, Alan, 4
Dodd, Chris, 14–16, 17
Dodson, Kellie, 71
Dole, Bob, 133, 147, 165–166
Dominican Republic, 53
Dow Jones Industrial Average, 115
Downey, Tom, 132
Drugs, 2–3, 149
Drug Enforcement Administration, 51
Dual use, 104, 140–144, 159
Dubinin, Yuri, 107
Duelfer, Charles, 39
Dumas, Lloyd Jeffry, 89, 98, 109
DuPont Corporation, 80, 83

EcoElectric Corporation, 90
Economic and community development, 86–87, 92, 97–98, 99, 101, 104, 105, 107, 108, 109, 111, 153, 168–169
community development corporations, 169

Economic Dislocation and Worker
    Adjustment Act (EDWAA),
    115, 117
Economic Policy Institute, 154
Economy
    global, 2, 9, 68, 69, 111, 149,
        157
    growth in, 84, 100, 117, 153
Education, 103, 117
    public, 165, 169
Edwards, Jack, 29
Egypt, 37, 151
    Cairo, 38
Eisenhower administration, 137
Eisenhower, Dwight D., 3, 5, 167
Electric vehicles (EVs), 58, 59–60,
    72, 82, 90, 119–120, 157–158
    batteries, 60, 119–120
    zero-emission, 59–60, 119
Electromagnetic Sciences, 76–77
Electronic Industries Association
    (EIA), 143
Electronics
    commercial, 141
    consumer, 149
    defense, 11, 22, 43, 60
Energy, 84, 88
    alternative-energy technologies,
        118, 145, 151
    efficiency, 86–87, 88
    renewable, 85, 118
    solar, 85, 97, 151, 158, 159
    wind, 159
Energy Conversion Devices, 60,
    119
    Ovonic Battery Company,
        119–120
English language, 76, 154
Environment, 84, 86, 87, 88
    depletion, 150–151
    environmental industrial parks,
        97
    investments in, 145
    nuclear/chemical pollution, 3, 45

nuclear weapons cleanup, 3, 84
pollution reduction, 119
products and technology for, 67,
    144
protection, 153
use of tax code, 161–162
Environmental Protection Agency
    (EPA), 86
E-Systems, 53
Europe, 15, 21, 35, 36, 39, 42, 82,
    121
Executive branch, 42, 168

Fallon, James, 68
Family planning, 161
Faulconer, Walter, 47
Federal Aviation Administration
    (FAA), 48–49, 54
Federal Bureau of Investigation
    (FBI), 7, 52
Federal Highway Administration,
    46
Federal Reserve
    District Banks, 117
    loans to state, local governments,
        169
Federation of American Scientists
    (FAS), 34–35, 40, 42
Feinstein, Dianne, 123
Fighter planes, 142
    F-4, 34
    F-14, 28–29
    F-15E, 34–35, 39, 40
    F-16, 20–21, 40
    F/A-18C/D, 29
    F/A-18E/F, 33, 129–130
    F-22, 20, 134
    F-117, 20
Fiji, 160
Filner, Bob, 99, 100
Finland, 38
Firefighters, 46, 51, 57, 67
First World, 151

Fischer Imaging, 82
Fitzgerald, A. Ernest, 5–6
Fitzgerald, Duane "Buzz," 61–64, 93
Flamm, Kenneth, 141
Florida, 46, 74, 82
Fonet, Inc., 82
Food, 151
   Food and Drug Administration, 50, 82
   stamps, 50
Ford Foundation, 95
Foreign aid, 166
Fortune magazine, 119
Foster, Gregory, 1
Foxwoods Resort Casino, 103
France, 37, 149, 151, 154, 160
Frank, Barney, 132
Franzone, Andrew, 76
French Guiana, 55
Frisby Airborne Hydraulics, 66–68, 121
   Frisby Technologies, 67
Frisby, Greg, 66, 73, 75
Frisby, Jeff, 66
Frost, Martin, 123
Furse, Elizabeth, 43

Galvin Commission, 84–85, 88
Galvin, Robert, 84
Gambling, 97, 103, 168
Gansler, Jacques, 7, 141, 154
Gejdenson, Sam, 15–16
General Accounting Office, 8, 30, 43, 65, 126, 130
General Dynamics, 6, 11–18, 19, 21, 58, 63–64, 115
   and A-12, 33
   campaign contributions, 16–17, 130
   Electric Boat, 12–18, 20, 147
   Fort Worth Division, 20–21, 27
   Land Systems Division, 12
   Space Systems Division, 19, 23–24

General Electric (GE), 69, 159, 166
   GE Aerospace, 19, 23, 48
   GE Engines of Ohio, 63
General Motors (GM), 55, 57, 58, 59–60, 64, 81–82, 119–120
   EV1, 120
   "head-up display," 57
   Impact, 59
   Oldsmobile Cutlass, 57
   Pontiac Bonneville, 57
   Saturn, 121
Geneva, 36
Georgia, 24, 47, 113, 125
   Atlanta, 76
Gephardt, Richard, 128
Germany, 54, 83, 145, 155, 160
   West, 37, 121
Gingrich, Newt, 133, 166
Global Engagement, 161
Global warming, 88, 151
   greenhouse gases, 161
   International Panel on Climate Change, 88, 151
Golding, Susan, 99, 100
Goodyear, 31
Gordon, Harvey, 108
Governments
   civilian agencies of, 45–54
   federal, 45, 150
   foreign, 45
   local, 45, 51–53, 105, 138
   state, 45, 50, 51–53, 105, 111, 115
Gramm, Phil, 131
Grassley, Charles, 135
Great American Lines, 63
Great Britain, 37, 160
   London, 38
Greece, 70
Gross national product, 2
Grumman, 19, 28–30, 45, 83
Guatemala, 37, 150

Gull Electronic Systems Division,
    Parker Hannifin Corporation,
    69–71, 121
Gund, Ed, 51
Guns and firearms, 3, 38, 52

Hafer, Tom, 6
Haitians, 76
Hansen, James, 151
Harley motorcycle, 64
Harman, Jane, 123, 128, 129–130
    constituents, 129
Hartung, William, 40, 42
Hatfield, Mark, 41, 135
Health care, 148
The High Priests of Waste, 6
Hispanics, 76
Hochbrueckner, George, 29
Hofstra University, 169
Hollywood, 28
Honeywell, 31
Hong Kong, 54
Hoops, John, 65
Horn, Steve, 128
Housing, 119, 169
Hubble Space Telescope, 22
Hughes/Hughes Aircraft/Hughes-
    GM/Hughes Electronics, 25,
    43, 46, 47, 52, 54, 55–60,
    63–64, 68, 72, 89, 91, 98, 166
Human rights, 38, 41
Humphrey, Hubert, 36, 137, 138
Humvee, 76
Hunt, Betsy, 104
Hunter, Duncan, 100, 135

IBM, 24, 30, 58, 137, 149
Illinois, 97
    East St. Louis, 97
    Northeastern Illinois
        Transportation Regional
        Authority, 53, 77
    See also Chicago
Immigration, 151, 154

Immigration and Naturalization
    Service, 45
Income
    erosion of, 2, 149
    worries about, 149
India, 54, 150, 151, 152, 160
Indiana, 76, 149
    South Bend, 76
Indonesia, 23, 37, 54
Industrial College of the Armed
    Forces, 1
Industrial policy, 100, 140,
    158–159
    community-based, 97–98
Industrial Solar Technology, 83
Industrial Tools, Inc., 81
Inflation, 149
Information, 142
    services, 22
    superhighway, 139, 143, 144
Infrastructure, 2, 97, 103, 139,
    150, 153
Inner cities, 3, 97, 117, 127, 149,
    163
Inouye, Daniel, 17, 132
In Search of Excellence, 66
Institute for Peace and Justice, 95
Insurance companies, 151
Intelligent Transportation Society
    (ITS) of America, 47
Internal Revenue Service, 46
International Association of
    Machinists, 61–62, 106, 120
    District 725, 72–73
    District 837, 95
    Local S6, 61–62
Investments, public, 2, 144–145,
    147
    in high-tech infrastructure, 144
    public-private, 139, 156
Iowa, 50
Iran, 34, 36–37
Iraq, 36, 37, 124, 127, 152
    Saddam Hussein, 36, 37, 42, 152

Ireland, 160
Isaacs, John, 15, 134
Israel, 21, 35, 70
Italy, 149
  Christian Democrats, 37

Jackson, Scoop, 105
Japan, 37, 68, 70, 83, 145, 149, 155–156, 160
Jewish, 31, 38
Job Corps, 50
Jobs, 126, 141, 146–147
  civilian vs. defense, 118–119
  loss of, 2, 12, 17, 20, 29, 34, 35, 42, 59, 63, 67, 70, 72, 77, 103, 109, 113–122, 128, 149, 150
  manufacturing, 116, 149
  new, 84, 94, 97, 104, 108, 116, 118, 119, 122, 136
Job Training and Partnership Act, 115
Johnson, Gary, 71
Johnston, Bennett, 131
Joint Chiefs of Staff, 28, 148
Jones, Keith, 86
Jones, Thomas, 30

Kaminski, Paul, 27
Kammer, Raymond, 141, 142
Kaplan, Robert D., 150–151
Kasich, John, 123, 148, 168
Kaufmann, William, 161
Kennedy administration, 137
Kennedy, Edward, 36
Kerr, Robert, 125
Khilewi, Mohammed, 38
Kidder, Ray, 80–81
Kiefer, Lou, 120
Klare, Michael, 36
Korb, Lawrence, 4, 146
Korea, 21, 127, 151

North, 128, 135, 152
South, 63, 70
Kotz, Nick, 125
Kourpias, George, 62
Krugman, Paul, 119
Kutler, Jon, 74
Kuwait, 37
KWMU, 97

Laird, Melvin, 28
LAU Technologies, 77
Lawrence Livermore National Laboratory, 79, 80, 81, 82, 83, 85, 87
Lester, Wayne, 67
Lewis, Jerry, 123
Lewis, John L., 95
Limbaugh, Rush, 96
Limited Nuclear Test Ban Treaty, 138
Litton Industries, 7
Livingston, Bob, 135
Lobbying/lobbyists, 125, 127, 128, 130, 132
Lockheed, 6, 18, 19–22, 24–26, 51–52, 89, 115, 126, 166
  and C-5, 128
  campaign contributions, 130
  European market, 37
Lockheed Martin, 20–24, 26, 28, 31, 33, 45, 47, 51, 54, 85, 166
  Automated Highway System Division, 47
  Information Management Services Division, 51
Logistics Management Institute, 74
Long Island, 29, 46, 67, 69, 74, 75, 76, 86, 108–109, 121
Loral, 25, 30–31, 47, 167
Los Alamos National Laboratory, 72–73, 79, 82, 83
  Industrial Partnership Office, 84

Los Angeles, 7, 72, 73, 83, 129, 142
  Economic Roundtable, 142
  Rams, 97
Los Angeles Times, 34
Lott, Trent, 134, 135
Louisiana, 135
Lowrey, Mike, 107
Lum, King, 71
Lumpe, Lora, 42
Lyons, Pete, 84

MacAulay Brown, 108
MacAulay, John, 108
MacLachlan, Alexander, 80, 83–84
MacNeil/Lehrer Newshour, 30
M/A-Com Microelectronics
  Division, 68–69, 121
Magnetically-levitated trains (mag-
  lev), 83, 99
  High Speed Rail Association, 145
Magnuson, Warren, 105
Maine, 18, 60, 92–95, 99, 100, 142
  Bath, 61
  Chamber of Commerce, 94
Maine Economic Conversion
  Project (MECP), 92–95
Manufacturing, 142
Marcos, Ferdinand, 37
Marguth, Gilbert, 80
Marines, U.S., 52, 124, 152, 161
Maritech, 63, 144
Marketing, 43, 142
Markets
  commercial, 8, 55–64, 65, 66,
    74, 77, 103, 116, 140, 142,
    145, 150, 166
  foreign, 135
  and national needs, 143
Markusen, Ann, 85, 158, 168
Marshall, Ray, 121
Martin, Lynn, 126

Martin Marietta, 18, 19–28, 45,
  48, 49, 51, 108
  campaign contributions, 130
  Electronics Group, 22
  Information Group, 22
  Technology Ventures
    Corporation, 85
Martin, William McChesney Jr.,
  137
Martino, Roger, 49
Maryland, 19, 23, 29, 110, 137,
  167
Mashantucket Pequot tribe, 103
Massachusetts, 24, 65, 68, 77,
  110–111, 116, 124, 151, 153
  Boston Harbor, 17
  Massachusetts Bay Transit
    Authority, 53
  Massachusetts General Hospital,
    82
  and zero-emissions EVs, 119
Mathews, Jessica, 59
Mayer, Kenneth, 131
McCain, John, 18, 132–133, 135
McCarthy, Lance, 97
McDermott, Jim, 132
McDonnell Douglas, 6, 33–35,
  38–40, 42–43, 98, 113, 114,
  115, 116, 128, 129
  jobs appeal, 34–35
  shareholders, 98
McDonnell, John, 33, 34
McGee, Joseph, 101
McGivern, Mary Ann, 95–98
McGovern, George, 137–138
McKeon, "Buck," 123
McKernan, John, 93
McKinney, Cynthia, 41
McKinney, Stewart, 132
McNamara, Robert, 37
McPeak, Merrill, 165
MedDetect, 23
Medicaid/Medicare, 50, 146, 148,
  166

Melkonian, Martin, 169
Mellor, James, 12
Melman, Seymour, 98, 137, 138
Mexico, 100, 149
  Tijuana, 100
Michigan, 59, 60, 98
Middle East, 34, 35, 37, 40, 127
Military bases, 4, 8, 99, 105, 109,
    116, 124
  Alameda Naval Air Station, 120
  Davis Monthan Air Force Base,
    89
  and pork, 133, 134
  reuse, 145
Military-industrial complex, 5, 113,
    166, 167
Military-industrial culture, 9, 65,
    68, 88
Military intervention, unilateral,
    152
Military personnel, 109, 113, 115,
    138, 144
  retirees, 98
Military readiness, 128
Military specifications ("milspecs"),
    7, 11, 63, 65, 143
Military spending, 1, 3, 4, 33, 42,
    72, 93, 127, 133, 146, 148,
    165
  alternative models, 152–153, 161
  Cold War levels, 152
  and jobs, 118–119, 123, 124,
    128
  local impact, 4, 98, 101, 105,
    109, 124, 125, 131
  "off the table," 135
  as share of world total, 163
MILSTAR, 133
Milwaukee, 14
Missiles, 2, 11, 35, 43, 72
  advanced cruise, 98
  defense system, 134
  guidance systems, 68
  Maverick, 58

MX, 156
  Patriot, 124
  Stinger, 37
  Tomahawk, 98
Mississippi, 134
Missouri, 50, 73, 123
MIT, 27, 119, 156
  Lincoln Laboratory, 27
Mitchell, George, 93
Mobutu, Sese Seko, 37, 152
Morgan, Dan, 134
Morrison Knudsen, 52
Morrison, Philip, 161
Mosbacher, Robert, 39
Motorola, 84, 142
Moukawsher, Thomas, 101
Mueller, Elizabeth, 115–116, 117
Murtha, John, 17, 131
Muslims, 38, 39

National Aeronautics and Space
    Administration (NASA), 20,
    22, 45
  Goddard Institute for Space
    Studies, 151
National Air Traffic Controllers
    Association, 48–49
National Commission for
    Economic Conversion and
    Disarmament, 34–35, 85–86,
    144
National Governors' Association,
    101–102, 111
National Guard and Reserves, 133
National Institute of Standards and
    Technology (NIST), 141, 144,
    145
National Laboratories, 79–88, 110
  civilian, 79
  community involvement, 86–87
  weapons labs employment, 79
National needs and priorities, 156,
    159, 167
National security, 2, 29, 84, 123,
    124, 126, 168
NATO, 133, 146

Navy Submarine League, 14
Navy, U.S., 18, 29, 33, 60–61, 74, 76, 106, 124, 126–127
air wing, 165
T-45 trainer, 33
Neal, Clifford, 104
Netherlands, 39, 40, 86
Community Research, Policy and Assistance Centers, 86
Prince Bernhard, 37
New England, 13, 15, 16, 69, 114, 116, 147
New Hampshire, 93
New Jersey, 86, 92, 115–116, 149
New London Day, 16, 17, 113
New Mexico, 79
New School for Social Research, 115
Newsday, 27
Newsweek, 134
New York, 24, 47, 48, 70, 76, 89, 92, 108–109, 118, 121
Republican governor and legislature, 109
and zero-emission EVs, 119
New York Times, 14
Nicaraguan contras, 14
Nielsen, W. R., 81
Nigeria, 152
Lagos, 150
Night-vision equipment, 55, 57
Nixon administration, 37
Nixon, Richard, 5
Doctrine, 36
Nolan, Janne, 44
North America, 121
North American Aviation, 125
North Carolina, 67
Northeast-Midwest Institute, 142
Northrop, 19, 29–30
campaign contributions, 130
Northrop Grumman, 29–30, 47, 83, 129, 136, 167
Norway, 54

Nuclear Non-Proliferation Treaty, 38
Nuclear weapons, 8, 79, 143, 153
bomb design, 79
hydrogen bombs, 1, 13, 82, 126
installations, 165
and Iraq, 36, 38
proliferation, 38, 84, 129, 135, 152
and Saudi Arabia, 38–39
testing, 79, 84
U.S. arsenal, 162
Nuclear Weapons Freeze Campaign, 64
Nunn, Sam, 134

Obey, David, 134
Office of Economic Conversion Information, 145
Ohio, 48, 75, 76, 77, 107–108, 123
Oil, 39, 67, 88
and coal industry, 151
depreciation allowance, 162
industry, 119, 120, 151
and Iran, 36
Oklahoma, 125
O'Leary, Hazel, 83, 84
Oman, 54
O'Neill, Tip, 124
Ornstein, Norman, 131

Pacific Northwest, 106
Pacific Ocean, 48
Packard, David, 27
Pages, Eric, 75
Pakistan, 152, 160
Panama, 151
Panetta, Leon, 129
Partnerships
consortia, 157–158
labor-management, 62
manufacturing, 69

public-private, 47, 80, 83–84, 88, 145, 157–158
Peace dividend, 2, 4
Peace groups, 93, 99, 100, 105
Peacekeeping, 134, 152–153
Pennsylvania, 131
Pentagon, 4, 7, 8, 9, 11, 12, 16, 18, 27, 31, 42, 43, 51, 52, 54, 70, 96, 97, 101, 114, 124, 125, 135, 139, 140, 142, 165, 166
and EVs, 158
inspector general, 33
International Logistics Negotiations, 37
and McDonnell Douglas, 33–34
share of budget cuts, 146
unrequested weapons, 161
Perkin-Elmer Corporation, 82
Perry, William, 24, 25, 26–27, 39, 133, 148, 159–160
Persian Gulf, 36, 158
Peters, Tom, 66
Peterson, Wallace, 2
Philippines, 23, 37
Physicians for Social Responsibility, 89
Police, 46, 51, 52, 57
Polish, 76
Political action committees (PACs), 130–132, 168
Population pressures, 150–151
Pork barrel, 123, 124, 148
military pork, 123, 126, 132, 133, 134, 136, 147, 166
Portugal, 53
Postal Service, U.S., 45, 58
Poverty, 2–3, 149
Powell Tate, 14, 16
PRC, 51
Princeton University, 19
Productivity, 2
Profits, 36, 126
Progressive Policy Institute, 40
Project Mercury, 45

Prudential Insurance Company, 63
Pryor, David, 14, 128
Public Broadcasting System (PBS), 30
Public opinion, 162
University of Maryland Program on International Policy Attitudes, 162
Puerto Rico, 50
San Juan, 49
Quality management, 62, 120–121
Quarterdeck Investment Partners, 74

Racial problems, 2, 149
Radar, 35, 55
automotive, 83
Doppler, 49
Forewarn, 57
motion-detection system, 58
Radiation experiments, 2
Rand Corporation, 6, 114
Ray, Jerry, 14, 16
Raytheon, 31, 47, 49, 52, 54, 60, 68, 77, 124, 166
RCA, 55
Reagan administration, 61, 126, 148
Reagan, Nancy, 14
Reagan, Ronald, 4, 72, 92, 125, 168
Refugees, 135
Regional Advanced Manufacturing Project (RAMP), 72–73
Reich, Robert, 117, 149
Republican National Committee, 132
Research/research and development (R&D), 75, 80, 84, 85, 110, 142
applied, 85, 139
civilian, 155–156
DoD-financed, 4, 141, 144, 146
fundamental, 84, 85
and weapons labs, 79, 87, 88
Rhode Island, 15, 101, 147

Richards, Ann, 109
Riggs, Frank, 135
Rivers, Mendel, 125
Rockwell International, 47, 125
  lobbying, 125
Rose Health Care System, 23
Rowland, John, 104
Ruenzel, Neil, 14, 17
Russell, Richard, 125
Russia/Russians, 13, 22, 35, 54, 70
Rutgers University, 85

St. Louis, 34, 40, 43, 95–98, 99,
    113, 114, 115, 116, 121, 128
  Economic Adjustment and
    Diversification Committee, 96
  Management Assistance and
    Technology Transfer (MATT),
    96
  mayor of, 97–98
St. Louis Economic Conversion
    Project (SLECP), 95–98, 100
Sampson, Anthony, 37
Sandia National Laboratories, 79,
    80, 81, 82, 83, 85
San Diego, 98–100
San Diego Economic Conversion
    Council (SDECC), 98–100
Sargent Controls, 90, 91
Saudi Arabia, 34–35, 37, 38–40,
    42, 152
  King Fahd, 38
Savimbi, Jonas, 37
Scandinavia, 160
Schools, 155
  buses, 57, 108, 142
  public, 153
Schwartz, Bernard, 30
Schweppe, Jesse, 93
Schweppe, Susie, 92–95
Scientists and engineers, 155, 167
Scowcroft, Brent, 29
Sealift, 11, 160

Sears, 149
Secrecy, 1
Securities and Exchange
    Commission, 37, 50
Sega Enterprises, 22
Sematech, 140
Semiconductor industry, 140
Seyer, Christopher, 96
Seyer Industries, 96, 121
Shantytowns, 150
Shipbuilding/shipyards, 60, 61, 98,
    105, 107, 134, 147
  Avondale, Louisiana, 63
  commercial, 144
  Finnish, 62
  Japanese, 62
  Newport News, 12, 17–18, 63,
    126–127, 147
  Philadelphia Naval Shipyard, 131
  Puget Sound Naval Shipyard,
    134
  Tenneco Shipbuilding, 126–127
  Todd, 107
Ships
  cargo, 62–63
  LHD, 133
  naval, 60–61, 98
Shortt, James, 66
Sisisky, Norman, 127
Sisters of Loretto, 95
SIVAM, 54
Skelton, Ike, 123
Sloyan, Patrick, 25
Small Business Administration, 75
Smaller defense firms, 65–77, 98,
    100, 103, 106, 107, 109, 121,
    145
  "flexible networks," 106
  needs of, 167
  and TRP, 140
Smith, Daniel, 153
Smog Dog, 54
Solow, Robert, 119
Somalia, 37
Sommers, Albert, 119
Sonalysts, 76
Sony, 55

South Carolina, 67, 125
South Dakota, 137
Southeast Asia, 23, 68
Soviet Union, 1, 13, 22, 36, 51,
    126, 128, 133, 147
  military power, 8, 127, 128
Space
  age, 45
  Apollo program, 69
  commercial, 43
  satellites, 49, 57
  systems and projects, 11, 43, 45
Specter, Arlen, 131
Spence, Floyd, 133, 134, 168
Spinney, Franklin C., 7–8
Stadelmann, John, 69, 70
Stanford University, 95
Stark, Pete, 132
Star Wars, 168
Stein, Rob, 157
Stevens, Roger, 47
Stevens, Ted, 131
Stone, Gregory, 113
Stonecipher, Harry, 43
Strategic Air Command (SAC), 29
Stubbing, Richard, 5, 7
Submarines, 11, 12
  anti-submarine warfare
    technology, 74
  attack, 13, 15, 18, 147
  Polaris/Poseidon/Trident, 13, 22,
    133
  Seawolf, 13–18, 90, 113, 133,
    147
Superconducting materials, 83
Sustainable development, 94
Sweden, 68
Swensen, Marvin, 52
Switzerland, 38, 54
Symington, Fife, 91

Taiwan, 21, 40
Tanks, 2, 11, 60, 128
  main battle, 12

Taxpayers, 28, 97, 124, 132, 142,
    163
Technology Reinvestment Program
    (TRP), 61, 62, 68, 104,
    140–141, 145
  Operation Restore Jobs, 140,
    141
Technology Strategies & Alliances,
    27
Technology transfer, 55, 72, 85,
    110, 141–142
Teegarden, Suzanne, 116
Telecommunications, 55, 143
Television, 56–57
  cable, 55, 56
  DirecTV, 55, 56, 57
  sets, 150
Tellep, Daniel, 20
Tennessee, 59
Terrorism, 129, 135
  in Saudi Arabia, 38
  suitcase bomb, 152
Texas, 58, 109–110, 123, 131
  Dallas, 21, 48, 52, 53, 109
  Fort Worth, 3, 21, 40, 48, 109
  Houston, 38
  Texas One, 109–110
  University of Texas-Dallas, 89,
    109
  Waco, 58–59
Texas Instruments, 57
Textron Corporation, 72
  HR Textron, 72–73, 121
Thailand, 23, 70
Theatre High-Altitude Area
    Defense (THAAD), 22
Think magazine, 137
Third World, 128, 150, 151, 152
Threats
  domestic, 149–150, 153
  global, 150–152
Thurow, Lester, 156
Titan rockets, 22
Top Gun, 28

Tour de Sol, 119
Town meetings, 99, 100
Trade
  environmental and labor
    standards, 161
Trade Adjustment Assistance
  (TAA), 115–116, 117
Training/retraining, 61, 99, 103,
  115–116, 138
  and Clinton administration, 145
  joint labor-management, 62
  on-the-job, 117, 155
Transportation, 139
  advanced, 118, 119, 120, 139,
    145, 146, 159
  air transport, 143, 145
  Amtrak, 145
  bridges, 127, 139, 159
  ferry designers, 106
  "intelligent," 46–48, 50, 139,
    143, 144, 145
  Intermodal Surface
    Transportation Efficiency Act,
    46
  passenger ferries, 106
  railroads, 48, 139, 145
  rapid transit, 95, 119
  regional mass transit, 145
  roads, 2, 139
Trost, Carlisle, 28
TRW, 43, 45, 46, 47, 49, 52, 60,
  166
Tsipis, Kosta, 161
Turkey, 37

Ukraine, 54
Unions, labor, 34, 61, 92, 93, 97,
  99, 103, 105, 106, 107, 109,
  114, 115, 120, 138, 157
  AFL-CIO Industrial Union
    Department, 159
  share of workforce, 149

United Auto Workers, 62
United Steelworkers, 62, 127
Unisys, 115–116
United Nations, 38, 41, 133, 160,
  161
  U.S. dues to, 162
United States, 1, 5, 22, 42, 54, 83,
  120, 127, 145, 146, 149, 151,
  152
United Technologies, 117
Universities, 47, 72, 73, 80, 86, 90,
  92, 140
  graduates, 149

Vaage, Robert, 48
Vanderslice, Thomas, 69
Van Dillen, Ken, 145
Vercelli, Tom, 81
Vessey, John Jr., 28
Vietnam, 36, 68
  North, 132
Vinson, Carl, 125
Virginia, 18, 52, 126–127, 147
  Quantico, 52
Vought Aircraft, 29
V-22 helicopter, 131

Walkup, Robert, 58
Wall Street, 24, 30, 149
Warner, John, 18, 133
Wars, 151
  civil, 1, 127, 152
  Gulf, 22, 34, 37, 39, 40, 55, 76,
    124, 126
  Iran-Iraq, 36
  nuclear, 13, 92, 133
  regional, 4, 146, 152
  Vietnam, 31, 47, 147
  World War II, 8, 15, 35, 72
Warsaw Pact, 152

Washington, DC, 4, 14, 39, 48, 50, 52, 72, 125
Washington Post, 4, 18, 30, 38, 45, 128, 134
Washington State, 105–107, 111, 123
  Bangor Submarine Base, 106
  Keyport Undersea Warfare Center, 106
  Legislature, 107
  Pacific Manufacturing Group, 106
  Shipnet, 107
  University of Washington Northwest Policy Center, 105
  Washington Aerospace Alliance, 107
  Washington Alliance for Manufacturing (WAM), 107
Webster College, 95
Weicker, Lowell, 101, 106
Weida, William, 85
Weinberger, Caspar, 8
Weiss, Ted, 138
Welch, Jack, 69, 159
Weld, William, 111
Weldon, Curt, 135
Wellins, Richard, 155
West Coast, 107
West, Karen, 106
Westinghouse, 30, 47, 139, 166

Whiteford, Fred, 43
White House, 34, 141, 143
  Clinton, 152
Wiesner, Jerome, 161
Wilcox Electric, 49
Williams, Cassell, 95
Wilson, Charles, 131
Wilson, Howard G., 57, 60
Wireless telephone service, 23, 54
Workforce, 149
  trained, literate, 154–155
Working capital, 67, 73–75, 77, 97, 104, 110, 142
Workplace organization, 155
  High Performance Work Organizations (HPWOs), 120–122
  joint decisionmaking, 61–62, 64, 77, 97, 121, 155
  work teams, 61, 69–70, 71, 96, 108

Xerox, 31

Young, C. W. Bill, 133
Yudken, Joel, 156, 158, 168

Zaire, 37, 152